WAR

The Natural History Press, publisher for The American Museum of Natural History, is a division of Doubleday & Company, Inc. Directed by a joint editorial board made up of members of the staff of both the Museum and Doubleday, The Natural History Press publishes books and periodicals in all branches of the life and earth sciences, including anthropology and astronomy. The Natural History Press has its editorial offices at The American Museum of Natural History, Central Park West at 79th Street, New York, N.Y. 10024, and its business offices at 501 Franklin Avenue, Garden City, N.Y. 11530.

MORTON FRIED, MARVIN HARRIS and ROBERT MURPHY are Professors of Anthropology at Columbia University. The contributors to this volume are affiliated as follows:

FRANK B. LIVINGSTONE, Department of Anthropology, University of Michigan;

FREDERICK P. THIEME, Vice-President, University of Washington;

RALPH L. HOLLOWAY, JR., Department of Anthropology, Columbia University;

C. R. CARPENTER, Departments of Psychology and Anthropology, Pennsylvania State University;

ALEXANDER ALLAND, JR., Department of Anthropology, Columbia University;

BENJAMIN D. PAUL, Department of Anthropology, Stanford University;

ANDREW P. VAYDA, Department of Anthropology, Columbia University;

ALEXANDER LESSER, Department of Anthropology, Hofstra University;

NAPOLEON A. CHAGNON, Departments of Anthropology and Human Genetics, University of Michigan;

ELMAN R. SERVICE, Department of Anthropology, University of Michigan;

ANTHONY F. C. WALLACE, Department of Anthropology, University of Pennsylvania;

STANLEY DIAMOND, Department of Sociology and Anthropology, New School for Social Research;

SOL TAX, Department of Anthropology, University of Chicago;

E. ADAMSON HOEBEL, Department of Anthropology, University of Minnesota;

MARGARET MEAD, American Museum of Natural History and Department of Anthropology, Columbia University.

WAR:

THE ANTHROPOLOGY OF
ARMED CONFLICT AND AGGRESSION

EDITED BY
MORTON FRIED, MARVIN HARRIS
AND ROBERT MURPHY

PUBLISHED FOR
THE AMERICAN MUSEUM OF NATURAL HISTORY
THE NATURAL HISTORY PRESS
1968 · GARDEN CITY, NEW YORK

ANTHROPOLOGISTS ARE POPULARLY REGARDED as students of primitive man and simple societies. This characterization has never been quite appropriate. Anthropologists concerned exclusively with so-called primitives have been far outnumbered in the last few decades by colleagues who have explicitly devoted their main research efforts to the analysis of aspects of complex, state-organized societies. Moreover, the number of anthropologists who lay claim to an exclusive preoccupation with primitive culture is larger than the facts warrant. Many anthropological studies of "tribal" populations have been shown upon re-examination to be concerned with colonial, refugee, peasant, and other non-primitive situations. Research carried out in a remote land inhabited by an exotic "nature folk" provides special professional and career advantages. This has led to a veritable "search for the primitive" which has further widened the gap between the ideal and actual in anthropology. Many field workers have been subtly encouraged to present their data as if the larger world of colonial wars, labor recruitment, taxation, indirect rule, forced migration, missionization, and other post-contact phenomena did not exist.

A devastating result of the premium status of research among "genuine" primitives is that it automatically legitimatizes the study of that which may be irrelevant or inconsequential for an understanding of matters of contemporary concern. But the present period of intense and growing national unrest brought on by our Vietnam involvement has produced a crisis of conscience which has called into question the right of anthropologists to remain aloof from the great issues of our times.

This book on anthropology and war is a direct product of that

crisis. It contains the expanded text of prepared papers and comments on papers as well as comments from the floor delivered at
an unprecedented plenary symposium held on November 30,
1967, in Washington, D.C., during the Sixty-sixth Annual Meetings of the American Anthropological Association. To understand how this book and the symposium upon which it is based
came into being and to judge its value as a contribution to the
confrontation between the discipline of anthropology and the
political and moral dilemmas of the modern world, we must return to another meeting of the Association, held one year earlier
at Pittsburgh, in December 1966. There, at an impromptu midnight caucus of anthropologists, most of whom had publicly identified themselves as opposed to the United States' Vietnam
policy, indignant voices were raised against the miniscule portion of the meeting's formal papers and symposia which had displayed any concern for the critical issues of contemporary society.
On the basis of this discussion, a petition was drafted, mimeo-
graphed overnight, and circulated the next morning. In a few
hours some three hundred and fifty members of the Association
had signed their approval to the text. It read as follows:

> In view of widely shared sentiment that anthropologists have both a
> moral and professional concern for the effects of war on the human
> species, an ad hoc committee has formed to organize symposia on
> this subject for the 1967 American Anthropological Association
> Meetings in Washington, D.C. Because we can no longer ignore the
> moral, biological, and social consequences of the present political
> situation, we, the undersigned, members of the American Anthro-
> pological Association meeting in Pittsburgh, 1966, urge that these
> symposia be included in the 1967 meeting.

The editors of the present volume undertook, in the name of
the Ad Hoc Committee which had sponsored the above petition,
to interpret and execute the petitioners' mandate. During the
preparations which ensued, we suffered no illusions concerning
the nature of the symposium which would best satisfy the majority of those who were dissatisfied with the inattention of the
Pittsburgh program to the problems of our time. For, at the meeting of the Fellows of the Association which took place during the
day following the midnight caucus, a resolution had been introduced, debated, and approved which testified to a widespread concern with the moral and political issues of the Vietnam war and

to a majority sentiment of opposition to the premises and conduct of that war. The resolution read as follows:

> Reaffirming our 1961 resolution, we condemn the use of napalm,
> chemical defoliants, harmful gases, bombing, the torture and killing
> of prisoners of war and political prisoners, and the intentional or
> deliberate policies of genocide or forced transportation of popula-
> tions for the purpose of terminating their cultural and/or genetic
> heritages by anyone anywhere.
>
> These methods of warfare deeply offend human nature. We ask
> that all governments put an end to their use at once and proceed
> as rapidly as possible to a peaceful settlement of the war in Vietnam.

The organizers of the 1968 Symposium were aware however,
that a large minority of the Association's members had passion-
ately dissented from the above resolution, not necessarily because they supported the Vietnam war, but because they believed
that the politicalization of a scientific association could only result
in its rapid demise.

It would have been possible to structure the Washington Symposium in such a way as to make of it a political act first and a
scientific meeting second. Topics and speakers could have been
selected strictly according to their conformity to our point of
view, and contributions could have been edited to emphasize
inflammatory political phrases. The Symposium could, in other
words, have taken the form of a teach-in. Indeed, several of the
principal innovators of the teach-in had helped to draft the enabling petition. Moreover, the Symposium's organizers happen to
respect the teach-in as a highly creative and effective educational
device. But it was quite clear in going over the list of signatures,
comprising an aggregate to which we were responsible, that many
of the Pittsburgh petitioners would have been dismayed and
shocked had political expediency been permitted to dominate the
Washington session.

Given the fact that the members of the American Anthropological Association do not profess any single political line with
respect to the war in Vietnam, we reached the conclusion that
our prime responsibility was to organize a symposium which was
consistent with the highest standards of scientific authenticity.
Every effort was thereupon made to invite the participation of
recognized authorities regardless of their conformity to a particular political position. Throughout the organization of the Sym-

posium, political instructions or innuendos were scrupulously
omitted from all correspondence with the participants. It thus
results that in the absence of specific remarks directed at alternatives in Vietnam, no conclusions are warranted concerning the
political positions of the authors who have contributed to this
volume. It cannot even be assumed that all of the contributors
agree with the enabling petition. Indeed, in one case—that of Professor Andrew P. Vayda—a specific disagreement with the petition's allusion to the study of war as a moral obligation must be
recorded.

The editors, for their part, wish to make it equally emphatic
that they have not capitulated to the point of view which either
recommends or asserts the possibility of politically neutral social
science. While we did not solicit political evaluations, neither did
we seek to avoid them. Each contributor was left completely on
his own to grapple with this problem as he saw fit. Our editorial
permissiveness thus led to the inclusion of several politicized
presentations to which segments of the Symposium's large audience responded with emotional applause and approval. These
manifestations led in turn to the inaccurate and unkind accusation that the organizers had in fact turned the plenary session
into a teach-in about the war in Vietnam. At the same time, the
conspicuous omission by several of the participants of any reference to Vietnam prompted the more radical members of the audience to conclude that the entire performance was nothing but a
diversionary tactic intended to occlude the need for more drastic
action. At a special session devoted to the need for "radical anthropology" the present Symposium was bitterly denounced not
as a teach-in but as a "fink-out."

The editors admit to neither charge. We reject the notion that
the study of war or of any other socio-cultural phenomena, even
of trivia, can be pursued without political consequences. Anthropologists who claim that they have attained the sanctuary of political neutrality are obviously deluding themselves. When one's
society arrives at a fateful crossroads, to stand still, to keep quiet
is no less politically decisive than to march loudly and resolutely
to the right or left.

On the other hand, we also firmly reject the insinuation that
the loudest political voices are necessarily the best informed scientifically. Those who seek a political justification for the subordination of science to politics, will find it at their peril. The

greatest danger confronting any political movement is for it to permit its analysis of reality to be contaminated by its own rhetoric. We know far too little about war, and the threat of war is far too great, for us to ignore or shut off scientific information which emanates from politically dissident or ostensibly neutral positions.

We should like this symposium to be judged, therefore, as a highly self-conscious attempt to survey what contributions have been made or can be made by anthropologists of diverse political opinions, specialties, and theoretical orientations to the scientific understanding of war and its causes. Anthropology, despite its unique strengths in biological, paleontological, archaeological, cultural, linguistic, ecological and psychological specialties, has been strangely inarticulate on the subject of war. Yet here is a subject in which the trivial cannot easily flourish, whose understanding will demand a mighty collective effort, and in which all of the specialties at our disposal may prove tragically inadequate to the task.

A special note of thanks is due to Professor Fred Eggan who consented to chair the Symposium, fully aware of the difficulties described above. Without dwelling further on the history of the symposium or the negotiations it entailed, it is possible to take a quick overview of the various contributions presenting a general picture of the proceedings.

The first paper[1] by Frank Livingstone started the symposium on a controversial note. According to Livingstone, war has few if any serious genetic consequences for the human species. At the core of Livingstone's presentation are two arguments. One of these has to do with the mechanics of selection in evolution. Livingstone asserts the insignificance of shifts in the gene pools of large societies through the action of war. The other concerns the question of population loss through warfare. Livingstone is convinced that modern wars reduce populations ephemerally; thus

---

[1] In this final version of the proceedings the order of original presentation of the papers has been disturbed by moving Chagnon from third to fifth and moving Alland and Vayda one notch forward in the final sequence. In addition, Margaret Mead's paper has been divided into two parts: first, remarks prepared in advance of the meetings and to which Seymour Melman responded as discussant; second, remarks prepared at the meetings and which in their concern with the nature of the symposium itself serve as a fitting epilogue to the present volume.

far, no matter how great the slaughter, populations have bounced
back with alacrity. Indeed, Livingstone asserts that even the population of Vietnam has continued to grow rapidly throughout the
present war. Fred Thieme, Livingstone's discussant, agreed with
the main substance of this view. From the floor, however, came
the charge that both Livingstone and Thieme had taken too narrow a view of war, that casualties comprised not only those
directly killed and wounded, but those who suffered disease, starvation, or other consequences of social disarrangement due to
war. Pushing beyond this point, it was also suggested from the
floor that both speakers had failed to project their views into a
future in which nuclear warfare might play a larger and larger
role.

Quite obviously, the area between the generally minimal and
moderate estimates of physical and genetic damage attributable
to radiation following the atomic bombings in Japan, and the
widespread lay belief that the consequence of nuclear warfare is
maximum and overwhelming damage to the living and the unborn, requires much more study than it has yet received, and the
results of such studies must be made widely available. In view of
the discussion of this symposium, it must be stated that the attempt to extrapolate from present knowledge to the probable future is completely proper as a scientific endeavor, provided that
the proper methods are used.

While Livingstone raises the problem of warfare as an expression of a postulated instinct for aggression, it is Holloway who
gives his major attention to this sort of approach. In the end, like
Livingstone, he rejects any such postulated instinct. Detailed consideration of the nature and evolution of the human brain and
behavior fails to support any such notion. Simplistic concepts
fail to do justice to the complexity of the phenomena that comprise human warfare. Once again it becomes obvious from the
unfolding of the paper that there are vast lacunae in the concrete
knowledge that must be amassed on these problems. At the present stage of research, Holloway is impressed by the significance
of the evolution of the brain as a basis for increasing potential
ability to find means for conflict resolution other than military
combat. Yet he recognizes a paradox which is manifest in the fact
that warfare, far from withering away, seems empirically to be
increasing. Thus as man's brain increased his facility for dealing
with some of his fellows more sympathetically, it also increased

his efficiency at dealing with others hostilely. Indeed, the human capacity for either positive or negative effect is such that Holloway has little regard for theories of human cultural behavior that emphasize origins in and continuities with primate or other mammalian ethology. Such a position, of course, immediately places Holloway at serious odds with certain scientists and popularizers who have been arguing the case for strong behavioral continuities between man and certain carnivorous and aggressive animal relatives.

Without declaring himself a supporter of the latter position, C. R. Carpenter, a pioneering student of primate ethology, takes exception to Holloway's demand that a framework specific to mankind be utilized for the discussion of drives toward aggression and warfare. On the other hand, in subsequent discussion, Carpenter makes it clear that he agrees that aggression and warfare in man are complicated and brought to a new emergent level by association with the phenomenon of symbolization and its cultural consequences. It seems that, lay opinion to the contrary, one of the areas of extensive agreement in the problem of understanding war has to do with the irrelevance of man's primate ancestry.

The question of a broader approach to the concept of war in assessing biological effects was raised early in the symposium by David Aberle, who spoke from the floor. In a prepared paper, however, Alexander Alland, Jr., goes more deeply and appropriately into detail. Alland's was the first paper read in the symposium to pay specific attention to the war in Vietnam. Perhaps for this reason it was the paper that received greatest attention from journalists. What helped focus further attention on this paper was its raising of the spectre of plague in Southeast Asia. It is important to note that beyond the intrinsic significance of the rise in plague is the parallel in everything but scale (which will remain uncertain at best) between the "natural" war-induced development of epidemics and the potential for "artificial" epidemics induced through bacteriological warfare. Alland seems to agree with Livingstone that in simpler societies with small populations the potential evolutionary consequences of population destruction through warfare are quite significant. On the other hand, there are the makings of a sharp disagreement between them with regard to the same proposition assayed for complex, modern societies.

Benjamin Paul, an anthropologist long known for his interest in public health, backs up Alland and raises again the question of effects of biological weapons, herbicides, and defoliants upon the Vietnamese population. This, of course, brings up matters that have confronted anthropologists before, as the previously cited resolutions have shown. Like Livingstone, Alland is overtly concerned with the life risks of individuals and of populations. He draws attention, however, not merely to the problem of maintaining or achieving certain population levels or gene frequencies but to the suffering produced by war and to the quality of the lives of war's survivors. Very clearly, Alland's approach leads to the conclusion that no matter what the long-term biological effects of war may be, biological considerations alone cannot justify the immediate physiological and psychological costs.

Andrew P. Vayda's paper may be viewed as an exploration of the question of the costs of war calculated from yet another perspective. Vayda's concern is to explicate various hypotheses which attribute to war life-sustaining functional consequences when war is considered as a component of homeostatic systems. Such systems relate human populations to their ecological matrix, and are functional in the narrow sense of acting to maintain or restore an evolutionarily selected equilibrium. Vayda very carefully insists that the varieties of functions which have been attributed to war and which he reviews, have only the status of hypotheses. His main explicit concern is a call for additional research in order to provide empirical tests of the diversity of functions which have been offered. Despite the cautious phrasing of Vayda's paper it is clear that he regards it as probable that some of the functions discussed are indeed empirically demonstrable. Vayda's concept of "function" however, does not commit him to the position that because war is part of a homeostatic system, it is therefore permanently adaptive. The homeostatic system which war serves may itself eventually fail to provide adequate biocultural rewards and become vulnerable to evolutionary replacement by more efficient systems. In this respect, Vayda's approach differs from that with which the much discussed *Report from Iron Mountain* is associated. Although there may be a stylistic resemblance, Vayda's dry calculations lead to fundamentally different conclusions from those attained by the anonymous defenders of the "war-system." The *Report from Iron Mountain* insists that there are no viable alternatives to war, if something which we may vaguely define as the American "way of life" is to be preserved. Vayda indicates that a comprehensive theory of the functions of war permits no such conclusion. If war is indeed "functional" and not a mere matter of caprice and madness, then and only then can we "proceed to try to prevent war either by seeking to eliminate the disturbances whereby the variables or activities in question are moved from their proper, desired, or acceptable state, or else by looking for alternatives to war as a counteracting response to the disturbances."

The discussant for Vayda's paper was Paul Bohannan. At the latter's request, this contribution to the Symposium has been deleted from the present volume. Remarks originally presented from the floor by Alexander Lesser in criticism of Vayda's concept of function have been expanded upon and substituted for Bohannan's critique.

The shift from the general models of the functional role of warfare proposed by Vayda to the specific model applicable to the combative Yanomamö, is the step from ethnology to ethnography. N. A. Chagnon's continuing investigation of warfare and its effects of the social structure of remote peoples in the Orinoco jungles is paralleled by a few other contemporary ethnographic studies of war, mainly in New Guinea. As Elman Service points out, this twentieth century work is of great importance for, paradoxically and despite its late date, some of it might throw light on conditions more pristinely "primitive" than those represented in monographs and other descriptions of many decades past. Service raises another problem which is of concern to a number of the contributors, authors, discussants and critics from the floor: this is the definition of war. Note, for example, that though Chagnon presents no definition of war, he plunges into warfare as an aspect of Yanomamö culture without apology. Enthusiastic as Service is about other aspects of Chagnon's paper, this failure worries him, and he compares Yanomamö "warfare" with youthful gang fighting or brawls between individuals, which are never considered "war" in our culture even by the greatest stretching of the concept. (This limiting case on the side of primitive society may be contrasted with its opposite phenomenon in complex society, as when a state attacks another with hundreds of thousands of full-time military specialists, and huge numbers of aircraft, warships, cannon, bombs, *et cetera,* yet cannot say for sure that a war does or does not exist because certain secular rituals, i.e., a congressional declaration of war, have not yet been held.)

Anthony F. C. Wallace begins the next paper with a further attempt to define war. (A similar but more sustained attempt to define war will be found at the beginning of Margaret Mead's paper.) Wallace emphasizes the sanctioned use of deadly force by trained and coordinated teams supported to some extent by a significant portion of the remaining population. From this basis Wallace launches into a general analysis of means of securing optimum mobilization of combatant and non-combatant sectors of society in the course of an episode of warfare. In the actual symposium Wallace's paper played an interesting role. After a long afternoon session, the audience was well into an equally long evening session. Yet, apart from Alland's paper at the end of the afternoon program, and apart from a few speakers from the floor, like David Aberle and Alexander Lesser, there had been little direct linkage between what was said at the symposium and the war in Vietnam, whose existence was the explicit stimulus for the meeting. Into the breach stepped Stanley Diamond whose emotional but elegantly controlled attack on Wallace's paper received the loudest and most prolonged applause of the symposium. To many in the audience, the main value of Diamond's attack was its timeliness and preoccupation with the moral problems of war in our own time, our own place, our own society. Yet even within this context there was a clash of other than moral and political views. Diamond challenged Wallace's basic definition of war. War has changed, in Diamond's view, for it no longer requires mobilization, and anthropologists had better begin to take note of this. This point was to become a major theme of the remainder of the session. It was featured in Sol Tax's remarks on the draft, E. A. Hoebel's review of the penetration of the United States Congress by the military, and Seymour Melman's detailed critique of the concept of military defense in the second half of the twentieth century.

The editors are grateful to all of the contributors for sticking their necks out. One paper, however, was perhaps particularly difficult to write, that on "Alternatives to War." In the past it seemed inconceivable that peace could exist in the presence of two or more organized religious systems. Our time is marked by the certainty that only limited coexistence is possible between two economic systems, even if one of them accepts a subordinate role. Yet Dr. Mead argues for the importance of momentarily ignoring such systemic clashes in order to offer a visionary program, "new models for world organization," that will make for denial-free distribution of life's essentials and remove the cancer of nationalism.

It is impossible to agree with all the notions and assertions of this book; similarly, it should be equally impossible not to disagree with many of the utterances which it contains. The editors are even prepared to admit the legitimacy of certain feelings of irritation over the failure of the Symposium to reach the kinds of firm conclusions which are desperately needed. But we would hope that those who are thus irritated will also accept our challenge to go ahead to better results.

December, 1967

M.F.
M.H.
R.M.

CONTENTS

FOREWORD Fink-out or Teach-in?   ix

PART I BIOLOGICAL EFFECTS OF WAR

FRANK B. LIVINGSTONE The Effects of Warfare on the
Biology of the Human Species   3
FREDERICK P. THIEME, *Discussant* The Biological Con-
sequences of War   16
General Discussion   22

PART II HUMAN AGGRESSION

RALPH L. HOLLOWAY, JR. Human Aggression: The Need
for a Species–Specific Framework   29
C. R. CARPENTER, *Discussant* The Contribution of Primate
Studies to the Understanding of War   49
General Discussion   59

PART III WAR AND DISEASE

ALEXANDER ALLAND, JR. War and Disease: An Anthro-
pological Perspective   65
BENJAMIN D. PAUL, *Discussant* The Direct and Indirect
Biological Costs of War   76
General Discussion   81

PART IV PRIMITIVE AND MODERN WAR

ANDREW P. VAYDA Hypotheses About Functions of War   85
ALEXANDER LESSER, *Discussant* War and the State   92
General Discussion   97

PART V   EFFECTS OF WAR ON
         SOCIAL STRUCTURE

NAPOLEON A. CHAGNON   Yanomamö Social Organization
and Warfare   109

ELMAN SERVICE, *Discussant*   War and Our Contemporary
Ancestors   160

General Discussion   168

PART VI   PSYCHOLOGICAL DIMENSIONS
          OF WAR

ANTHONY F. C. WALLACE   Psychological Preparations for
War   173

STANLEY DIAMOND, *Discussant*   War and the Dissociated
Personality   183

General Discussion   189

PART VII   WAR AND RECRUITMENT FOR
           A WAR SYSTEM

SOL TAX   War and the Draft   195

E. ADAMSON HOEBEL, *Discussant*   The Draft and the
United States Congress   208

General Discussion   211

PART VIII   ALTERNATIVES TO WAR

MARGARET MEAD   Alternatives to War   215

SEYMOUR MELMAN, *Discussant*   Decision Making on War
and Peace   229

EPILOGUE   235

BIBLIOGRAPHY   239

INDEX   255

WAR

Part I | BIOLOGICAL EFFECTS OF WAR

THE EFFECTS OF WARFARE ON
THE BIOLOGY OF THE HUMAN SPECIES

FRANK B. LIVINGSTONE

WARFARE, HOWEVER DEFINED, includes many different kinds of conflict. Even for the primitive Murngin of Australia, Warner (1930) lists six different kinds of "warfare," and other cultures have been equally inventive. The great technological changes in the last few hundred years have also markedly affected the nature of modern warfare. Thus, it would seem likely that there are few, if any, biological effects common to all these different warfares. "Intergroup aggression" is perhaps closest to defining my subject since I will be concerned with both the possible effects of modern, "civilized" warfare on present and future generations and the effects of past warfare on the present composition of the human gene pool. To be sure, warfare is a cultural phenomenon, but genetic change takes a long time; so that our present genes may be due to adaptations of our pre-human ancestors. Hence the genetic and demographic aspects of aggression in other animals may be of use in an analysis of human aggression.

Several possible biological effects of the various kinds of warfare come to mind, but it should be emphasized at the outset that many are only possibilities. Hence this paper, and others like it, are speculative for the most part. Wright's (1965) massive compendium contains the available demographic statistics on wars of the last few centuries—and there are many—but I know of no study which demonstrates with any certainty a specific genetic change attributable to warfare. For the most part I will be concerned with the genetic and demographic effects of war; that is, whether war has altered the gene frequencies of any population or has been a factor controlling the size of the population, but first the biological effects on the combatant populations, some of which are obvious and others not, should be outlined.

First, and most obvious, the death rate of young males is increased by warfare, and usually also the death rate of the rest of the population, particularly the weak and very young. Presumably, the birth rate should decrease for the same reasons, and this often happens. But it is a fact that the birth rate actually rose in England and some other European countries during World War II, and such a rise invariably occurs after a war. The frequencies of birth malformations also has increased during wars (Stott 1962), which seems plausible since such results can be obtained by subjecting animals to similar environmental stresses during pregnancy. The two World Wars have even had an effect on the average stature of the combatant populations. Despite the great increase in stature which has occurred in most European populations in the last eighty years, Chamla (1964) has shown that in the two decades of war there has been a decrease in stature, and Kimura (1967) has recently shown that the same decrease occurred in Japan. In all cases, however, the populations have recovered rapidly from these reversals and continued to increase their mean stature.

With the introduction of atomic weapons, the hazards of previous wars have been increased by the deleterious effects of radiation. The numerous studies of survivors of the atomic attacks on Hiroshima and Nagasaki indicate an increase in leukemia in those exposed to radiation (summarized in Neel 1963). There is an association between leukemia and chromosomal damage, so it would seem reasonable to assume that the gametes, particularly the sperm, are also affected. But detailed studies of the offspring of atomic bomb survivors produced no evidence for genetic damage by radiation (Kato, Schull, and Neel 1966). Children exposed in utero however have a much higher rate of mental retardation (Wood et al. 1967), and recently survivors of the bombing have had a very high rate of malignant lymphoma ten to fifteen years after the explosion (Shimizu 1966). The increase in radiation by military operations and testing, as well as the peaceful uses of atomic energy, have undoubtedly increased the rates of mutation to deleterious genes in the human species, but this effect of atomic warfare seems to have been overestimated, particularly by the press, political pressure groups, and in novels such as Huxley's *Ape and Essence.* In fact, evidence seems to be accumulating that changes in food habits and the increased use of a multitude of new drugs has had more effect in increasing mutations than has radiation. Recent studies on the effects of LSD on leukocytes, for example, show enormous chromosomal changes. If similar damage is present in the reproductive cells and the reports of the widespread use of this drug among college students are true, this one drug has probably caused more mutations and affected future generations more than all the atomic explosions thus far.

The last two World Wars have been responsible for enormous numbers of deaths, but it is nevertheless questionable as to whether they have had any permanent effect on the demography of the populations involved. Certainly the effects of war on the birth and death rates have caused a populational decrease. In the case of Russia during World War I and the subsequent revolution, the deficit between expected population and the actual figures was about 5,000,000 during the height of the fighting and famine, but even with Communism the population had recovered by 1927 (Lorimer 1946). In World War II approximately 9 percent of the U.S.S.R.'s and 5 percent of Germany's population were killed, while for England and France it was only 1 percent, and for the United States an infinitesimal 0.2 percent. When we consider that these slaughters only occur about once in a generation, the conclusion seems inescapable that they have no effect on the population growth or size and do not act as forces controlling the population despite the enormity of the slaughter in round figures—for the world it comes to about 51,000,000 in World War II. For Europe and the United States, the economic depression of the 1930s had almost as much effect on the birth and death rates. Today one hears frequently that the population of South Vietnam is being annihilated, but a comparison of the UN 1964 estimate and a recent one in the *New York Times* (Sunday November 26, 1967) indicates that the population has grown by about 1,700,000 or about 3 percent per year, which is average for underdeveloped countries. Furthermore, Wright's (1965) statistics show that the twentieth century has been the most lethal both in terms of numbers and percentages; so that during the Christian Era, warfare has not been a major force controlling the size of human populations. Even today the number of young men killed in automobile accidents in one year, which is about 12,000 and is less than 0.1 percent of the age group, is greater than all the American deaths in the Vietnam War up to September 1967. This limited participation of the population in wars and the extremely low percentage which are either killed or wounded has been characteristic of the United States since its birth. I'm not sure that this indicates a lack of patriotism, but it is a fact that when the capital was burning in 1814, only 0.2 percent of the population took up arms to save the country. Only in the Civil War did 10 percent of the population become engaged in fighting each other, and 1.3 percent of the population was either killed or wounded.

Given the negligible effects of modern warfare on the size of human populations, it would seem to follow that it has little effect on genetic evolution. As Haldane (1953) has emphasized, those forces which tend to limit the size of the population have the greatest effect as agents of natural selection. Aside from the effects of ionizing radiation on mutation, warfare would most likely influence the two other forces of evolution, natural selection and migration. The World Wars have been one of the major factors causing the huge migrations within and from Europe (Kulischer 1948). In this way warfare can account in part for the variability and distribution of genetic characteristics among human populations, but marked genetic differences, whether actual or postulated, must be due to natural selection.

Natural selection changes the genetic characteristics of a population by either a differential mortality or fertility of the specific genotypes. In order to be an effective agent of natural selection warfare must thus account for a significant amount of mortality or differences in fertility. Crow (1958) has devised an index which measures the amount of selection that can occur, but this does not mean that it necessarily will. It is necessary to show that different genotypes actually have fertility or mortality differing from the agent in question. The differences in mortality or fertility are expressed by differences in fitness, which is defined by geneticists as the individual's or genotype's contribution to the next generation. The problem then arises as to the magnitudes of the differences in fitness within the human species and those caused by warfare.

There are some genetic conditions, such as sickle cell anemia, for which the fitness is 0 or close to it. However, for most genetic differences, such as the blood groups, body size, or intelligence, the differences in fitness among most genotypes is perhaps 10 percent at most. With fitness differences of this order of magnitude, genetic change or evolution is much slower. For example, the sickle cell gene, for which sickle cell anemia is the homozygous state, is quite common in Africa and is generally considered to be present there because the sickle cell trait carrier or heterozygote for the gene has a relative resistance to falciparum malaria. If we assume that the high frequencies of this gene in Africa are close to equilibrium, then the sickle cell heterozygote must have a fitness of about 1.25 times that of homozygous normals. This relative fitness of 1.25 is the highest which is known for any human genotype. Under these conditions of extreme selection, it takes the sickle cell gene about 1000 years to increase from a small amount up to its equilibrium, and in order to accomplish this change malaria must have killed about 15 percent of the population every generation during those 1000 years. It has been said that malaria has killed more human beings than any other single disease or cause, and this is perhaps why we are beginning to find genetic conditions which are adaptations to this scourge.

In contrast, the previously quoted figures indicate that modern warfare could not have had much effect on the ongoing evolution of man. Even if selection was maximum or only one genotype was selected out by warfare, it could not change the fitness of a common genotype by more than perhaps 5 percent. For example, if all the selection was against the homozygotes for a particular allele and the selection was about 2 percent of the total population at the beginning, it would take about 1250 generations or 25,000 years for this allele to be replaced, or in other words, for the homozygotes to decrease from over 90 percent of the population to less than 1 percent. This emphasizes the point that most genetic change takes a very long time, and, secondly, that the human species hasn't been "civilized" long enough to have much genetic adaptation to this environment.

I think a further implication of this analysis is that the eugenists are unduly worried. It is frequently said that modern war, by selecting the healthiest and most intelligent for combat, is selecting for deleterious genes. First of all, however, the amount of possible selection is small since the percentage of the population killed in warfare itself is so minimal as to be ineffective. In addition, this percentage was highest during the Civil War, for which Hunt (1930) estimates that out of a total of 5,281,683 males in the North between eighteen and forty-five years old, 316,937 or 6 percent were killed. But, as Hunt shows, only 4 percent of Harvard graduates died in the war; so that intelligence does not seem to be decreased by war if we assume that Harvard

graduates have more than average intelligence and behave in the
same way as the population. On the other hand in World War I,
only 0.6 percent of the male population between twenty-two and
forty-nine years old died, while 1.0 percent of the Harvard graduates did (Hunt 1930:76). The patriotism of Harvard graduates
may have increased, but the genetic effects of the war on the level
of intelligence were surely minimal.

Although the genetic effects of modern warfare may not be
very great, the same may not be true for the second topic of this
paper, the effects of past warfare patterns on the present composition of the human gene pool. Since warfare is so ubiquitous
in the human species, there may be common genetic characteristics which have been selected by warfare. Human behavior has
included internecine fighting since the time of Sinanthropus and
perhaps from the time of the Australopithecines almost 2,000,000
years ago as indicated by Broom and Schepers (1946) who found
a skull with a large rock imbedded in it. During the long time
when man was a hunter, the social organization of the entire human species and consequently the warfare patterns were probably
more similar. The warfare patterns among shifting agriculturalists also seem to be more comparable throughout the world, and
most of the world's populations were at this cultural level for
some 5000 years.

In contrast to modern warfare, the continuous feuding among
hunters and shifting cultivators seems to have accounted for a
much greater proportion of the deaths and thus could have been a
major factor controlling the size of human populations. For the
Murngin, Warner (1930) estimated that there were 200 deaths
from fighting in a population of 700 adult males or 28 percent,
while accounts from New Guinea, such as Pospisil's (1958) of
the Kapauku or van Baal's (1966) of the Marind Anim, seem to
indicate an enormous toll from warfare. I have been able to find
few quantitative estimates, but Bennett, Rhodes, and Robson
(1959) have recorded a death rate from tokabu or ritual killing
among the Fore of 14 percent for adult males and Meggitt (1958)
estimated from genealogies that 25 percent of the adult males
among the Enga died from fighting. Matthiessen's (1962) account of the Dani of the Baliem River Valley also indicates a
great toll from fighting and in addition emphasizes the ritualistic
nature of warfare in New Guinea. For any one encounter or skirmish a single death on one side would frequently end the hos-

tilities, but the biannual occurrence of these wars and the intermittent raiding result in a very considerable percentage of the deaths.

Among the Indians of the Americas, warfare, although still surrounded with ritual, seems to have been to a much greater extent an attempt to annihilate the enemy. Of course, the extent of warfare varied considerably. For the late prehistoric site of Madisonville, Ohio, Hooton (1920) estimated that 22 percent of the adult male skulls had wounds and 8 percent were fractured. On the other hand, the evidence for warfare from early sites such as Indian Knoll (Snow 1948) and protohistoric sites such as Pecos (Hooton 1930) is much scantier. Ethnographically, for the Yanomamö of Venezuela a death rate of 24 percent among adult males from fighting has been recorded by Chagnon, although he thinks this is an underestimate. The Mohave of the Colorado River Valley also seem to have spent most of their time fighting, and Stewart (1947) indicates that five to seven were usually killed in a war party of fifty to one hundred, which fought perhaps once a year. For nomadic pastoralists, Wissler's (1936) compilation of population estimates of the Plains Indians shows a deficit of 50 percent for the adult males in the Blackfoot tribe in 1805, a 33 percent deficit in 1858, while during the reservation period the sex ratio rapidly approached 50-50. Ewers (1955) lists many of the recorded battles on the Northern Plains and estimates a loss of 1 percent per year for the Piegan, which would amount to perhaps 25 percent per generation. Finally, for the intensive agriculturalists of the Valley of Mexico just prior to the Spanish conquest, Cook (1946) estimates that for a population of 2,000,000, the annual death rate was about 115,000 with 15,000 due to warfare and the subsequent human sacrifice.

Cook concludes for Mexico that the 15 percent increase in the death rate due to warfare was sufficient to act as a major controller of the population. I think the evidence from areas still inhabited by hunters or primitive agriculturalists who are not under the control of a national power indicates the same conclusion, and thus by implication that warfare has been a major agent of natural selection. Warfare could also have been a major factor determining the dispersion of human populations at this cultural level, so that it would affect the other forces of evolution. The population size and consequently the amount of genetic drift, the amount of inbreeding, and the amount of gene flow among groups are all effected by population dispersion. In addition, cannibalism, which is also an ancient human trait and a frequent practice in warfare, could have been a means of transmission of a newly discovered group of virus infections which act like inherited traits (Gajdusek, Gibbs, and Alpers 1965). One, kuru, is found among the Fore tribe of New Guinea and was originally thought to be due to a single gene when it was discovered some ten years ago, but is now known to be due to a virus. However, its transmission is still a problem, and cannibalism is one possibility.

Despite these other means by which warfare may influence the genetic evolution of man, nevertheless, its major effect would presumably be by natural selection. So the question arises, selection for what? The obvious answer seems to be fighting ability, which would include both physical and psychological characteristics. Either intra-group or inter-group conflict within a species would probably lead to selection for size and strength. For humans, as well as most animals, the strong, silent? genotypes are given the most opportunities to mate. Fighting in animals leads to threat behavior, and thus threat features such as beards, manes, and natural warpaint in the form of brightly colored faces are selected for and become exaggerated. Large body size, sexual dimorphism, and these threat features tend to occur together as in the baboons who have a rigid dominance gradient and more intra-group conflict. Goodhart (1960) has proposed that beards and the distribution of body hair in man, which is similar in all human groups although the amount of hair may vary, can be interpreted in terms of threat displays. Beards cannot be explained by climatic adaptation since women and children suffer as much from cold. Neither can axillary and pubic hair, and they seem to be unexplainable in terms of any other function. But they do seem to contribute to the threatening appearance of an adult male.

Some of the body size differences among human populations may also be due to selection by intra- or inter-group conflict. The Nilotic peoples of East Africa and the Vikings of Scandinavia are among the biggest human populations and do seem to have been fighters to a much greater extent than the Pygmies of the Congo or the Bushmen, who, however, did have wars when they had the Kalahari to themselves (Schapera 1951). Of course, in order to be a selective factor success in warfare has to be related to size and strength and not to ability to ride horses, shoot poison arrows, or sneak quietly through the jungle. In any case, warfare may have been one contributing factor to body size differences, but there were surely other selective factors such as climate or nutrition.

Finally, the problem as to whether warfare has selected for any psychological characteristics, in particular aggression or bellicosity, raises the question as to the future of warfare and its inevitability. This has always been a popular topic for discussion and never more than at present. Recently two books have appeared which attribute to man an aggressive or killer instinct (Lorenz 1966; Ardrey 1966). This view has been widely publicized and implies that the solution to the problem of stopping warfare is to divert this instinctive aggression to other pursuits, for which there have been many suggestions. Sports seems to be a favorite (Lorenz 1966), but as Haldane remarked (1952:45) some time ago, "sportsmen are not usually conspicuous as pacificists." Haldane's own suggestion was "an organized struggle against the natural forces which are adverse to men," and more recently, the space race (Storr 1964) has been added to the kinds of competition which are thought to be substitutes for war.

Implicit in these suggestions is the assumption that innate aggression is the major explanation for human warfare. If this is accepted, then it implies further that differences in the amount of warfare among human populations is due to varying amounts of this genetic trait. So we are back to the explanation that the Plains Indians waged war because they were warlike. In the past this has not been a useful approach to the problem, but to reject this as an adequate explanation of human warfare, does not mean that there are no genetic differences in behavior which are due to selection by warfare. Obviously societies have to recruit individuals for the roles that are necessary for the society to survive. They do this by placing high value on these roles, which usually leads to greater procreation by the individuals who fill them. Thus, Lorenz (1966: 236) can be absolutely correct in his assertion that the Plains Indians' behavior is unduly "aggressive" due to selection by warfare because the warriors did seem to have higher fertility rates. But it still doesn't explain the presence of warfare. As a comparable example for a known genetic trait, the sickle cell gene is found in high frequencies in Africa *because* malaria is endemic there, but it is not true that Africans have survived in a malarious region *because* of their high frequencies of the sickle cell gene. The presence of this gene has little effect on the average fitness or reproduction rate of the population. And it also has little effect on the transmission of malaria despite Weisenfeld's (1967) recent effort to demonstrate such an effect. Sickle cell trait carriers get malaria but just do not die from it. In fact, there is some question as to whether they produce more gametocytes (the forms of the parasite infective to the mosquito) than normals and thus increase the transmission of the disease.

Just as there may have been some selection in some societies for aggression, there may have also been selection at other times and places for the "instinct" of non-aggression. But all human societies have had little trouble teaching their members to kill other human beings and especially those of another society. And contrary to resolutions by anthropologists there seems to be no moral revulsion involved. Man can be trained to kill as easily as other animals. Accounts of attacks by gorillas in zoos seem to indicate the same lack of revulsion or "morality," but frequently there seems to be no pleasure or viciousness either. Perhaps the fact that man has been a carnivore for a considerable length of time can account for an ability to kill efficiently, but other carnivores do not kill members of their own species as man does so often. As Scott (1962:168) says, "The comparative physiology of fighting behavior in animals yields the extremely important conclusion that the primary stimulation for fighting behavior is external; that is, there is no spontaneous internal stimulation which makes it necessary for an individual to fight irrespective of the outside environment. The physiological and emotional factors involved in the agonistic behavioral system are thus quite different from those involved in sexual and ingestive behavior."

If we conclude with Scott that human warfare is not due to any instinct, then we should be able to outline the environmental conditions that lead to warfare and explain why man kills his own species in such great numbers. Very simply, the major environmental factor is an unstable ecological community. When it invades a new area, any animal population will increase up to some optimum density and then fluctuate around this value which is approximately the carrying capacity of the population's ecological niche. Any animal population that is still expanding its range or population is thus unstable, and this has been characteristic of the great majority of human populations in the last few hundred years. This is perhaps just another way of stating a *Lebensraum* argument for war, but it raises the question as to what happens when the species runs out of *Lebensraum*. In these ecological circumstances territoriality, the defense of which leads to fighting, begins to control the size of the population. The behavior associated with territorialism evolves into all kinds of rituals, which establish a winner and a loser with little loss of life. As Wynne-Edwards (1962) points out, conventional competitions substitute for contests over real rewards, and these select for display characteristics of the competitors. Society can be viewed as an organization which provides for conventional competition.

If we apply these concepts to man, I think that first of all much of human fighting has been found in unstable ecological circumstances such as the Plains of North America after the introduction of the horse. The head hunters of many parts of New Guinea and the Iban of Sarawak also seem to be in unstable environments since some populations were expanding until recently. But the elaborate conventions involved in head hunting or coup counting, like the Geneva conventions, indicate that cultures have evolved ritual competitions which include killing members of the same society by which I mean those individuals subscribing to the same conventions. This is quite different from the competition of other animal species. It is probably due to the recent evolution of man's conventions in the last 2000 to 3000 years, but it may also be due to man's unique ability to symbol. Many anthropologists have commented that man is the only animal who knows he is going to die, which also implies he alone knows a vanquished enemy can return older, wiser, and bigger in the future.

Man's ecology is different from that of other animals in another way. He alone seems to occupy many different ecological niches, which have very different behaviors and optimum population densities associated with them. Thus, one human population very frequently eliminates or displaces another one with a different way of life. Among other animal species there is often a considerable amount of fighting among close ecological competitors, and much human warfare has been due to competition between different cultures for the same area. However, it is not usual for one group of animals to replace another of the same species. The fact that man occupies many different ecological niches with different behavior associated with them has prompted Erikson (1967) to refer to human cultures as pseudo-species. Ecologically they do act like different species, which, I think, is another reason for the great prevalence of fighting among populations of the human species. Genetically, of course, man is one species, and there are no circumstances at present where human populations seem to be undergoing the process of speciation which results in one area being shared by two genetically closed populations with different ecological niches. I don't think there is any doubt that sooner or later all mankind will be participating in a single world culture.

Most human ecological diversity has occurred since the evolution of agriculture, which is still spreading to some areas of the world inhabited by hunters. Hence, taking the world as a whole, this ecological niche is not at equilibrium. As our estimates show, warfare seems to be a major factor controlling the size of human populations among many primitive agriculturalists. Despite Warner's (1930) figures for the Murngin, the Australian Aborigines seem to have evolved a social organization which controlled the size of the population without warfare. For the most part the control of population in Australia, as well as among the Bushmen, was by infanticide. With a stable population all the territory was divided into ritually owned home bases of patrilineal kin groups whom no one would think of displacing by fighting. Each family had on the average one son and one daughter who was exchanged by various marriage systems for a wife for the son. Among the Murngin and other tribes, this was not a direct exchange but involved the participation of many other kin groups. As Warner (1937) points out, most of the fighting was over women who were not exchanged properly. But there was little warfare over space. At equilibrium and with constant resources, this social organization would appear to operate without a formal pattern of warfare as an integral, functional requisite for the maintenance of the social system. The prescriptive marriage system formed a set of rules for the allocation of women, and it was only when the rules were broken that conflict ensued.

On the other hand Matthiessen's (1962) account of the Kurelu of New Guinea and Chagnon's account of the Yanomamö seem to indicate an absence of such rules. The dominance gradient within the society was maintained by the ability of the individual male to rape or steal others' wives, which seems quite comparable to the social organization of the Hamadryas baboon. In these individualistic societies there are fewer formal rules for the allocation of women or for the rights of marriage partners. Relations between groups are also characterized by feuding and warfare, although there do not seem to be many disputes over territory. Given a stable ecological setting, a social structure will evolve rules governing interpersonal behavior. Obviously there are other causes of aggression apart from ecological instability, and such feuding seems to be found in many different human societies. The Kurelu of New Guinea, the Hatfields and McCoys of Appalachia (Jones 1948), and the Albanians (Hasluck 1967) evolved very similar social organizations. In the absence of a social structure and its rules, there will be an increased amount of aggression among the individuals of any animal species. What happened among the baboons of the London Zoo after the introduction of several females and among the mutineers on Pitcairn Island are two instances of such aggression. But the Pitcairn Islanders evolved a social organization, and I see no reason why the human species as a whole will not control its population in the near future, and then, with ecological stability, evolve a social organization with non-lethal competition for the regulation of behavior, resources, and territory.

THE BIOLOGICAL CONSEQUENCES
OF WAR

FREDERICK P. THIEME

F RANK LIVINGSTONE'S PAPER on the "Effects of Warfare on the Biology of the Human Species" can be summarized, using a simple classification, as testing the relevant data on the biological consequences of warfare in either genetic or demographic terms, and measuring the consequences in past and recent periods. He indicates distinctly different effects of warfare on the demographic and possibly on the genetic characteristics of early human populations compared to the absence of discernible effects on recent populations. My study of the subject leads me to the same conclusion Livingstone presents; namely, that modern warfare has no perceptible genetic or demographic long-term effects in the distribution of genes, sexes, age groups or other biological features of the involved populations. The effects at worst are only temporary. The technological innovations, which have changed the nature of modern warfare, make it most likely that the damage to populations in the future will be random in respect to age, sex, and genetic constitution of the affected populations. The demographic effect of future warfare, then, would be to decrease the numbers of mankind and possibly even, of course, to annihilate life. But as long as selection is random, the survivors not reduced to numbers below a few thousand in each breeding population, and no real mutational effect results from irradiation, it is difficult to see how modern warfare will have a sharp genetic effect. The eugenists of a few decades ago saw young men in the prime of life rushing into battle and being eliminated from the breeding population with dire genetic consequences. It is hard, after reviewing Wright's *A Study of War* (1965), to find that this ever was the case. Livingstone makes this clear, at least as far as the last century or so is concerned. This applies to Western European societies and their wars as well as the wars that were conducted in areas under their control. It was not so, however, for wild human societies outside the reach of Western European domination. In pre-conquest Mexico, warfare and associated slavery had a clear effect in reducing or controlling the numbers of the population. However, the length of time in which the practice was intense is probably so short as to make it ridiculous to think that any of the unique characteristics of the descendent populations can be attributable to any non-random, selective effects of human sacrifice in that area. S. F. Cook (1946) ("Human Sacrifice and Warfare as Factors in the Demography of Pre-Colonial Mexico," Volume 18) combining data from a host of historic sources and recognizing the relative unreliability of these sorts of data nevertheless arrives at some conclusions as to the demographic effects of war and sacrifice in Central Mexico. He concludes that the intensity of warfare and the institution of human sacrifice took on an almost pathological development just prior to conquest, yet the demographic consequences were small. For the century prior to 1519, the annual war losses based on his calculations were approximately one-quarter of one percent and the death rate was fifty per thousand in that population of approximately two million. The death rate was increased by warfare to the extent of only five percent. This conclusion at first glance seems at odds with reports on the rate and number of sacrificial victims. Cook refers to a ceremony reported by Duran in which the king started the sacrificial event but soon tired. He was replaced by teams of priests and helpers who worked in shifts and handled captives in four lines some two miles in length. The ceremony lasted without break for four days. The victims were done away with at the rate of about two per minute with the result that approximately 12,000 were sacrificed in this one ceremony. For all the hard work involved, the demographic consequence of this event and the century of sacrifice and warfare was merely to decrease the rate of increase of the population.

I agree with Livingstone as he speculates about the genetic consequences of warfare in certain living wild populations, such as is found in New Guinea or was known in certain Plains Indian groups prior to conquest. Indications from archaeological skeletal remains, discrepancies in the sex ratio, and other evidence suggests that there could have been significant genetic consequences of war in such populations. Whether these selective patterns existed for a period of centuries, which would be necessary to bring

about significant changes, is not known; but if so, and if warfare
in these preliterate hunting and gathering or in early agricultural
societies was as drastic as these few instances indicate, we can
conclude that in the early history of man war was possibly a significant determinant, through selection, of genetic characters of
such groups.

In view of the variety of topics to be covered by other speakers
in this symposium it would indeed be brash for me to enter into a
lengthy discussion on the nature and the purposes of warfare.
However, in order to evaluate the relative consequences of warfare on the biology of man, a few remarks are in order. First, the
difference must be noted between predation and aggression. Predation is fundamentally used by animals to supply food for themselves
and for their immediate families. Predators may hunt in packs, as
the wolf does; however, it is seldom a social activity but more
frequently an individual one. War is not an extension of predatory
behavior. Aggressive behavior, on the other hand, can take a number of forms and organizational features. It may, of course, be
interpersonal, between groups, between classes or sub-groups of
the society, and, of course, between societies. Warfare, it seems, is
fundamentally one of a group of patterns of aggressive behavior
between societies. However, cold wars, the fiscal actions of De
Gaulle, the devaluation of currency, tariffs and customs, and other
forms of intersocietal or international aggression are all too well
known to us. But when one attempts to evaluate the role of warfare in biological or genetic terms, compared to the consequences
of the whole range and types of aggressive behavior, it is clear, at
least to me, that racial discrimination, selective immigration policies, imperialistic exploitation of peoples, and a host of other
forms of behavior by societies have had a much more significant
effect on the demography or genetics of many populations than has
warfare.

Konrad Lorenz in his book *On Aggression* deals extensively with
the role of aggression in animal behavior and at the same time
with those inhibitors that make aggression selective and useful but
which control it when it becomes socially dangerous or harmful.
Lorenz contends that man is the heir of the same instinctive aggressive behavior patterns that characterize all animals. By virtue of
certain elements in his evolution—namely having been arboreal,
omnivorous, and relying on wits and cunning rather than predatory
power—he did not need to develop the inhibitors which are so

characteristically found in the fiercest of animals. Thus, he contends, we suffer from uninhibited aggression. One way of looking at our society and the condition of the world today certainly would support this point of view. Historically, some nations have been more peaceful and unaggressive than others, but this pattern does not seem to be spreading; instead, it appears that the less aggressive nations of the past are showing a great capacity for learning how to be more aggressive than they had been. New nations show this same capacity. Western European society at the same time has developed patterns of uninhibited aggression to previously unseen levels. From my point of view, however, the biological or genetic consequences of this aggressive behavior has not been from warfare but the result of other forms of social actions.

To see this from another perspective, let us look for a moment at what keeps man from achieving his full potential. We have only suggestions of what the full biological capacity of man is. In a study done in Ann Arbor, we discovered that fourteen-year-old boys seventy-five years earlier were approximately six inches shorter and thirty-one pounds lighter than the sample measured in 1953 (Martin 1953). Changes in stature of a significant amount occurred in the United States between World War I and World War II, and, of course, we are all aware of the changes that have taken place throughout the world where better nutrition, more effective public health, and improved environmental qualities have been experienced. Yet we still don't know what freedom from deprivation, from neglect, and from a host of other traditional malfunctions in our society would bring in biological development. As a side note, in 1967 we live in a society where it is probable that the highest cause of infant mortality is parental abuse. We can all list a number of other social disabilities arising from behavior that I associate in Lorenz's terms with uninhibited aggression. The degree to which I do feel this is a major factor does, however, lead me to disagree with Livingstone's conclusion that an unstable, ecological community is a major environmental factor which may explain why man employs warfare. Often territorial demands are much emphasized and appear to rationalize the occurrence of wars. The need to occupy some other nation's ecological niche, however, is not useful in explaining warfare. The desire for domination and aggression coming from nationalistic pride and other basic aggressive motivations makes warfare individually and socially satisfying and consistent with the aggressive behavior one sees played out in many other spheres of life. In a number of species, angry, aggressive acts and domination are followed by social grooming and other behavior in a friendly fashion —a moving and satisfying form of peacemaking. We had our Marshall Plan following victory and domination. Throughout our own history we have taken the view that if our enemies would but bend to our view we would then be loving and clutch them to our bosoms and overwhelm them with friendly behavior. This behavior is consistent with aggressive animal patterns and in man is a cultural complex inexplicable in terms of territorial needs. This takes me to another step, and to another point on which I do not agree with Livingstone. He seems to infer that if some form of social organization for controlling the size of populations were to be developed, warfare would be unnecessary and also the need for it would vanish if competition for territory could be reduced. In my view, the purpose of war has never been to limit the size of populations, and while this has occasionally been a momentary side effect, it is not an efficient mechanism in this regard nor can its occurrence be explained by overpopulation and territorial needs. If indeed Australian aborigines have used infanticide to control population size, I find nothing to suggest this was devised as a substitute for warfare. Certainly whether we do or do not manage to control the numbers of people in the world is irrelevant, I feel, to the question of why we do or do not have wars. The corollary to this is the irrelevance of the need for territorial expansion as an explanation for war. Protection of territory is a powerful motivation for resisting aggression, but, in my view, the motivation initiating wars and inspiring the troops can seldom be attributed to any appeal to the men to march away from their familiar territorial home to provide *Lebensraum* for their compatriots. They march off—now fly off— and, to the extent that they have a cause, with other things in mind.

In conclusion, I agree with Livingstone that the demographic or genetic consequences of warfare, *per se,* are minimal, unless we postulate an annihilating hydrogen bomb war. On the other hand, it appears to me that the biological consequences of social malfunction associated with aggression and which lie behind warfare, can and do have deep-seated consequences on the biology of our own population and of mankind, past and present. Improvements in the conditions which will enhance the quality of the lives of men the world over will do more to change the human biology than has been done by warfare.

Frederick P. Thieme

21

As a loyal Darwinist, I have left unanswered, as has Livingstone, the question "What does war do?" "Why does it exist?" I am confident, however, in leaving these questions open for others in the symposium to attack, that the answer, or answers, are not likely to be found in any biological function or natural selective role of warfare. That, to me, is the major conclusion of Livingstone's paper.

ROBERT M. ADAMS (*University of Chicago*): It was asserted by the speaker that the demographic effects of past wars involving civilized, urban societies have been not only short-lived but very small in relation to the scale of those societies. It seems to me that this judgment rests upon an excessively narrow definition of the effects of warfare, and hence that it should not be allowed to pass without question.

A measure in terms of casualties directly resulting from warfare is misleading in that it reduces the entire syndrome of militarism to acts of organized physical violence. To be sure, without at least the threat of such violence, the remainder of the syndrome would have little meaning. But as anthropologists we ought to be concerned not merely with "body count" but with the broad deformations produced by militarism in the whole range of political, social and economic institutions. And the suggestion that the total demographic impact of militarism is slight only can arise from a willingness to disregard those of its effects which were not the direct consequence of hostilities but were mediated through other institutional changes.

For example, consider the frontier zones of the great empires of antiquity. I think it can be shown beyond any reasonable doubt that massive shifts in settlement patterns were imposed by long-standing imperial rivalries, in spite of the fact that only occasionally were these rivalries punctuated by campaigns resulting in significant numbers of casualties. In the interim, populations were induced—whether voluntarily or not is immaterial—to abandon zones of danger and resettle elsewhere, leading to radically different densities of settlement, forms of urbanism, and associated policies of state and private investment. This may be seen in a contrast of the imperial heartlands of Rome and Byzantium, as well as their Parthian, Sassanian and Arab adversaries, with the deep, disputed region in Armenia and Mesopotamia over which they contended.

I will freely concede that the example is a somewhat specialized one. But the underlying criticism of the approach of the speaker is general.

ALEXANDER LESSER (*Hofstra University and Columbia University*): If our two speakers are correct, then a lot of time and effort has been wasted in achieving a nuclear test ban treaty—wasted because apparently in their view the radiation that nuclear tests release in the atmosphere is of no importance genetically or biologically to the present and future of the human race (and by implication to life on earth). Does this also apply by implication to current efforts to secure international agreements to restrict or limit nuclear arms escalation? And in this nuclear age does it also apply to nuclear war itself?—that is, is their thesis that war (based on their evidence from past wars) has no appreciable effect on man genetically or demographically an assessment of any and all wars—those to come as well as those of the past? A good many biologists and other scientists have taken a position opposite to theirs, and in so doing contributed greatly to the achievement of the nuclear test ban treaty. I cannot understand how "The Effects of Warfare on the Biology of the Human Species" can be discussed without meeting the questions raised by biologists involved in that achievement and the universal recognition that Hiroshima and Nagasaki and the nuclear age have changed for all time the relations of warfare to the biology and the very existence of man. I do not see how these questions can be simply disregarded and avoided in a symposium on war that has anything to do with the realities of 1967.

DR. THIEME: I don't want to apologize for my point of view. I was discussing a particular paper and didn't try to extend myself beyond that. But I must say that data supporting the point of view that there are genetic, biological, or demographic consequences for failing to have a test ban are non-existent. We can speculate that one consequence of hydrogen bomb warfare would result in the annihilation of all living fauna. One can, I suppose, assume less totally destructive consequences. But if the consequences of such an intermediate war are non-random in their selection and if the number of individuals remaining in each breeding population are over 5000 or so, and the effects of this radiation are not damaging to the genetic qualities, then the damage of this sort of limited war will not be seen in genetic terms. By contrast, the consequences of such a war in social terms, in terms of the *quality* of lives, in terms of all the things that make life meaningful, would of course be immense. But if you are talking solely about genetic damage, the consequences, I say, are beyond our power to determine. This is *not* to say, however, that I condone such a war or even anticipate that it will be somewhat less in importance because it may not have serious genetic consequences.

DAVID RABOY (*Rhode Island College*):   I would like to point out the various implications of your discussion of nuclear warfare, particularly in regard to small populations (a point that was omitted in both presentations).

If populations are affected biologically by nuclear warfare to any extent, and if certain basic foods, such as lichens in the northern areas of the globe, attract certain kinds of nuclear radioactive material, i.e., Strontium 90, then it is likely (and there is some evidence for this) that certain groups of eskimos, for example, would be severely affected. Now, my question is this: is it not conceivable that smaller, isolated populations like the eskimos, would be more directly affected by this radioactive material than large populations? And, if this is possible, might it not be important to look at *segments* of a large population rather than at the population as a whole (segments, for example, of the Japanese population rather than the population of Japan as a whole)?

DAVID ABERLE (*University of British Columbia*):   Although I feel a little bit confined by the question as to whether warfare causes genetic changes, I will nevertheless address myself to it. The matter of biological warfare has not been mentioned and yet we know that preparation of biological warfare exists. Presumably, the effects of such warfare on a population would not be random; so it might turn out that war *does* have some genetic effect after all.

STEVEN POLGAR (*University of North Carolina*):   I believe that Professor Thieme has somewhat simplified Professor Livingstone's ecological argument and I would like to hear Professor Livingstone rebut on that particular point.

DR. LIVINGSTONE: My paper was an attempt to assess the genetic effects of warfare on the human species. For this reason it was deliberately confined to the warfare which has or is occurring. But it did not imply that all kinds of warfare now imaginable or possible would have no genetic or demographic effects. Obviously an H bomb holocaust could exterminate mankind; that it would have no effect is Lesser's generalization, not mine. Given the many different kinds of biological organisms which have been mentioned as possible agents in biological warfare, obviously there could be many different genetic effects, depending on which was used and on the mortality rate. We do know instances in the human species of genetic resistance to disease. Atomic warfare would also have effects on Arctic populations but on everyone else too, and I am not sure the Arctic would suffer more proportionally.

My disagreement with Thieme is to a great extent the age-old argument in anthropology concerning the consciousness of function. Does the population practicing a cultural trait such as infanticide, aggressive warfare, or abstention from eating pork comprehend the adaptive value of their behavior? I don't want to defend the functions I attributed to the first two nor even the usual one attributed to the third, but in general I think the answer is no. Anthropologists or scientists in general develop functional explanations which are a part of their scientific models, and neither man nor the other animals have any idea as to why they act the way they do. The ordinary activities of any animal population are such that they usually result in at least a doubling of the population every generation. It is thus a legitimate scientific question as to why most animal populations are comparatively stable and what factors contribute to this stability.

Finally, Adams' comment is quite correct. There are many other consequences of warfare. There seem to be instances such as Northern Ceylon and parts of the Middle East, where the destruction of warfare was so great that the area never recovered from the devastation. But I also remember the graphic pictures of the front lines in France in World War I which are now as green and lush as ever; so that there seem to be other factors involved in the recovery of the land as well as of the population. But this also raises the point that some wars in the past have had grave consequences for specific human populations. For the most part I was concerned with how the selective effects of warfare could change the genetic characteristics within a population. But one can also consider selection to operate among populations; so that if one is completely eliminated there is considerable genetic change. Such wars of extermination have been common and perhaps the Indian Wars of the United States are the best examples of the extermination of whole peoples, which certainly have genetic consequences in the sense of the loss of a whole population of genes.

Part II | HUMAN AGGRESSION

HUMAN AGGRESSION:
THE NEED FOR A SPECIES-SPECIFIC FRAMEWORK

RALPH L. HOLLOWAY, JR.

INTRODUCTION

THIS PAPER IS BEING WRITTEN in a surrounding aura of violence, for it is Summer, 1967. Has there ever been an era without aggression and violence, and are not these a natural penumbra of the human condition? History surely indicates that violence and conflict have been a constant concomitant of the human condition, although the tempos have varied considerably between allegro and adagio.

My tack in this article is to compare the aggressive components of man's behavior with those of other animals. There is hardly any question that academic and public interest in this theme is very pronounced—a rash of biologically oriented books have been placed before the public treating this very issue: Konrad Lorenz's *On Aggression* (1966), Robert Ardrey's *The Territorial Imperative* (1966), The Institute of Biology's Symposia, *The Natural History of Aggression* (Carthy & Ebling, 1964) are a few examples. The major issue that comes from these efforts revolves about the very nature of human aggression. Is it innate, an instinct, or is it learned? Do animal studies provide us with illuminating frameworks to further our understanding of human aggression, or not? Do we need a species-specific theory of human aggression? Can anthropology, particularly the study of human evolution, give us any insights into these important questions?

Actually, what is said about human aggression in this paper is

Part of the literature research for this paper was supported by the Council for Research in the Social Sciences, whose support is gratefully acknowledged. I also wish to thank Professors Marvin Harris and William Torrey, Columbia University, for reading an earlier version of this manuscript and offering many helpful criticisms and suggestions. Naturally, I am responsible for any inaccuracies or fallacies in this paper.

somewhat irrelevant to the theme of this symposium. Let me explain. War is, after all, as von Clauswitz wrote long ago, simply an organized extension of politics carried to a different level. It is an organized activity directed by rational decisions by political bodies whose membership is infinitesimal compared to the aggregates involved in actual combat. Abel (1941) showed very clearly in his study of factors operating in several European wars that warfare cannot be understood by recourse to individual psychology. Aggression, outside of how politicians use the term, is an individual act presupposing some emotional basis. Abel showed that rational decisions to make war go well in advance of the emotional, aggressive exacerbations usually thought of as the direct cause of war. (For an excellent discussion of this, see Burton 1964.) Furthermore, human aggression cannot be discussed without reference to the kinds of socio-economic conditions under which men live, or better, try to live.

This is one of the most disappointing and infuriating aspects of the recent attempts by a few biologists and dramatists to explain human aggression and violence by reference to animal studies, instincts, death drives, and the like. Lorenz (1966) for example, claims that we must understand our animal nature and phylogenetic experience before we are engulfed in a species-wide disaster. Ardrey (1966) re-echoes this line and draws a convenient equation between private property and territorial behavior in other animals. Some writers have called for standardized displacement activities patterned after many ethological examples, e.g., worldwide games, Olympics, et cetera. This is to let the animal aggression in us spill over into nonviolent beneficial activities rather than in harmful aggression. Few have had very much to say about the social and economic conditions confronting most of the human race, and this symposium is not exceptionable in that respect, aside from Professor Alland's contribution.

In other words, if man goes about killing off his own species, let us look to lower animals that show far more biological wisdom in their social habits. Or, let us make sure that private property (free enterprise) stays as it is, since it is obviously distributed justly, according to evolutionary and biological principles. Or, let us institute displacement games for everyone to play to dampen our aggressive overdrive.

To be frank, such lines of reasoning often seem like rationalizations for the status quo. These formulations are, in spite of the possible well-meaning intent, conservative forms of evading the central critical issues concerning the human condition. What faces most humans is poverty, starvation, substandard health, exploitation, increasing relative and absolute deprivations, disease, poverty of self-identification and evaluation, and little if any chance for meaningful self-participation in the "grandeur of human adaptation, civilization."

To put the matter in more simple relief, the problems of human aggression and violence are not up for academic grab-bagging along ethological, psychoanalytic, or displacement lines of research. We know that man has awesome potentialities for aggression and violence, and we know a great deal about the inequities of socio-economic distribution. The real problem facing men is not to better understand lower animals, but to implement drastic social changes throughout the world; to find a way to structure power on a world-wide sharing basis, to prevent the social conditions that lead to violence and war. This problem is a political one, not a biological or psychological one.

Nevertheless, insofar as other authors have made claims about equivalence of human and other animal aggression (and these are few) and its relation to the theme of warfare, there is an academic responsibility to provide a counterreaction against such views. I hope my own academic grab-bagging will be seen in this light. For what I suggest is hardly unique or original, and is only relevant to the major theme of this Symposium in the terms I have already discussed. The study of human aggression, like the phenomena itself, is beyond the competence of any one individual or discipline. Psychology, sociology, anthropology, zoology, ethology, anatomy, and physiology, and even political science have contributions to make. Since I am a physical anthropologist, concerned with man's evolution, I will concentrate on this area, and following a brief critique of certain recent biological writings declaring human aggression as instinctual, I will argue for the need for viewing human aggression in the context of a larger framework, and finally present a few ideas concerning man's earliest adaptations (biosocial) and their possible place in the development of a theory of human aggression and violence.

HUMAN AGGRESSION: INSTINCTIVE, INNATE, OR LEARNED?

Most discussions on the nature of human aggression have tended to gravitate between two poles: viewing it as direct (sometimes identical) *instincts* inherited through evolution from other animals; and viewing aggression as learning or cultural conditioning. Neither extreme viewpoint seems to fit the human case, or that for any other vertebrate animal. An enormous amount of zoological, psychological, and sociological literature provides examples of the manipulation of aggression through physiological, psychological, ecological and social psychological restructuring. Proponents of both extremes have usually ignored the greater weight of evidence from many disciplines that aggression, however defined, has both physiological and learning components involved in its genesis and expression. For reviews on this controversy and empirical findings from different disciplines, the reader is referred to Scott (1958); Berkowitz (1962, 1965); Buss (1961); Lorenz (1966); Ardrey (1966); Carthy and Ebling (1964); Bernard et al (1957); Durbin and Bowlby (1937); McNeil (1965, particularly 14–41); Masserman (1963). (See also Leach 1966, 1967, for critique of ethological positions, and Holloway, in press). (I am not including the psychoanalytic frameworks of Freud and others in this paper. It should be obvious that these positions are very close to some ethological positions, particularly in terms of instincts, death wishes, and so on.)

Aggression is most often defined as "behavior where goal is the injury of some person or object" (Berkowitz 1965:302) which stems mainly from Dollard et al (1939) treatise on aggression and frustration. Scott (1958:1) uses the word to refer to fighting, or the act of inflicting attack. Buss (1961:1) defines aggression as a response that delivers noxious stimuli to another organism. Note that neither Buss' nor Scott's definition includes any explicit or implicit reference to intent. As human beings greatly concerned with aggression, its genesis, and hopefully its control, we are concerned very much with intent. Whether other animals engaged in aggressive actions harbor intents in the manner we are accustomed is an unanswerable question. It seems reasonable that actions may occur that do not harbor aggressive intent in terms of injury, but which are interpreted as such. On the other hand, it seems pointless to deny that much aggressive action has the intent of injury behind

it. The reason for discussing this aspect of definition is not to quibble whether or not this or that instance of defined aggression was
intended on the part of the actor. The reason is to point out but
one tricky aspect of studying aggression: interpreting an action as
aggressive depends on an appraisal of the cue functions or environmental stimuli which help to activate an animal to an aggressive
action, and also depends on the internal state of the animal in terms
of its readiness for action and *its* appraisal of the outside cue or
stimulus. To some extent, this is an artificial problem with human
beings because we have some basis for sharing our human experi-
ences. When we are talking about nonhuman behavior, however,
the cue definitions or appraisal of the environmental stimuli (such
as one animal's motor actions toward another), the definition is
ours, not the animal's.

This would be a minor quibble were it not for the fact that
there appears to be a recrudescence of the idea that humans
possess an instinct toward aggression and warfare. Both Lorenz
(1964, 1966) and Ardrey (1966) have tried to re-establish this
instinct in man.[1] An instinct is generally understood to be a quite
specific response pattern, invariant in its development, maturation, and expression, which occurs in the presence of a quite specific cluster of stimuli from the environment. As such, it is
regarded as an innate, genetically determined pattern, which
comes about without reference to, or in absence of, learning.
(See Thorpe 1963 for a review on the history of this concept;
also Lehrman 1953 for a critique.) The success and increasing
sophistication of the ethologist school has focused on the innate
and relatively fixed action patterns of numerous animals, and
elaborate studies have been attempted to demonstrate the almost "key-in-lock" relation between certain stimuli and fixed ac-

[1] On the other hand, it is curious to read Lorenz's (1967) remarks concerning ritualization in animals and man. In this publication Lorenz is careful to
state that the ". . . role played by genetic inheritance in the evolution and
maintenance of phylogenetically evolved rituals is, of course, taken over by
tradition in cultural ritualization" (p. 280). For Lorenz (see also Huxley,
1967) the functioning of rituals in human groups are analogous with those
occurring in lower animals. I am not sure whether this means that Lorenz is
not as adamant about human instincts or whether he regards ritualized behavior patterns as exceptions to human instincts inherited from other animals. For Ardrey (1966) the behavioral dynamics of human adaptation are
given as identical homologies with other animal patterns.

tion patterns of motor sequences. The example of the male stickleback responses to the red belly of another male is well known. In addition, there has been a great deal of success in interpreting such behavior patterns, in terms of the environmental releasers within the framework of adaptation and natural selection. It is particularly this latter emphasis, that of adaptedness of behavior in the ecological context, that augurs such optimism for the study of animals other than man.

It should be noted that I have been discussing *instinct,* not *instinctual,* which seems so loosely defined (see Huxley 1967 and Lorenz 1967) as to include any aspect of behavior involving drive or central states of motivation. If it is this loose, what utility does the concept have, and how does one avoid the Aristotelean fallacy of labeling differently organized processes with the same rubric? If one man attacks another because the latter trespassed on his "territory," and a baboon attacks another because it takes a peanut outside of "prescribed" limits, are we to say that in both cases there is the same *instinctual* basis for aggressive response? Motivational or drive states don't operate in vacuum: cue stimuli are necessary, and how these are defined by an animal depends on how the animal has organized its experience, and how it has been programmed both biologically and socially. One cannot realistically argue for cue-sameness between man and baboon (or other animals) simply by noting the response. One must know the proximal stimulus for each beast, before one can argue for sameness.

Most of the criticism directed against the ethologists have revolved around the importance of learning in the genesis of fixed action patterns. While there is still debate, there appears to be a greater appreciation that both innate and learning phenomena must be taken into account in the behavior of all vertebrates and possibly those lower in the animal kingdom. Does man have an instinct toward aggression? Does he have any instincts? If understood in the usual sense of a fixed invariant pattern of action directed toward some definite invariant cluster of stimuli, there appear to be precious few (if any) examples of instincts in man, and no evidence for an aggressive instinct.

This does not mean that the human infant, however, does not possess fixed action patterns. The sucking reflex, seeking or head-turning toward a source of stimulation, the smiling response, crying, possible grasping and walking, are examples of relatively fixed action patterns that undergo wide changes as the animal matures (see Eibl-Eibesfeldt 1967). These types of patterns seem equally applicable to other animals with the exception of smiling, crying and walking. But the important question is: to what extent are the adult responses the same kind of fixed action patterns? It is precisely here that the anthropologist, and indeed other social scientists and biologists, part company with the more adamant ethological frameworks.

Human aggression shows neither motor nor sensory constancy in the ethological sense. The range of stimuli that can produce acts of aggression for man is enormous, as are the ways in which he can manifest his aggression. What are the critical sign stimuli for the human which act to release stereotypical adaptive responses? What are the invariances of the cue functions in the human environment not mediated by arbitrary symbols that help to release specific motor patterns built up through evolution by natural selection? Red feathers, blue gewgaws, green turf, butyric acid, white eyelids, the exposed neck, white tails, et cetera, et cetera, have been identified for numerous animals. What are the critical sign stimuli that make up the human "unwelt"? The question is not about human aggressive responses to various stimuli. The sordid history of man attests well to the fantastic plurality of stimuli that can be cooked up to elicit aggression. How natural are they? Skepticism about human instincts is not any attack on the animal nature of man or an arrogant claim that man does not act according to natural and man-made laws. Such skepticism need not blind anyone to the possibility of innate dispositions in man to define certain environmental contexts as inimical to their interests and to act aggressively toward such clusters.

Man, like any other animal, is an evolutionary product. It would be a strange exception indeed if natural selection during the last two million years had not acted on behavior, particularly since man is a highly gregarious animal as are most of his closest relatives, the apes and Old World monkeys. Numerous animal studies on both wild and domesticated forms show conclusively that temperamental variables are operative in all species and can be varied through training, or heightened or lowered through genetic selection (see Hafez 1962). The biological basis for such variations, as for example between basenji or terrier dog breeds and cocker spaniels have not been demonstrated (see Scott and Fuller 1965). Indeed the actual biological basis for differences in aggression between wild and domesticated rats, mice, or different species of primates have yet to be demonstrated. This hardly means that biological variables do not exist that help account for the differences. While there has been much fruitful work on the anatomical and physiological underpinnings of behavior, such as rage and attack, there is precious little in the way of relating these in a comparative way to different animals and anchoring these to concrete anatomical and physiological differences.

While we often think of aggression as maladaptive, it is obvious that under certain conditions aggression is an asset to an animal when it prolongs its life and opportunities for passing its genes to the next generation. Animals are up against things from members of their own species as well as from different species, e.g., predators. Man is hardly an exception, and it should occasion no surprise that he is biologically capable of perceiving threat to his existence and reacting to such threats aggressively.

While man evolved in a social context, as did many other animals, his social adaptations were of supreme importance in his evolutionary history, and perhaps unique in their manifold complexity. Selection operated not only on his aggressive potentialities, but on the rest of his social behavior as well. Man is capable of great degrees of cooperation, empathy, sympathy, sacrifice, the deferment of gratification, exceedingly strong bonds to others closely related to him, and extraordinary ties with numerous symbolic constructs involving religious, ideological, and material matters. In other words, man's evolution has involved a number of complex interacting variables, and we cannot hope to understand man or his evolution without reference to his social matrix. One of the major tasks facing the anthropologist is to unravel this matrix and relate the numerous variables to adaptive and selectional processes.

NEED FOR AN EXPANDED FRAMEWORK

Looking back at the definitions of aggression mentioned earlier, these are mainly drawn from works that have a highly experimental bent. I think that our understanding of human aggression must encompass more than the laboratory demonstrations compatible with or dependent upon the definitions give. This is hardly meant as any slight to the empirical studies that are able to delimit and vary external and internal variables in their study of human and other animal aggression. It is argued here, however, that we need a species-specific framework[2] of aggression, and such a framework must integrate the aggressive components of man's behavior with the rest of his social and psychological, and biological matrix. Man is the only animal with language and an adaptation based on the sharing and use of arbitrary symbol systems. He is the only animal with plural role responsibilities and the animal who lives under differential power allocations that can be decided arbitrarily, i.e., without reference to biological attributes. His brain is unique as are his behavioral processes, albeit he shares many aspects of his behavioral processes with other animals. The organization and ontogenetic development of his brain is unique—or better—species-specific, as Lenneberg (1967) has so well argued. His development and behavioral expression is species-specific, just as the development of a cat's behavior differs from that of the dog, mouse, chicken, or the chimpanzee differs from the baboon. In addition, man is in constant interaction with his peers, himself, a material world, symbol systems, strangers, enemies, friends, and kin. (See Mead 1963b, particularly pp. 93–99.)

Nonhuman animal studies show that all animals are capable of aggression. There seems, however, to be fair agreement that animal aggression is not constant but fairly rare and that the stimuli evoking aggressive responses are specific to the animal's habitat and involve discrete cues associated mostly with mating and territorial behavior (see Collias 1944, Eisenberg 1966 for reviews; also Schneirla 1965 for a general theoretical treatment in terms of approach and avoidance; for specific examples relating to primates, see Hall 1964, DeVore 1965, and Southwick 1964). There seem to be no animals who attack purely for attack's sake, the

---

[2] I am using *species-specific* in the sense of special characteristics for different animals (see for example Rheingold 1967, p. 288) to underline the point that not only are the biological attributes of man unique, particularly his brain, but also ontogenesis in terms of interaction with a cultural milieu, and the nature of his social relations are also unique—that is, specific to man. This does not mean that other animal studies cannot be used for purposes of comparison, or that they cannot provide heuristic frameworks with which man may be examined. I do mean that man's behavior, in the holistic sense, cannot be reduced to the same frameworks available for describing nonhuman animals, including primates.

attack being related to the quest for food, as in canids and felids, or when challenged by predatory species or by members of their own or different species for territory or mates. As Lorenz and others have pointed out, most animals enjoy the possession of behavior and sometimes structural mechanisms which serve to inhibit further attack that might be injurious, as in the wolf which bares its neck to inhibit the onslaught of its opponents.[3] Perhaps there are postures and vocalizations that have an appeasement function in man, such as the averting of eyes, cringing, tears, et cetera, but it should be equally clear that these do not offer any guarantees against further aggression or injury from an opponent. There are several studies on facial and bodily gestures in different primate species which demonstrate a wide range of adaptations serving to communicate possible aggressive intent and submission on the part of the actors (see Altmann 1962, 1967, Andrews 1963, Hall 1964, Struhsaker 1967). It does not seem unlikely that we retain, as Darwin suggested, some of these non-verbal communication devices to allay violent actions and reactions, but it also seems certain that there is a heavy cultural or learning component in the genesis of such gestures, and it remains a problem to decide which are universal or specific for different cultures. The fact that they exist in all cultures suggests that conflict is a structural property of human societies. In the human case, the range of stimuli that can evoke aggression is exceedingly varied and complex, and aggressional tendencies can last long beyond the emotional state of anger, and can continue to occur in the absence of the attitude of hostility.

Perhaps analogues to the "displacement activities" of other animals often discussed by ethologists (e.g. Lorenz 1966) fits in here. Activities such as sports, hobbies, et cetera, probably aid in "draining off" heightened levels of arousal or excitation that involve the degree to which the central nervous system is "tuned up." The state or pitch of excitement can be increased by a fantastic plurality of stimuli (even writing a paper), however, many of an internal symbolic nature, such as in ego-evaluation, paranoia, et cetera. However, even if "displacement activities" do have this function, it is doubtful whether one can claim that they solve the problems of human aggression. Certainly the matter of

---

[3] This view is, however, open to question (see Scott, 1967, in Symposium on Canine Behavior, in the American Zoologist).

vicarious substitutes for aggression, as in movies depicting violence, boxing matches, working to decrease aggression is an issue open to question (see Berkowitz, op. cit. for review).

The major framework in psychological thought regarding human aggression revolves about the "frustration-aggression" hypothesis offered by Dollard et al in 1939. There seems to be little doubt that frustration is a major stimulus for provoking aggressive responses, but it is debatable whether the original formulation that all aggression stems from frustration, or that aggression always follows frustration is accurate (see Berkowitz 1962, 1965 for critique).

Several studies of primate behavior (see DeVore 1965, Mason 1967, Schrier et al 1965) show that monkey and ape offspring are highly motivated toward play and contact with peers, adults, and inanimate objects, and are highly curious, observations which apply to man and other young mammals. Through play and mock combat, the young animals learn skills of social interaction, and eventually their position in dominance terms relative to their peers. They enlarge their sphere of knowledge about their environments, and part of this enlargement is the outcome of aggressiveness. The human animal is hardly an exception. In line with the concept of species-specific behavior, the ontogenetic or developmental tendencies (how behavior changes with maturation) offer the best evidence for species-specific patterns of organ development and functioning. The so-called critical periods of birds, sheep, dogs, et cetera, are familiar examples. In the human case, a child acquires different behavioral patterns as it passes from birth to adolescence (see Gessel 1950). The language abilities, starting at about one to two years are a good example of species-specific patterns of neural and behavioral development. These also involve a species-specific pattern of social and emotional nurturance for their healthy development. Associated at least in part with the specific neural events that accompany human development, there are patterns of psychological development centering about the construction of the child's ego, his moral sense, his reality picture and abilities for concrete and abstract thought, his pleasure in controlling his body from proprioceptive impulses, and his aggressiveness. The studies of Goodenough (1931), Bender & Schilder (1936), Schilder (1942), and the numerous studies of Piaget (1926, 1929, 1954) are definitive in this regard.

Goodenough (1931) for example, found definite developmental patterns of rage expression and control during the course of child maturation. In general, as the brain grows and so does the child's reality picture of the world, his expectations of his parents' and peers' behavior, and his control of rage. In early stages, rage is sudden, explosive yet quick to subside and be forgotten. With maturation the thresholds for such expression rise, but once exceeded, the rage and anger are longer in duration, and subsequent brooding or hostile periods are prolonged. These changes point to neural and ego variables, involving components of inhibition and facilitation, as well as an enlarged capacity for sustaining particular memories. I will return to this aspect later when I discuss the early evolution of man as a set of strategies to promote a longer period of dependence and nurturance so that the enlarged brain had time to mature.

Other authors have studied children's aggression, and there seems to be wide agreement that aggression increases during the early years, reaches a peak, and then tapers off as social control factors and the child's realization of deferment of gratification by the environmental surroundings come into play. It is worth stressing something that Schilder pointed out some time ago: that much of the destructive elements of child playing has natural concomitants of learning and is often accompanied by a constructive aftermath.

Allied with this explorative and constructive aspect, there is yet another realm of species-specific development of the human child—that of his ego structure, his self-concept, his evaluation of self-worth, in an ever-changing external (and internal) environment. *As definitions of the child change through a constantly interacting feedback process of his own development and how adults and other peers perceive and treat him, so do the demands made upon him. It is in this area that frustrations are practically impossible to avoid—they are structured into the process.*

There is another aspect to human species-specific behavioral organization, particularly at the social structural level, which must enter into any framework of human aggression. The cohesion of human societies depends on mutual cooperation in economic tasks, and these require different degrees of role affiliations. A man often has three roles—those of father, husband, and worker. If the social structure has additional complexities,

the roles proliferate, and the complexities and contingencies of
each role enlarge. Roles depend on tasks, and roles place commitments and burdens upon people. The human animal, because
of his social adaptation, is perhaps unique in the fact of plural
role responsibilities, each attended by symbolized, arbitrary
codes for conduct. These provide a natural structure not only
for beneficial adaptation to varying difficult environments, but
also for the production of frustrations (see example, Cartwright
1950, Coser 1963, Mead 1963, Murphy, 1957).[4] As animals,
humans are highly egoistic, emotional, and dependent. His closest relative, the chimpanzee, evokes the greatest amount of empathy among its human observers. Moods, personal attachments
to objects and other peers, infants, dominant males, et cetera,
seem to be a common theme in the primate literature, and these
effects seem particularly heightened and expanded to symbolic
stimuli when one deals with man. In other words, there is a matter here of what might be called (to reflect our lack of understanding and ignorance) a "sentiment structure"[5] which figures
in the species-specific patterns of human behavior, both socially
and individually. The task is to define this structure, understand
its components and their interactions, and place this structure in
an evolutionary, adaptive framework. This is why our framework
of human aggression must be enlarged; why we must reject any
simplistic incantation of direct instincts. It is largely through his
"sentiment structures" that man is capable of the frantic antics
of cathection upon diverse symbol clusters, is able to fan up and
maintain hostilities in thought and deed toward symbol clusters
and their human associations, and can be manipulated by those
who understand too well what men need, and what frustrations

---

[4] I am not concerned here with the possible eufunctions of conflict and aggression as derived from Simmel by Coser 1956, and elaborated by other
social scientists. For a recent survey into this problem, see Zawodny 1966
Vol. I and II.

[5] Lorenz (1966) uses the concept of "militant enthusiasm" to imply a sort
of collective or individual increase of tonicity to the body which can be
brought about by certain symbol clusters and which figures so heavily in
fanaticism and aggression. I believe this concept is one of the most important
topics raised in Lorenz's book and hope that he will pursue this topic further
in later publications. My use of "sentiment structure" would include this
proclivity or phenomenon.

are most capable of diminishing the individual evaluation of himself. These considerations lead to the following formulation that the capacity for human aggression is an outcome, in part, of natural selection for heightened sentiment structures focused about self-identity and cooperative social structure. Natural selection for complex and prolonged cooperation has endowed man with greater degrees of affect interplay than in other animals. These are necessary for other-commitment which develops through self-commitment. But the social and symbolic structures which permit him to perform shared tasks to insure his existence also insure frustration, pain, and group conflict. In short, groups mean conflict. Groups mean figure and ground, where each sees the other sometimes as a figure, sometimes ground. Perceptions are selective and structured, and then become foci for resistance. Conflict, or forays of imposition, are structured into existence by the very fact of group identifications. Aggression may be defined as the imposition of the self (either individual or group identity) or any definition of the self, on another (individual, group, object, abstraction). Imposition may be defined as any statement (speech, motor act, gesture, action) which acts to maintain figure from ground against resistance.

The human brain might be viewed as an organization of tissue and its programming which evolved to cement environmental stimuli into figure-ground anchorages, where symbol systems are the basis for organizing experience into anchorages that facilitate social control through communication. Symbol systems permit arbitrary figure-ground representations to be defined. The adaptiveness of this rests in the fact that power relations can be established which provide social solidarity and implementation of cooperative tasks, *and these can be defined independent of biological variables.*

HUMAN EVOLUTION AND AGGRESSION

It is impossible, however, to do more than speculate about human origins and make educated guesses about the mechanics and dynamics of early human adaptations. This section is thus admittedly speculative, but it is hoped that the speculations might lead to some critical thinking and dialogue about the nature of man and how he came to be.

It is convenient to start with what seem to be reasonable conclusions of some important variables that were involved in the early evolution of man. No attempt is made here to produce a complete list (see Count 1958, Hockett and Ascher 1964, Spuhler 1959).

1. The evolution of the brain, mainly involving an enlargement of the cerebral cortex. The brain enlarged from roughly 500 cc 1.75 million years ago to about 1450 cc at present. (For details, see Holloway 1966; in press, a; in press, b, concerning the significance of this parameter.) It is important to note, however, that this evolution involved more than simple expansion; it also reorganized the different neural tracts and nuclei that make up the brain. While there are no new structures in the human as compared to ape or monkey brains, quantitative shifts between different neural components (i.e., reorganization) resulted in both qualitative and quantitative differences in behavioral processes. This reorganization involved more than the cortex; it also involved the sensorimotor nuclei in the brain stem, the reticular formation, limbic and septal nuclei. It is probable that the cerebellum, which helps to integrate fine motor movements and proprioception, was enlarged, if not reorganized.

Appreciation of this cannot, of course, be based on appraisal of the cranial capacity alone, but must be based on logical considerations of comparative neuroanatomy and the obvious musculoskeletal changes known from early hominid fossils. Of particular interest is the fact that the major expansion of *cranial capacity* occurred after the Australopithecines, i.e., after stone tools were already being produced according to standardized patterns. This, however, does not mean that brain evolution had not occurred before this; only that cranial capacity was the major change after the appearance of these hominids.

2. The morphological remains of the fossils, particularly the teeth, suggest that sexual dimorphism had decreased significantly in comparison to other terrestrial primates. This decrease must have involved more than simply the structures used aggressively, such as the canines. Other aspects of sexual dimorphism, such as body build and shape and fat deposition, may have increased. Such a change would have involved endocrine-target tissue interactions, probably involving androgens, and it is suggested here, speculatively, that behavior was also effected (e.g. raising thresholds to intragroup aggression; see Holloway 1967).

3. Associated with the above, full-time sexual receptivity of the female and domestication of the male would have been important behavior adaptations, related both to economic activities, e.g. hunting, and social structure (see Etkin 1954, 1963 for elaboration). This would have meant division of roles, the male securing added amounts of high protein resources through hunting.

4. To effect an increase in brain growth there was an increase in the dependency period for infants and children. This must again have meant some alteration in endocrine-target tissue interactions suggested in (2) and implied in (3), either involving growth hormone and target tissues, or a synergistic relation between growth hormone interactions and those androgens related to growth of musculoskeletal parts of the body. Such a change or group of changes would have meant concomitant adaptations in terms of nuclear family structure, and very possibly affect-interplay ("sentiment structure") between offspring and parents, and between peers.

5. A cognitive reorganization related to brain growth and organization, resulting in tool-making, and a shift in the nature of social relations involving the use of arbitrary symbols for communication. This last supposition is based on the assumption that stone tools made to a standardized pattern presupposes a cognitive basis in symbol-using, i.e., it is cultural behavior in the peculiarly human sense. Obviously, both tool-making and symbol communication would have been highly adaptive and under intense positive selection. Tool-making alone suggests some basic shift in the nature of social relations to a more cooperative and sustained type.

Thus four main aspects were involved: reorganization of the brain, endocrine relationships (in the broadest sense), and social and individual cognitive behavior. The brain, and its added growth was the key element in these changes, and its evolution brought on the veritable "revolution" suggested by Hockett and Ascher (1964).

With this basic but incomplete list, it is possible to move to a more detailed consideration of aggressive behavior. The evolution of human social structures was essentially a strategy to engender cooperation for survival. Both intellectual and emotional attributes were involved in human brain evolution and in an integrated fashion. The following discussion makes only an analytic separation for heuristic purposes.

The kind of brain changes leading to increased efficiency of intelligent behavior, e.g. complex stimuli appreciation and task performance are easiest to appreciate. Increases in neuron number, expansion of cortical areas, dendritic branching and possibly neural/glial ratios, can be related to increased adaptive behavior from comparative and experimental neurological evidence (see Holloway 1967 for further details and an expanded framework along these lines). Such increases would have facilitated memory storage, recall, communication, and *both* inhibition and facilitation of certain responses of an affective nature.

The fossil record surely attests to an ever-increasing degree of material complexity (e.g., stone tools, shelters, types of animals hunted), and this in turn suggests an attending increase in social complexity. Symbol systems are usually seen as processes to aid in cognitive optimization, allowing for increased communicative facility. It is suggested here, and this is surely not original, that one of the prime functions of the development of symbolization was *social control*. Fearing (1950:455) has suggested that "communication, as a human activity involving the production and utilization of significant symbols, is *always* a part of the process through which the field is cognitively structured and operates to increase or decrease group tensions." (See also Holloway 1967, for nonverbal communication as a set of redundancy operations to avoid ambiguities; see also Ekman 1965).

Thus, symbolic communication is a device for reducing and/or increasing distortions, ambiguity, and emotions as well as a process that increases memory (amount, storage, permanence), and facilitates recall (see Brown and Lenneberg 1954 for experimental evidence on how language facilitates cognitive operations). Selection for neural reorganization leading to increased behavioral efficiency would also be selection for *facilitation* of attention and inhibition of second-to-second monitoring of other actors' personal qualities—a condition particularly developed in some of the most aggressive of the terrestrial primates, the baboons and macaques (see Southwick 1967, Altmann 1962, 1967, for examples of such constant monitoring of gestures and the penalties paid for inattention by other troop members).

Experimental evidence is very clear that there are optimal levels of arousal of the organism associated with the appreciation of cue complexity and task performance (see Hebb 1966 for examples). This relationship is known as the "inverted U function" because there exists an optimal state of arousal, mediated through the reticular formation and possibly the limbic lobe, which facilitates intellectual functioning. Too much or too little arousal results in a drop-off in perceiving cue complexity and task performance.

Surely, in the evolution of the human animal, natural selection did not militate against the ability to appreciate cue complexity (the many and ever-increasing attributes of the physical and social environments), or task performance. The increasing complexity and sophistication of stone tools during the Palaeolithic (concomitant with brain size increase) attest to this. This all suggests another possible relationship:

Natural selection favored the development of a large cortex to handle environmental complexity (see Holloway, in press, for extensive discussion) and task efficiency, at the same time selecting for optimal arousal patterns. Such selection for optimal arousal patterns very likely also meant selection which resulted in temperamental differences, thus adding another sector to the complexity of the environment in social terms. If the adaptation of early man was heavily in the social realm as suggested here, increasing inhibitive controls would have been highly beneficial. In other words, not only was intellect enhanced, but also the ability to get along in groups through positive affects, in part based on more optimal arousal mechanisms which would also have been advantageous for intellective function, e.g., concentration at some task.

Admittedly, the above framework is speculative, but it does allow for a considerable degree of synthesis between neural and behavioral changes and processes at the individual and social-psychological levels. The species-specific attributes discussed earlier involved neural, endocrine (and certainly neuroendocrine), and social structural changes. These processes, taken in concert, produced the human condition.

Let us now ask the question we have been leading up to: would an increase in positive effects or "sentiment structures" help in any way to achieve these improvements through evolution? The argument offered in the early part of this section, and that in the last part of the "need for an expanded framework" suggested that the social nature of man and his social adaptations *were* facilitated by an increase in the emotional sector, associated with what has been loosely termed as "sentiment structure," where these facilitated both the task of cooperative enterprises and care of the long dependency time of the child with its increasing brain growth.

But what of aggression, particularly human aggression? The hypothesis I offer here is as follows:

Human evolution has been the evolution of a paradox. The evolution of the brain and social structure, and symbol systems has also meant an increase in frustration and aggression. The meaning of symbols in the adaptive evolutionary sense is at least two-fold: they aid in cognitive optimization, and also, they mediate the social controls necessary to stem what arises out of the human condition, frustration and aggression. The same symbolism that enhances sentimental bonds between kinsmen, and symbolically defined groups outside of biological relationships (clan, tribe, state, nation, ideology), bring in their wake its antithesis: extra-group aggressional tendencies. Role differentiation and intra-group commitments generate frustration and power allocation. Man is up against himself—he is up against social structure —he is up against culture.[6] These are his costs as well as his gains. The structures, social and symbolic, which permits his adaptations and the execution of shared tasks to insure his existence, also insure frustration, pain and conflict.

And what about warfare? Warfare at the level of mass societies cannot be explained by this framework or recourse to individual psychology. (See Abel 1941 for example.) This framework does provide a basis, however, for understanding how states can utilize the aggressive components of man's nature for their own ends, and how hostilities at all levels can be perpetuated through time. This framework does not explain revolutions either, but does provide a basis for understanding the absolute necessity of providing all with a chance to realize their full human potential, which includes the very important sector of self-evaluation and opportunity for self-participation in any culture.

Animal studies both in the field and laboratory are of great interest and are to be encouraged for their heuristic value. They suggest mechanisms and give us some idea of the range of stimuli that interact with species-specific organizations of genetic and

---

[6] Freud said much the same thing in *Civilization and Its Discontents.*

social programming to elicit behavioral patterns. They (animal studies) are not, however, some kind of panacea for human ills. Claims that we need to study lower animals to find out about human aggression seem to me as dangerous as simply attributing human ills to a few instincts or need for increased displacement activities. It is power, organizations, socio-economic conditions and symbol systems that need study.

THE CONTRIBUTION OF PRIMATE
STUDIES TO THE
UNDERSTANDING OF WAR

C. R. CARPENTER

THE DISCURSIVE AND PROVOCATIVE PAPER, by Ralph L. Holloway, Jr., provides the departure point for constructive discussions of many fundamental issues of the behavioral sciences. Included are the subjects of evaluation, ecology and population dynamics as well as aggressive behavior.

A revision of his title, which I shall propose, reflects a different but not entirely a contrary view of the area of life sciences. The subject of aggressive behavior can and should be brought into a conceptual system that is useful for understanding, and when necessary, regulating the aggressive activities of organisms, man included.

The preferred title would read *Aggressive Behavior of Organisms, Including Man: The Need for an Integral System of Information.*

We must use correctly defined terms in the beginning or explicitly assume a shared understanding of them. Our stated hypotheses should be clear and subject to proof if our conclusions are to be valid, meaningful and useful. Faults and errors at the beginning of a discourse are multiplied and increased during the development of a theme and are reflected in the formulation of conclusions. Let us avoid these errors in discussions of the paper by Holloway in this very important symposium on "Anthropology and War."

The terms *aggressive behavior* or *aggressive activities* are more accurate than *aggression*. Aggressivity is a quality of action; it is a qualifying adjectival term. It is not a substantive term nor should it be used as a noun. It is suggested that the focus of attention and thought be on *patterns and networks of actions,* either gross or fine, molar or molecular, and that we then consider the action attributes of *aggressive behavioral characteristics.*

Terms are also needed that objectively and without bias refer to the wide range of *organisms* which are being discussed as reference subjects. The nonhuman primates will be used mainly throughout this discussion. For objective study, however, the term organism is general, neutral and inclusive. Let us use it.

An integral system of information and interpretation is needed; substantive, solid, extensive and complete information and not merely a "framework"—not merely a frame-of-reference. We urgently need a full system of information that is *relevant* to the vastly complex qualities of behavior that we know as aggressiveness. Fortunately this body of information is accumulating rapidly. Many recent books deal with the central theme of aggressiveness in animals (Ardrey 1966; Carthy & Ebling 1964; Lorenz 1966; Scott 1958) while there is deep concern everywhere about human wars.

The term "species-specific" is widely used, and it is a popular though somewhat pedantic term. It is disturbing to observe, furthermore, that many structural-behavioral traits that are described as being "species-specific" are actually characteristic of the genus or even family of organisms rather than of a species. Should we revise the term to become genus- or phylum-specific or perhaps should we drop the term altogether? The ethologists have emphasized and extended the concepts of "species-specific" activities especially in fishes and birds—organisms that are more remote in any evolutionary scheme and more specialized than the nonhuman and human primates. It is doubted that the term "species-specific" can be applied accurately to big brained, adaptive and time-binding man.

Dr. Holloway is less tolerant of our colleagues, the ethologists, than an objective scientist should be and therefore, it is somewhat surprising that he would argue for a "species-specific framework" for Homo sapiens. Human aggressive behavior is adaptive, elusive of expression and control, and ubiquitous. I must argue, as I am expected to and as the vast body of observation shows, that the aggressive behavior of man has deep roots in biotic history.

OBJECTIVE OF DISCUSSION

My intent in this discussion of Dr. Holloway's paper is to be as constructively critical as possible and to emphasize areas of agreement that are supported by evidence or that summarize evidence. I propose to support the sub-theme that aggressive behavior can be adaptive and nonadaptive, and that on some levels of semanticity there are homologies which can be compared from animals to animals and from animals to man.

Permit me to formulate in developing this discussion and in attempting to be constructive a set of hypotheses, propositions and assumptions which, I believe, can be supported by evidence and become rationally deductive thought systems. These propositions may usefully supplement and help to reorganize the basic structure and thrust of Dr. Holloway's discursive and multi-faceted paper.

TWELVE PROPOSITIONS

1. Assuming the validity of presently conceived phylogenetic and evolutionary relationships based on comparisons of structures, it is logical to assume, since structures and behaviors co-exist, that there are similar relationships for behavior and physiological functions (Fuller & Thompson 1960; Hirsch 1967; Mayr 1959; Schiller 1957; Wynne-Edwards 1965).

2. *Comparative studies of behavior,* as of structures, must describe accurately the *full ranges of variability* of the defined characteristics and of the organisms that are being compared. Comparisons of *different* categories of behavior with each other should be avoided as an error of the first order and comparisons made only of behavior that is in the same or in similar categories.

3. In view of the fact that a sound, validated and systematically complete taxonomy of behavior does *not* exist, we are at a great disadvantage in comparing the same or similar behavioral characteristics across orders and genera of organisms. For example, comparisons of what seems to be *aggressive behavior* of rodents with hostility and war in humans is fraught with vast risks and possibilities of error. Dr. Holloway's paper reflects this concern for the errors of inappropriate comparisons.

There would seem to be two possible and acceptable approaches to the comparative studies of aggressive behavior, given the dilemma of needing to have comparisons but wishing to avoid the possibilities of serious errors of set orders and of extrapolation:

The first involves making comparisons of micro-behavior patterns that are clearly of the same kind involving the same physiological mechanisms and manifest the micro-behavioral levels of observable actions. This can be done on the endocrine and neurophysiological levels and with fine patterns of expressive behavior such as the threat patterns of nonhuman primate behavior.

The second approach involves making comparisons at a general functional level of considerable complexity and on a high level of general abstraction which can be generally and usefully descriptive even though many specifics are lacking. It is this level of comparisons that Dr. Holloway may have found very satisfactory for this Symposium. These comparisons may also be useful for developing an integral conceptual system for understanding and analyzing aggressive behavior in animals and man.

The proposal is that we describe the *design characteristics* of aggressive behavior in a manner similar to that of scholars in linguistics who describe the design characteristics both of languages and of primate vocalizations. Furthermore, the general design characteristics of the behavior and grouping structures of nonhuman primates living in undisturbed natural habitats can also be studied relative to the general design characteristics of corresponding human behavior. More specifically, the design characteristics and functions of aggressive behavior of nonhuman primates could be compared with similar characteristics of aggressive behavior of the human primates.

4. There is no avoiding a confrontation with the problem of dealing with both the comparisons of *kind* or *quality* and comparisons of *amount* or *quantity* in studying the natural history of aggressive behavior (Darwin 1872; Huxley 1967; Lorenz 1967; Southwick 1967). However, on the levels of physiological functions and behavior as on the levels of structure or anatomy, homologies, analogies, sequential and parallel classes of processes and phenomena are necessary qualifying and descriptive concepts. It would seem logical in terms of available evidence and what we think we know of phylogenetic orders and relationships, to view aggressive activities as being *homologous* across the mammalian phyla including that of the human primate.

5. All behavior is the product of a plurality of determinants and of additional contingent conditions, of genetic elements, ontogenetic or developmental factors, of ecological and of biosocial

contingencies. This proposition is surely as true for nonhuman as for human primates, and when accepted, it invalidates arguments which swirl around the simplified and false dichotomies of "instinct" and "learning." Tinbergen and Lorenz can be forgiven their uses of the term "instinct" because they clearly use it as a translation of "genetic factors" or of basic biological states and stereotypical persistency behavior. Perhaps Dr. Holloway would agree with this general proposal.

6. The ecological context or ecosystem should never be ignored, nor can the biological basis and the biosocial components of the full ecological context be neglected, when systematic valid information is sought for understanding aggressive behavior, or for any other major modality of activity. Furthermore, the "sameness of sensory cues of baboon and man" cannot be argued, as Holloway points out. Nor can perceptual-cognitive and associative selectivity be the same even in different species of nonhuman primates. It is agreed also that responses *alone* should not be observed nor should such data be used as a basis for generalization. The full relevant stimulus conditions to the instigation of behavior must be described. Likewise *releasors* or *excitors* of aggressive actions, as well as *inhibitors* of pugnacious or aggressive activities, must be included in systematic studies of behavior and social interactions whether they are conducted in the laboratory or in the field. There is no doubt from the evidence arrayed by Scott (1958) and others (Fuller & Thompson 1960; Schiller 1957; Scott & Fuller 1965) that animals, especially dogs, can be bred for different kinds and *amounts* of aggressive behavior. It is equally clear that animals, including man, can be trained to fight, and as Southwick (1967) observes, once fighting is learned it is most difficult to extinguish.

7. Biosocial organizations and the structures of troops, groups, and colonies of nonhuman primates are observably affected, shaped and patterned by ecological and biotic factors and also by the aggressive components of appropriate activities. The organizational structures, interactional possibilities and the stimulus-sign-signal systems exert, in turn, *regulatory effects* on the arousal and expressions of tensions, hungers, needs, drives and other physiological states. The organizational structure and composition of individual organisms in mammalian groups generally regulate, for example, what animals will reproduce them-

selves and when this is done. In this context aggressive behavior
is a two-edged sword. It operates to implement the regulation of
grouping structures and composition, and, conversely or reciprocally, aggressive activities are regulated by the organizational patterns of a primate population.

For example, I deliberately controlled the level of aggression
in the Santiago Island colony of rhesus monkeys by arranging
the original socionomic sex ratio to be one male to five females.
Later the ratio was changed to one male to twenty females and
aggression was further reduced (Carpenter 1942, 1964).

8. The aggressivity components of many modalities of behavior like feeding, mating, playing, tutoring, spatial and status
positioning, serve regulatory functions as the inhibitory counter-
poise to the operating system of *rewards* and *reinforcements*.
Without aggressive behavior as regulators, territories could not
be established or maintained, groups structured or controlled,
young included or eliminated from the organized groups, or dominance orders arranged and sustained. Nor without aggression
could the stimulus-cue-sign-signal networks of communicative
behavior be made operationally effective (Altmann 1967; Berkowitz 1962; DeVore 1965; Hall 1964; Imanishi 1957; Wynne-
Edwards 1964).

This proposition suggests that aggressive behavior is not as
modal as feeding, mating or grooming, but like signaling, aggressive behaviors operate as components in other behavioral modalities. While studying the mating behavior of rhesus macaques on
Santiago Island, I observed that injury is a most frequent sign of
estrus and consort formation.

9. Aggressive behavior is most frequent, diverse and extensive when a sample population of animals of the same species
has no organization or is in the process of becoming organized
into grouping structures, or when groups are threatened by others
of the same species, or when there are unresolved drive tensions
within organized groups as during the early phases of the breeding
season. The animals of the Santiago Island rhesus colony fought
persistently during the early stages of that colony's organization.
Many individuals, especially infants and early juveniles, were
killed. Some were driven into the sea (Carpenter 1942, 1964). A
further example was the Choshi Japanese macaque colony on
October 1, 1966, at the beginning of the breeding season:

peripheral males surrounded the colony, there was a high incidence of driving attacks, and the whole colony was in a state of great tension.

10. Molar aggressive behavior of nonhuman primate groups living under natural conditions becomes progressively mediated by fine, limited, economical action patterns such as threat gestures, stereotyped movements and patterned vocalizations. Signs and signals substitute for raw aggressive actions and contact control which involves driving threats, fighting and killing. Treetop signaling in the macaques and the calls of gibbons and siamangs or the roars of howlers replace and function like intergroup conflicts and fighting. Signaling and fighting serve similar regulatory functions.

11. The strength or intensity of aggressive behavior during normal states of excitement of low intensity is released so as to correspond to the demands of stimulus conditions and to the functional requirements of a place and time. However, at high intensities of aggressive excitement in primates the aggressive behavior is all-out and full-charge. Kill or be killed is its design characteristic. Usually also, aggressive behavior is fittingly displayed, directed and gauged to fit circumstances but, at levels of high excitement, aggressiveness may be *displaced* from the instigator, or the provocation to another animal or object. Furthermore, in complex social interactions attacking, charging and fighting constitute alternatives among other possible courses of action. When wrong alternatives are selected and followed, or the wrong objects attacked, then aggressive behavior becomes maladaptive or even pathological.

What behavior is adaptive or maladaptive must be judged by criteria from the biotic levels of ecosystems and defined population dynamics. In many nonhuman primate populations the number of males is reduced by fighting and some are excluded from reproductive groups. Thus, the efficiency of the population biomass has improved reproductive efficiency.

12. In free-ranging and organized populations of animals conflicts and the consequent aggressive behavior occur most frequently and are most intense between or among animals of the same species. Gibbons, the small anthropoid, may feed in the same trees with siamangs or langurs, and do this without serious

conflict. Howlers may tolerate a group of cebus monkeys filtering through the trees in which the howler group is feeding. Neither gibbons nor howlers would similarly tolerate the near presence of groups of their own species without strong aggressive vocal action. When the aggressive vocalizations fail or are inadequate as buffers, then actual fighting will occur as the means of regulating spacing of groups.

This intraspecies antagonism of nonhuman primates is not fully accounted for by the ecological niche theory. Siamangs and gibbons eat the same foods, live in the same tree areas and altitudes and otherwise occupy the same ecological niches, yet aggressive conflicts between the different species are rarely observed.

These highly generalized propositions, assumptions, summary statements and hypotheses urgently need to be supported more fully by details of evidence and observations, only some of which are available. The rest remains to be discovered by research. The generalizations also need to be applied in papers like that of Dr. Holloway's in order to deepen and broaden our understanding of those factors, at all the levels of biotic complexity and organic evaluation, that instigate and shape aggressive activities in both animals and men.

I agree with Dr. Holloway that a theoretical system for aggressive behavior urgently needs to be formulated and tested by logic, by laboratory research, and by field studies within ecosystems which are not seriously disturbed.

THE REGULATION OF AGGRESSION

I concur with Dr. Holloway in proposing the effects of emergents like the enlarged and elaborated central nervous system, developments in reproductive physiology and behavior and extended care of young, the emergence of a truly symbolic language, and also, or consequently, an elaborated social structure. I must demur, however, to separations, except for purposes of analysis, of the "emotionality sector over that of the more rational, intellectual attributes—" Affectivity and rationality have developed as operationally inseparable characteristics of organismic behavior on all evolutionary levels. Furthermore, I strongly support Dr. Holloway's deductions about the possible modification of intellectual functions as a consequence of the enlarged brain. I especially like

his emphasis on elaborative development of two sets of mechanisms—those of *facilitation* and *inhibition*.

The issue and the overriding question before this Symposium
is how can man employ his newly acquired brain power to design
strategies for regulating aggressive behavior. I repeat, the issue
is that of developing and using strategies for *regulating* and not
eliminating aggressive behavior. Perhaps, therefore, the most important result that we can expect from the study of the aggressive
activities of animals is to discover *models of aggressivity regulation* and to test these adaptive models for usefulness in regulating the aggressive activities of man.

What can an observer of nonhuman primate societies say
about war? War is institutionalized aggressive activity. War is
extra-legal. War is a cultural and technological phenomenon including vast new destructive capabilities. War is both a raw power
struggle, and it is a symbolic sub-system. Institutions, law, culture and true *symbolic* systems are emergents that occur beyond
the highest evolutionary developments of even the anthropoids.
The observer of animals can report little about human war.

I shall conclude this discussion with a brief report of an event
that happened in the Takasakiama macaque colony in Kyushu,
Japan in the summer of 1966. The colony of about 950 animals
was then organized into three distinct groups; A, B, and C. The
intergroup dominance order that had prevailed for many years was
A>B>C. This was the order in which groups came on the feeding ground and fed for years prior to an intergroup battle.

In July 1966 a serious and protracted fight occurred between
groups B and C. A sub-group of 10–12 young adult and fighter
males belonged to B-group and played a leading role in the aggressive crisis. However, the smaller C-group won the conflict
and gained priority over B-group to the feeding ground and to po-
tatoes, wheat, soya beans and peanuts. The subgroup of young
adult males left B-group, the loser, and joined C-group, the victor.
Henceforth, and until now, the intimidated B-group needs to be
coaxed and led each day by a kind of primate herdsman from its
forested territory on the steep mountainside to the shared area
of the feeding grounds.

In summary, using Dr. Holloway's stimulating paper as a basis
for discussion, I have (1) attempted to sharpen definitions of
terms contending that aggressivity is a characteristic associated
with many modalities of behavior; (2) warned against wasting

efforts arguing about oversimplified dichotomous terms, especially "instinct—and—learning," and "emotional—and—rational";
(3) stated twelve propositions which I believe both summarize
available information and can be supported by additional evidence; (4) proposed under proposition 3 two ways to make comparisons of aggressive behavior across animal and human phyla;
and (5) proposed that the central problem under discussion is
one of *regulating and managing aggression,* and that the study of
such regulation cybernetic mechanisms in the biotic levels within
ecosystems, especially of nonhuman primates, may serve as models for regulating some of the many types of aggression on the
level of the human primates.

General Discussion

JOSEPH C. FINNEY (*University of Kentucky*): I should like to comment on this excellent paper by adding some psychological considerations that are related to what the speaker said. I have five points to make. The first is that, when we consider a particular emotional reaction—anger, for example—which is a response that each person learns to attach to cultural situations, there are two aspects of learning to be studied: the input and the output. Input involves the question of how children learn to attach the emotional response to different kinds of situations. The stimuli evoking the emotion, such as anger, will vary from one person to another and from one cultural group to another. On the other hand, for output, we should study the different behaviors which satisfy anger, for example.

A second point is that we may have some difficulty in defining unequivocally what we mean by war. In a small tribe, if 50 people get together and attack 50 other people, it would be considered war. In the United States, however, such an action would not constitute "war" because we define it only at a national level involving a much more highly complex system of interrelated behaviors. Are we all talking about the same thing?

The third point is that anger is by no means the only urge that is satisfied by war. To one person, war may mean the satisfaction of his aggressive urge. To another, it may be an opportunity to prove his manhood, and to take pride in his fighting ability. To still another, the war may bring a quite different kind of satisfaction, such as an opportunity to make money. These things vary with one's status and situation. The fears, frustrations, and satisfactions offered by a war are quite different for the President and the people who are making decisions about war from those of the man in the street or the footsoldier in the front line.

The fourth point is that one important function of war is to reassure a person by expressing and strengthening his identification with his own country, and with his friends and neighbors. War reinforces this sense of identification and solidarity.

The last point is that we have known since Freud that the behaviors that are most strongly reinforced are those that offer a compromise by managing to symbolize and satisfy two or more urges that are generally opposed to each other. Such may be the case with war. On the one hand, war satisfies hostile, aggressive drives, the urge to attack people. At the same time, war gives opportunity to satisfy an urge that is apparently opposed to aggression, namely, the urge to sacrifice oneself unselfishly, on behalf of one's fellow man, or at least those within one's own country. In the end, a man can make the ultimate sacrifice, laying down his life for his fellow men. Perhaps this is an important reason why people resort to war: it can satisfy at the same time their hostile, aggressive urges, and their altruistic, self-sacrificing ones. This is all the more so in groups of people who have a missionary or crusading spirit, and who believe that they are fighting for right and justice. People who are inspired by a charismatic political or religious movement not only believe that they fight to benefit the people of their own side: they may also believe that victory for their side will ultimately benefit the misguided people of the enemy nation. When they believe that, they need suffer no pangs of guilt for their warlike acts. The same effect can be achieved in a less sophisticated way by the belief that the enemy is pure evil. Or one may have a split image of the enemy nation: its leaders are pure evil, to be destroyed, but its common people are only misguided ones, to be redeemed and re-educated. (As you can see, the defense mechanisms of repression, dissociation, and projection make it possible to perceive things in this way.) Belief systems of this kind are effective in providing a rationale and a justification for war.

JOHN ALLISON (*University of Indiana*):   I think that Dr. Carpenter neglected what I considered to be the main point brought up by Dr. Holloway, namely that at least "modern war" is often the result of a conscious manipulation of shared symbols by a limited group within the society, perhaps for social, political, and/ or economic ends. I wonder why Dr. Carpenter did not respond to this except to say that war was extra-legal. Would he care to comment on this now and also on the implicit suggestion that there is a certain responsibility on the part of anthropologists that goes along with this knowledge?

DR. CARPENTER: In view of the time limitation, I tried to abbreviate references to human wars. Dr. Holloway did a very good job explicating the shared symbol concept. Furthermore, I was concerned especially with concepts of emergent evolution. I did not talk about symbol systems; rather, I considered the evolution of communication only up to the level of animal signalling where there is accumulating an abundance of evidence and observations. Semantics goes beyond the level of animal evolution and on to the human level.

I have no further reason for not discussing the proposal by Dr. Holloway that war is a power struggle or a function of shared symbol systems. War is certainly a multifaceted, extra-legal institutionalized human development. It is not *only* a conflict in symbol systems, it is not *only* a power struggle, and it is not only determined by a *sentiment* structure. There are other explanations and contingent factors.

Part III | WAR AND DISEASE

WAR AND DISEASE:
AN ANTHROPOLOGICAL PERSPECTIVE

ALEXANDER ALLAND, JR.

WARFARE AND DISEASE ARE CLOSELY LINKED. The historical record is crowded with associations between war and the outbreak of major epidemics. The reasons behind such associations, both biological and behavioral, are far more complicated, however, than is generally assumed.

This paper is an attempt to clarify such relationships, particularly in the context of the war in Southeast Asia. In addition, I shall extend my arguments to the potential effects of overt biological warfare on civilian populations. This is done specifically to counter the suggestion of certain individuals in the military that biological weapons represent a breakthrough in the direction of "humanitarian" warfare.

While public health as a matter of policy is new to most countries, all human groups, even the most primitive, have made considerable behavioral and genetic adjustments to the common diseases in their environment. The genetic adjustments result from the selective effect of disease on populations, and more than one author has suggested that disease has been a powerful agent in the course of human evolution (Haldane, 1959; Barnicot, 1965). Behavioral adjustments to disease are of two sorts: preventive and therapeutic. Effective therapeutic procedures require conscious effort including both the development of accurate diagnostic techniques and the discovery of curative agents. In many, if not most, primitive and peasant societies the diagnostic process is concerned primarily with etiology. Disease may be linked to transgression of the moral code, to social enmity, or to supernatural power, with consequent treatment of these "causes" rather than of the disease-producing organism. More often than not primitive medical opinion fails to produce a consistent therapeutic orientation.

On the other hand, many non-Western societies do have pharmacopoeias that are quite effective in the treatment of local irritations and certain general symptoms such as fever, aches, and pains. A few good vermifunges exist, and of course, there are known cases in which primitive or peasant remedies have been demonstrated to contain powerful agents capable of ameliorating such serious conditions as malaria (quinine) and heart disease (digitalis). In general, however, "native" drugs have little effect upon specific disease agents.

I submit, therefore, that of all the adjustments that a prescientific population can make to disease, the most effective are genetic in origin or involve behavior that can be classified as preventive medicine. The term "preventive medicine" is used here in a special sense to include any medically or non-medically directed behavior that, in fact, has a positive or disease reducing effect on the epidemiological patterns of a population (for example, bathing).

Many behaviors among prescientific peoples are effective in combating or preventing disease. These range from cooking procedures, which lower the risk of intestinal parasite infestation, to customs that require individuals to defecate away from habitation sites and trails. Quarantine for at least some infectious diseases and avoidance of contaminated water are also widely reported.

This is not to say that all behaviors are positive in their effect. Indeed, many customs increase medical risk for particular groups. Certain subsistence techniques, for example, while they represent an economic advance for a population, nonetheless produce new routes for infectious agents.

Certain cultural practices that are relatively safe under one set of conditions increase risk if the conditions are changed. Small populations are less likely than large populations to be subject to epidemics, and nomadic groups are less susceptible to auto-contamination than settled groups, which live in constant contact with their refuse. However, the sudden migration or displacement of populations from one ecological zone to another may expose them to diseases against which they have no genetic protection.

In general, health patterns depend upon ecological relationships between man, disease organisms, and vectors, as well as upon their reservoir populations. These must be considered as part of the behavioral framework rather than as part of the "natural setting" of a population. Such relationships are always tentative considering what man can do to his environment, and there is much evidence to show that the natural setting is rarely natural.

It is unfortunate that no studies exist that weigh positive and negative behaviors against each other. There is evidence, however, that disturbances of normal (meaning long term) ecological and/or behavioral patterns usually lead to increased disease rates and lowered viability. This certainly suggests that the net effect of socially established genetic and behavioral adjustments undergone by prescientific societies is, in fact, positive.

In sum, genetic and behavioral adjustments to disease are part of a general process of adaptation to environment. Public health, particularly in prescientific populations, depends upon such accommodations. I am convinced that the view of public health outlined above is necessary if we are to understand the dynamics of adjustment to disease and the effects of war on such adjustments.

An example from European history has implications for the present situation of war in Southeast Asia. I have chosen plague for illustrative purposes because (1) its occurrence is well documented, (2) its etiology is complex but nonetheless well understood, and (3) it serves as a good illustration of a severe, highly contagious disease that is sensitive to ecological variation.

The agent of plague is the bacillus Pasteurella pestis. It is a disease with a short incubation period, florid symptoms, and a high mortality rate. Plague has a complicated etiology involving wild and domestic rodents and a flea vector, with the normal endemic focus located in wild rodent populations (sylvatic plague). Epidemics occur when the bacillus is passed on to highly susceptible domestic rodents, which rapidly die out. When this occurs their fleas are forced to search out new hosts, the most common of which is man. While there has been some dispute over whether the European plague was a cause or an effect of social disorganization, most authors today feel that the great epidemics of the thirteenth to sixteenth centuries were the outcome of Malthusian pressures and followed in the footsteps of social, political, and economic troubles. R. S. Roberts (1966), a medical historian, writes:

"Plague was endemic for a long time . . . as we shall see, (it) was a disease which could become epidemic only at a particular stage of socio-economic development, which demographers call 'oriental.'

"At the beginning of the outbreak, England was much more densely populated than is usually thought. From 1086 (Domesday Book) the population seems to have trebled from 1.0 to 3.5 million. In the absence of technical advance or import of foodstuffs, this greatly increased population could only be fed by a commensurate increase in the area of cultivated land. The inclosure of waste land and the settlement of new villages in the thirteenth century shows that this indeed was done on a large scale.

"It was the social and economic crisis of the 1340s, however, which seems to have created the necessary conditions—rats brought into closer contact with man in the search for food after bad harvests, movements of populations after famines and epidemics, overcrowding in certain areas, and a general decline in health and resistance to disease."

Judging from Roberts and other sources, the maintenance of plague in England, and perhaps other parts of Europe as well, for over three hundred years, was facilitated by the destruction of woodland, which was converted for agricultural purposes. Such incursions into the native habitat of wild rodents, the endemic reservoir of plague, brought these animals into closer contact with the domestic rat population. As I have noted above, domestic rats are highly sensitive to plague, and as they die out, the human populations among whom they live rapidly pick up the infection. Probably the epidemic cycle was completed when the natural habitat for wild rodents was reduced to the point where it could no longer support the reservoir population. In this case it would appear that the partial destruction of an ecological zone increased disease risk although further incursions into the same zone eventually led to an extinction of the endemic focus of the disease.

The parallel between this situation and Southeast Asia is striking. Plague and other acute infectious diseases exist in endemic focuses throughout the area. The flood plains of the Mekong Delta support one of the highest population densities in the world. In addition, the agricultural complex constitutes an ecological niche quite apart from the wild mountains zone. Until recently, Vietnamese from the plains were afraid to venture into the mountains, often citing exotic diseases as the cause of their anxiety.

Hygiene and public health measures are primitive, but under normal conditions, severe epidemic outbreaks are limited in their distribution and scope. While the population is certainly not the healthiest in the world, a delicate balance exists that has allowed humans to survive and multiply in great numbers. This is due in part to the incredibly productive nature of the delta area.

Although epidemics of the plague have not occurred for some time, the number of cases in Vietnam has mounted steadily and sharply over the past three years. On August 20, 1966, the *New York Times* noted that at that time the plague had infected 22 of 29 provinces stretching north of Saigon, but that in 1961, plague was reported in only one of those provinces. The same article presents the following statistics on plague incidence in South Vietnam: 1954–1962, less than 40 cases per year; 1963, 119 cases; 1964, 290 cases; and 1965, 4453 cases. The Reverend Do Van Quy, chief of the Pasteur Institute's plague laboratory predicted that "This problem will not be solved until the war is ended." Dr. Joe Stockard, chief of the United States aid mission's preventive medicine section, said, "Now that the disease has become so widespread, a high incidence may be expected to continue for an indefinite period."

Extremely crowded conditions in the cities with overstrained and primitive sanitary facilities are no doubt a major factor in the statistical increase. U.S. and South Vietnamese authorities are aware of the problem, at least insofar as it relates to cities, and a program of rat elimination is under way. The dangers inherent in such a program are minimized by the existence of a relatively effective plague vaccine and effective antibiotic therapy. Nonetheless, a case of the plague in an American serviceman was considered important enough to be included in the AMA *News* for December 1966.

Rat elimination is a rather quixotic pursuit in Southeast Asia. The ability of rats to survive even in the urban areas of the United States attests to their hardiness. Rats flourish in the primitive sanitary conditions on the slums and *bidonvilles* of Vietnam. It would seem, therefore, that an effective antiplague program should be more concerned with interrupting the routes of infection from the endemic focuses to the domestic rodent population. What has happened may be the reverse! Defoliation and extensive napalm attacks may have produced disturbances in plague reservoir areas sufficient to increase the contact between wild and domestic rodents. While I must stress that this is mere conjecture, such an explanation fits well with current theories of plague epidemiology. In addition, the fact that plague is virtually absent in the Mekong Delta region for "reasons [according to the *New York Times*] that scientists are unable to explain" lends support to the theory that plague will tend to break out more readily in regions where there has been severe environmental disturbance. Until recently the delta has experienced only limited warfare and no major defoliation programs.

One major difference between the English plague and the Vietnam situation is that in England it was the English who changed their environment, while in Vietnam it is we who are doing so. We are therefore largely responsible for the potential consequences that may now affect a large segment of the population. The U.S. military can easily vaccinate its soldiers and a good part of the urban population, but what of the civilian village population, particularly in uncontrolled territory? According to Vietnam government statistics only about a quarter of South Vietnam's population has been immunized with plague vaccine (the *New York Times*, August 20, 1966).

Plague stands only as a model for what can happen when a natural setting is disturbed. Such waterborne diseases as typhoid and cholera, as well as various forms of dysentery and intestinal parasites, constitute a constant danger in Vietnam. Even malaria is sensitive to environmental changes that effect the breeding grounds of vector mosquitoes.

The ecological situation in Southeast Asia, as in any tropical area, is quite complex. This has two major implications for epidemiology: (1) The climate, both warm and humid, provides a benevolent setting for a wide range of infectious parasites. Organisms that would under other conditions have difficulty surviving outside of their human hosts remain viable for long periods in water supplies and in the soil. (2) Disruption of the ecological balance within either the settled and/or less densely populated areas can produce changes in both floral and faunal composition that, at the very least, are difficult, if not impossible to anticipate. Some of these changes are bound to have their effect on epidemiological patterns.

Extensive warfare in any part of the world has always had the side effect of producing severe impairment of public health facilities and of disrupting normal life patterns for civilian populations, which, in turn, are often correlated with rising disease rates (Zinzer 1934; Ackerknecht 1965). The imposition of modern warfare on Southeast Asia, particularly a war that is fought prin-

cipally against guerrilla forces with no distinct battle lines, creates
serious problems for the health of the entire population. Taking
the tropical ecology and the type of warfare into account, the following factors can be expected to affect epidemiological patterns.

1. With vast areas of the country under only tenuous control, it is impossible to impose any effective public health measures on the population at large. Potential epidemics are difficult
to check, and the endemic focuses of disease cannot be wiped out.

2. Defoliation of forest land in guerrilla-held territory drives
wild animal populations into new areas, increasing the risk of contact between animal reservoirs, potential domestic animal carriers, and human populations.

3. The dislocation and relocation of large segments of the
population increase the possibility that groups from different ecological zones will cross-infect each other with exotic diseases
against which they have no genetic or acquired immunity.

4. Both relocation camps and cities become overcrowded. Increased population densities and poor sanitation, combined with
inadequate diets, increase the risk of epidemics.

5. Disruption of the local ecology and indigenous behavioral
patterns leads to the breakdown of existing barriers to disease.

6. The stress associated with relocation, lowered nutritional
standards, and cultural deprivation due to changes in traditional
life patterns is sure to lower resistance to common diseases. Under such conditions, normally benign diseases can become serious
health hazards for the population.

7. The increased disease risk produced in such groups may
last long after a return to normal conditions. Wolf (1960) cites
evidence that a prison-camp experience can have a striking effect
on the continuing life chances of exposed individuals:

"A recently completed study of the effects of imprisonment on
Americans during World War II furnished revealing information
about approximately 94,000 United States prisoners of war who
were taken in Europe. These men were imprisoned for about ten
months. Less than one per cent of them died before liberation. In
contrast, in the Pacific theater, about 25,000 Americans became
prisoners of war. They remained in prison four times as long as

those captured in Europe, and suffered far more threats, abuse, and humiliation. Their demoralization was often extreme. More than one third of them died in prison.

"Six years after liberation, the fate of those that survived the Japanese prison experience was investigated. In the first place, the total number of deaths in the group during these six years was more than twice the expected incidence for a similar group not so exposed and three times as great as the group of United States prisoners of war in Europe. Moreover, the causes of death included many diseases *not directly related to confinement or starvation* [italics mine]. Twice the expected number died of heart disease, more than twice the expected number of cancer, more than four times the expected number of diseases of gastrointestinal tract. Twice the expected number died as a result of accidents. Nine times the expected number died of pulmonary tuberculosis."

Now one might argue that the Vietnamese peasant relocated to camp or city has had a more rugged initial life experience and therefore is more immune to stress than his American contemporary. One might also argue that life in Vietnamese relocation camps is not comparable to life in Japanese prisoner of war camps. It must be admitted that we do not know what effects, if any, will appear in the incarcerated segment of the Vietnamese population several years from now, but published descriptions of the camps suggest that severe stress is an everyday experience.

It is therefore possible that we are risking the health of relocated and incarcerated individuals, possibly for a long time to come. Furthermore, this concerns a very large segment of the South Vietnamese population. Countless people have become refugees from American bombing and/or Vietcong attack. At least 2,000,000 of these have been or are in relocation camps while the remainder have been left to their own devices (*New York Times*, October 28, 1967). This is perhaps the first war in which a major segment of the civilian population has been so uprooted for so long. (One must include the Japanese occupation and the war with the French along with the present episode.)

8. The life risks of individuals not directly involved in relocation or evacuation may also be increased. According to Wolf:

"The main point is that the great majority of the clusters of illness occurred in the lives of the members of every group (an experimental study of life stress in civilian populations) at times when they perceived their life situations to be unsatisfying, threatening or overdemanding and productive of conflict, and they could make no satisfactory adaptation to these situations. These situations were in general those which arose out of disturbed relations with family members and important associates, threats to security and status, restrictions and limitations which made it impossible to satisfy important personal needs and appetites."

This kind of dislocation certainly occurs in all war, and even in normal circumstances, but the Vietnam conflict, which has dragged on for so long, is particularly contributory. The new weapons used in Vietnam today, with the exception of defoliants, are merely an extension, albeit a terrible one, of "conventional" weaponry. But their vast destructive power, combined with our efficient, varied, and numerous delivery systems, used over and over again, year after year, is bound to have new and unhappy consequences for the entire ecology of Vietnam and for the majority of its civilian population. While I do not believe that the United States has used or intends to use biological warfare in Southeast Asia (it is perhaps of more strategic value for an area in which there is little or no troop commitment), I submit that the kind of conventional warfare that has been raging for the past three years is, intentionally or not, a kind of covert biological warfare. The continued imposition of stress conditions upon an area with a delicate health balance will, in a variety of direct and indirect ways noted above, subject the inhabitants to the same type, if not the same degree, of pathological devastation as that brought about by overt action involving biological and chemical agents.

Overt chemical and biological warfare has been described by its advocates as "war without death." Soft sell lobbyists have emphasized research on incapacitating chemicals and the limited use of crop diseases as the ultimate in humane weaponry. Yet Elinor Langer in her important and enlightening series of articles in *Science* (13 and 20 January 1967) points out that considerable effort has been expended at the Fort Detrick center for biological warfare research on such diseases as anthrax, bacillary dysentery, brucellosis, glanders, plague, tularemia, Q. fever, Rocky Mountain spotted fever, viral encephalitis, psittacosis, yellow fever, and coccidioidomycosis. In addition, the center is involved in experimentation with botulism toxin. The list speaks for itself. None of these diseases can be described as mild; in fact most are highly contagious and extremely lethal. Bacillary dysentery is a major killer of children throughout the underdeveloped world. Plague, anthrax, encephalitis, and botulism are likely to kill quickly, if not painlessly, while Rocky Mountain spotted fever, brucellosis, and tularemia produce long term, painful infections with poor prognoses. Coccidioidomycosis is a peculiar disease in that it may occur in either acute or chronic forms with startlingly different symptomologies. The chronic type which is "highly malignant" occurs in higher frequency in Orientals than in Caucasoids. Dengue fever does indeed have a low mortality, but it is an extremely painful and debilitating condition.

Langer informs us that in addition to research on specific diseases, the Detrick center has a large investment in aerobiology, the study of airborne infection.

"Aerobiology is of particular importance to biological warfare, however, because the idea of disseminating infectious agents by aerosols—suspensions of small particles in air—seems to be displacing earlier notions about how to transmit disease. Conventional images of biological warfare—the overt 'man with the suitcase' or the poisoning of water supplies and ventilation systems —seems to have been discarded, partly because the number of people who could be subjected to infection at any one time is too small" (Langer 1967:176).

A biological weapons arsenal, including the diseases described above and delivered as aerosol infections, is certainly as indiscriminate a technique of warfare as the atomic bomb. The major difference between such weapons and explosives is:

" 'Their ability to accomplish their effects . . . with little or no physical destruction. This constitutes an advantage both in combat operations . . . and—from a longer viewpoint—in postwar rehabilitation, where over-all rebuilding requirements would be reduced' " (Langer 1967:299; quoting from Military Manual FM-3-10). It would appear that the humanity involved is extended to buildings rather than to human beings.

But what of less lethal conditions? Is it not possible that certain diseases could be used selectively or with reduced pathogeneity? These are naïve questions. Less severe conditions will, it is true, produce little mortality in a healthy population. In populations with poor diets or with no history of exposure to a particular condition, however, the mortality rate in general is likely to be much higher than in a control group of relatively healthy Americans. In addition, the old and infirm, as well as the new born, are likely to continue as a vulnerable group. If disease organisms are distributed unselectively throughout a population, they will have nonetheless, a selective effect, in most cases increasing risk for noncombatants in the population.

Furthermore, in areas with a delicate health balance, the introduction of new or increased frequencies of pathologies may upset the biological defenses of individuals. All epidemics produce at least short term changes in the behavioral system, and even a change in daily routines may open a population to the further incursion of disease.

Because biological weapons of the type described are difficult to control, and because selective delivery is a difficult proposition, it would appear that their use on other than a grand scale is out of the question. The threat therefore, that such weapons pose to civilian populations and to the state of world public health cannot be minimized. To date, the most apt description of the potential situation has been offered by the Department of Health, Education and Welfare, which has defined biological warfare as "Public health in reverse."

THE DIRECT AND INDIRECT
BIOLOGICAL COSTS OF WAR

BENJAMIN D. PAUL

IN ANALYZING THE RELATIONSHIP between war and disease, Alland adopts an ecological stance. Man is bound up with his environment in an ecological system, and the observer can study the workings of this system objectively. In terms of Pike's catchy contrast, this outsider's view constitutes an "etic" frame of analysis, as distinguished from an "emic" or insider's outlook. It represents one of several approaches to problems of health and culture. I will name four approaches, for present purposes, labeling them the "emic" approach, the applied approach, the behavioral approach, and the "etic" approach.

By the *"emic" approach* I simply mean the classic and common ethnographic procedure of describing illness in terms of the natives' culturally transmitted understanding of illness: its causes, categories, cures, and curers. The description may be coarse-grain or fine-grain, it may be based on traditional techniques of observation and interview or on the use of "eliciting frames," but the general aim is the same: to give readers an insider's perspective. These descriptions of ethnomedicine may be useful to academic anthropologists but they are only of limited use to medical personnel and others involved in social action.

More meaningful to men of action is the *applied approach* as exemplified by detailed studies of the process and outcome of interaction between particular health improvement projects and their personnel, on the one hand, and the beneficiary population and its customs, on the other. Attention to such case studies can have the favorable effect of sensitizing professional change agents to the significance of culture factors in shaping both their own behavior and the response of the target group. Nor is the applied approach devoid of theoretical implications. Studies of the impact of health programs can be grist for academic mills grinding out general propositions about the dynamics of acculturation. For the most part, however, this payoff remains unrealized.

What is here called the *behavioral approach,* unlike the applied approach, does not require the introduction of or presence of an action program among the people under observation. It does demand a substantial sampling of episodes of illness behavior. Collecting and analyzing such behavioral data is no simple assignment and has not often been undertaken. The few studies along this line now beginning to appear indicate that knowledge of native disease theory and of the cultural prescriptions for coping with illness goes only so far in explaining or predicting the actual behavior of individuals. Many factors of context and circumstance control the choice of alternative responses to illness, complicating the relationship between collective precepts and individual action, between culture and behavior. The behavioral approach remains an inviting one for enterprising medical anthropologists.

Equally attractive and similarly little tried is Alland's *"etic" approach* to phenomena of health and illness—his perception, from the vantage point of an expert outsider, of culture as a generally adaptive mechanism enabling human groups to remain reasonably healthy and hence viable in their accustomed habitats. Viewing culture, or some of its aspects, as ecologically adaptive is nothing new. Alland's contribution lies in spelling out some of the implications of this view of culture for public health research and for analyzing the effects of war.

His emphasis on ecology and adaptation facilitates cooperation and communication between scientific disciplines by providing a link to biology. It also tunes the medical anthropologist into the wave length of the medical epidemiologist seeking out the determinants and distribution of disease and disability.

Peering through his "etic" glasses at instances of culturally conditioned behavior, Alland looks past explanations offered by informants; he fixes instead on the practical effects. Men's actions speak louder than their words of explanation. Wearing a charm to ward off illness is not an instance of preventive medicine, despite cultural claims, because the detached scientist realizes that germs scoff at charms. Conversely, the practice of avoiding pork on religious grounds would qualify as an act of preventive medicine if in fact it averted trichinosis. This is tantamount to saying that in the scales of preventive medicine, latent functions weigh more heavily than manifest functions, to use a paired distinction made popular by Merton.

Alland's special definition of preventive medicine is valid in principle, but by this broad interpretation countless practices and prohibitions await inspection to see whether they qualify as instances of disease prevention. Where should a medical anthropologist begin to look and when does he finish? Moreover, a particular practice may have more than one latent function by different "etic" experts. How does one rate an item of culture if one of its functions serves to reduce, while another serves to induce, disease?

Alland makes short shrift of native therapies. Occasional folk remedies may be efficacious according to scientific criterion, but by and large, folk medicine and folk healers are ineffective, in Alland's "etic" estimation, because the ascribed causes of illness are usually irrelevant and because "symptoms are treated rather than diseases." This may all be true if we confine our attention to the explanations provided by the culture and proceed to evaluate them in our own scientific terms.

It would be more consistent with Alland's approach, however, to judge the efficacy of curative usages in terms of their latent rather than manifest functions. A function often attributed by observers to folk medicine and folk healers is the reduction of anxiety. I need not belabor the familiar proposition that unchecked fear and anxiety can wear down a person's emotional and physical health and impair his capacity to perform his social and economic roles. Alland may be overstating the case when he says that it is "an equally romantic and distorted view of primitive man" to credit the folk healer with real curative powers. Dr. Morris Carstairs, a sensitive observer who ran a medical dispensary in rural India, was told, "No matter how rare a medicine you give a patient, unless you and he have faith in it, he never will be cured." Faith may not deter a bacillus but it gives a sick man hope, and often raises his level of resistance. The expectation of recovery can have a self-fulfilling effect.

In arguing that native therapy systems often do in fact serve the cause of health regardless of their manifest doctrines, I am not trying to impugn Alland's approach but rather to extend its range of application. Alland is surely right in holding that all human groups have made behavioral adjustments to the common diseases in their environment. And it is true that any serious disturbance of the group's normal ecological and behavioral patterns, like a mutant gene, is more likely to be injurious than beneficial.

Nothing disrupts normal patterns so much as sustained and large-scale warfare. War and pestilence are two of the apocalyptic horsemen that ride through history together. Technological advance gives each war a new twist. Now we can seed disease germs among the enemy. A resort to microbiological warfare would indeed be "public health in reverse" almost by definition. Far from being humane or amounting to "war without death," the release of biological weapons, as Alland indicates, could have the severest consequences, given the lowered resistance of the civilian population, and the lethal power of the many disease agents being cultivated at Fort Detrick. Thus far, germ warfare is only a possibility, but ever since 1961 the biological and social imbalance produced by *chemical* warfare has become a grim reality.

There is little evidence that spraying of herbicides is achieving its stated tactical objectives of starving the Viet Cong and exposing their trails. Less doubt exists, however, about the unintended effects. Spraying has caused widespread destruction of commercial and food crops in friendly lands. American planes have spread more than a million gallons of chemicals over more than half a million acres of land, defoliated a thousand square miles of Vietnam and ruined 70,000 acres of rice. Referring to the current situation in Vietnam, Jean Mayer, a Public Health expert, states:

> "The examination of past wars and famines makes it clear that the food shortage will strike first and hardest at children, the elderly and pregnant and lactating women; last and least at males, and least of all at soldiers."
> [*Scientist & Citizen, cited 11/13/67 in news item, Times-Post service*]

In addition to the crop-reduction route, herbicides threaten to come at civilians from at least two other directions. The chemicals may linger in the soil for more than a year, as well as leaking into streams and killing fish by poisoning the microscopic fauna on which they feed. Second, by disturbing the environment niche of rodents and other wild animal reservoirs of disease, defoliation may set off a chain reaction in plague and other epidemic diseases. Alland draws an alarming parallel between ecologic changes

and conditions now prevailing in Vietnam and those that prevailed in the Middle Ages when plague swept through Europe.

To the threats of famine, poison and infection, one should add
the debilitating effects of social disruption, enforced migration,
and life in relocation camps. Surveying this battery of assaults
on the civilian population, with worse blows in store, one begins
to wonder how many sound civilians will be left to save when
and if we win the war. Some terrible danger must be lurking in
Vietnam to warrant the awesome price people are paying to be
saved. Whatever that danger may be, it must indeed be a fate
worse than death.

General Discussion

STEVEN POLGAR (*University of North Carolina*): Earlier in the
discussion, Adams criticized Livingstone and Thieme for taking
too narrow a view of the mortality that is consequent upon warfare, and Alland has amply illustrated the point that warfare and
disease are indeed inseparable. There are some good historical
studies on the relationships between social instability, war, disease, and life expectancy, which bear on this matter e.g., by
Angel in Greece and Celli in Italy.

What of the question of biological warfare in the future? The
attitude of many Americans today may be seen in the light of
attitudes that led to the biological warfare waged against Indians
during the Colonial-Indian wars: giving them blankets infected
with smallpox. The definition of the Indian at that time as a lesser
order of creation can be carried forward to the dropping of the
atomic bomb on Hiroshima and Nagasaki. Many people have
commented that the bomb might never have been dropped on
Germany—Germans, after all, are Whites, whereas the Japanese
are not. This kind of thinking is currently reflected in the news-
paper reports on how many Viet Cong were "bagged" or on how
many hostile villages are "softened up."

Dr. Alland was very careful, and I would be too, not to predict
what is going to happen in Vietnam; I think, however, that increasingly people are defining the opponents to the war at home,
as well as a large proportion of the population of Vietnam, as
specimens of lesser humanity towards whom the basic standards
of our society need not be applied. By the same token, it also appears that a few of the young people opposing the war are beginning to read out of the ranks of ordinary society such people as
representatives of Dow Chemical Company, denying them some
of the rights that should belong to all persons in this country.

Biological warfare, like so many other features of human
society, has evolved from less conscious, perhaps accidental, behaviors to more and more conscious policies. Public health, the
opposite of biological warfare, has also evolved from less deliberate acts, and, as Dr. Alland pointed out, very often from
such ordinary behavior as bathing. Alland's paper points to a
situation where diseases and malnutrition among non-combatants

are an unintentional byproduct of the way we are waging war. The more we define our opponents as subhuman, the smaller the step from an indirect effect to a deliberate policy.

DR. ALLAND: This has to do with the theory part. I agree with Ben Paul completely about latent functions and the psychosomatic elements of disease. I didn't put it in the paper because I felt that I was dealing with a specific ecological situation. As far as the problem of "etics" is concerned, if we say that all behavior is disease-orientated in one way or another, I would then suggest that we look at the behavioral and biological characteristics of disease organisms first. Understanding them fully will help us narrow down the behavioral framework that we want to look at. This is what I have tried to do in my research. Thank you.

Part IV | PRIMITIVE AND MODERN WAR

HYPOTHESES ABOUT FUNCTIONS OF WAR

ANDREW P. VAYDA

IN ANALYZING THE FUNCTIONS that war may have, we are trying to show the systemic antecedents and consequences of organized armed conflict. More specifically, analyzing possible functions of war involves us in considering hypotheses to the effect that war constitutes a counteracting response made by a system when a variable or activity within the system has been disturbed from its proper, desired, or accepted state. In other words, the "function" attributed to war in these hypotheses is the maintaining of one or more variables or activities in a certain state or within a certain range of states.

That war should have functions at all is of course in itself a hypothesis, and alternative hypotheses, e.g., to the effect that war is a nonfunctional pathological condition of society, may be and indeed often have been presented. One reason for the examination of particular hypothesized functions of primitive war is that such an examination may help to provide a basis for assessing the more general hypotheses about whether war is or is not, in some significant way, functional. The examination of hypothesized functions may also have practical implications for the prevention of war. If we should indeed find that war constitutes a counteracting response made by a system when a variable or activity within the system has been disturbed in some way, we can then proceed to try to prevent war either by seeking to eliminate the disturbances whereby the variables or activities in question are moved from their proper, desired, or acceptable state or else by looking

Much of this article has appeared in my earlier paper, "Research on the Functions of Primitive War," *Peace Research Society* (*International*), *Papers,* Vol. 7 (1967). I thank the Peace Research Society for permission to reprint this material.

for alternatives to war as a counteracting response to the disturbances.

My primary focus in the paper will be on the functions of what may be conveniently designated as "primitive war," i.e., organized armed conflict among members of the relatively small, stateless societies traditionally studied by anthropologists. However, brief comparisons with civilized societies will also be made. Diverse hypotheses will be considered but with no intention of presenting an exhaustive review. To indicate that the hypotheses need not remain idle speculation, I will close the paper by briefly considering the possibilities of testing them.

Functions of Primitive War

Hypotheses presented by various writers concern the functions of primitive war in maintaining (or, we might say, "regulating") certain economic variables. According to these hypotheses, war breaks out when the inequalities between groups in their possession of or access to certain economic goods or resources reach a certain magnitude. Such hypotheses are "functional" ones if they go on to state that the effect of the warfare is to reduce the inequalities to a point where they do not exceed a proper or acceptable level. Examples are hypotheses to the effect that the distribution of camels among Bedouins and of horses among Plains Indians is regulated by having groups with too many animals become the victims of stock-raiding activities of enemy warriors (Sweet 1965a; Sweet 1965b; Vayda, Leeds, and Smith 1961:73, note 14). With respect to certain primitive people who are not pastoralists, similar hypotheses have been presented but with land rather than camels or horses as the resource being redistributed as a result of warfare. Meggitt (1962:162 and 1965:81–82) has offered such a hypothesis with reference to the Mae Enga, a horticultural people of the New Guinea highlands, while I myself have offered it as possibly applying to the warfare of various primitive people who have in common the practice of swidden or slash-and-burn agriculture (Vayda 1961).

Similar to these hypotheses about the functions of primitive war in the regulation of economic variables are certain hypotheses about the regulation of demographic variables. In these latter hypotheses, the "resources" redistributed as a result of warfare are human beings, especially, in some cases, human beings belonging to some particular age or sex category. Autonomous local groups are small enough in much of the primitive world to be subject to considerable fluctuations in size, sex ratio, and age distribution as a result of chance variations in natality and mortality. The taking of war captives is one possible means of counteracting the imbalances resulting from such chance variations, and the capture of women in particular is mentioned in the traditional accounts of primitive warfare in various parts of the world (Davie 1929:89–102).

The redistribution of land as a result of primitive war can, of course, equally be seen as a redistribution of people upon the land, a process involving a victorious group's movement into a vanquished and dispossessed enemy's former territory. Should there be no place to which the vanquished can flee, the answer to problems of local population pressure may, it has been suggested, be heavy battle mortality rather than simply a dispersing or redistributing of people as a result of warfare. This familiar Malthusian hypothesis, attributing to war the function of reducing population pressure through effects on mortality, receives some support from accounts of primitive warfare in such regions as New Guinea. I myself know of one New Guinea local group of some three hundred people which was literally decimated in a single campaign, and there are other reports of entire village communities, both in New Guinea and elsewhere, being exterminated in fighting (e.g., Bureau 1959:149; Krzywicki 1934:101–108).

Another hypothesis in the study of primitive war is a hypothesis of deterrence or "preventive war." According to this, warfare undertaken by a group to avenge an insult, theft, nonpayment of bride-price, abduction, rape, poaching, trespass, wounding, killing, or some other offense committed against its members deters members of other groups from committing further offenses. Putting it in more explicitly functional terms, we can say that the hypothesis is that when some such variable as the number, frequency, or magnitude of the offenses committed against a group exceeds a certain value, then the group goes to war and thereafter, at least temporarily, the number, frequency, or magnitude of offenses committed declines. The hypothesis focuses attention on what has been called "fighting for revenge" among primitive societies. The reports of this from numerous societies of swidden or shifting (slash-and-burn) agriculturalists in various parts of the world (see the references in Vayda 1960:2) and even from

some of the simplest societies of hunters and gatherers (Hobhouse 1956) often emphasize the role of the fighting in helping
to satisfy aggrieved people's desire for revenge. However, the
possibility of deterrence—the part that the fighting may play in
maintaining the integrity of groups and their possessions—clearly
needs also to be considered.

Hypotheses about functions of primitive war in regulating psychological variables have often been presented. The notion that
primitive war may operate so as to keep such variables as anxiety,
tension, and hostility from exceeding certain limits is implicit in
the statements of anthropologists who speak of primitive wars
as "flight from grief" devices (Turney-High 1949:142), as "enabling a people to give expression to anger caused by a disturbance of the internal harmony" (Wedgwood 1930:33), and as
serving to divert intrasocietal hostility onto substitute objects
(Murphy 1957:1032, citing Coser 1956:41). Some support for
such hypotheses or generalizations is provided by native informants' accounts of the antecedents of wars in which they themselves or their ancestors have been involved. A good example is
an account given to Whiting (1944:142) by one of his informants
in the Sepik District of New Guinea. The man said that he had
organized a raid because his wife had made his "belly hot with
anger" by taunting him. Whiting presents this as an illustration
of aggression being generated within a group and then finding an
outlet against another group. I obtained a number of similar
accounts from informants in 1963 in the course of field work
among the Maring-speakers of the Bismarck Mountains in Australian New Guinea (see Vayda 1967).

So far, I have, for the most part, presented each hypothesis as
being concerned with the regulation of a single variable. It should,
however, be noted that there also are hypotheses concerning the
relation between functions in the regulation of one variable and
functions in the regulation of another. Thus, a more elaborate
hypothesis than those previously given would be the following:
(1) a diminishing per capita food supply and increasing intra-
group competition for resources generate intense domestic frustrations and other in-group tensions; (2) when these tensions
reach a certain level, release is sought in warfare with an enemy
group; (3) a result of the warfare is reduction of the pressure
of people upon the land, either because of heavy battle mortality
or because of the victorious group's taking its defeated and dis-

persed enemy's territory; (4) the reduced pressure on the land means that the diminution of per capita food supply and the increase of intra-group competition over resources are arrested and that domestic frustrations and other in-group tensions can be kept within tolerable limits. It can be seen that, according to this hypothesis (or set of hypotheses), psychological, demographic, and economic variables are all being regulated, with the regulation of one variable being dependent upon the regulation of another.

Comparisons with Civilized War

Most of the hypotheses noted in the foregoing review may be —and, indeed, often have been—stated (even if not proved) with respect to warfare among state-organized societies also. This is so, for example, in the case of the hypotheses about functions of war in the regulation of population size, population dispersion, intersocietal offenses, tension or aggressiveness, and inequalities in goods or resources. It should, however, be noted that some hypotheses about functions of primitive war have a prima facie inapplicability in the study of civilized war. A case in point is the function of regulating the sex ratio. We would not expect this to be significant in civilized warfare, for we know that, when there are numerous people settled over an extensive territory under a single government, adjustments of any local demographic imbalances can be handled within the larger socio-political unit through movements of people. Reciprocally, some possible functions of civilized war are hardly to be expected in the warfare of primitive societies. Thus, any functions dependent on the subjugation and subsequent economic exploitation of enemy populations cannot obtain in the truly primitive world where neither food production nor political mechanisms are sufficiently developed for the support and control of economically exploitable classes of laborers or slaves (cf. Hobhouse, Wheeler, and Ginsberg 1915: chap. 4; Nieboer 1900). Similarly, the frequently encountered hypothesis which attributes to civil or intra-societal war some functions in checking or stopping abuses of political power cannot apply to primitive societies in which no persons or groups are sufficiently powerful for the abuse of power to be a problem. It is true that intra-societal wars in Polynesian chieftainships prior to European discovery (Sahlins 1963:298) and in African kingdoms (Beattie 1959; Gluckman 1963; Worsley 1961) may have functioned to check abuses of power, but these societies, with their elaborate hierarchies of authority, are not truly primitive in terms of political criteria, even if the trait of writing, sometimes regarded as the diagnostic of civilized status, was not part of their cultures.

Tests of the Hypotheses

Two things need to be emphasized: first, that what we have been describing are hypothesized and not necessarily empirically validated functions of war, either in general or even as practiced by particular societies; and, second, that there is nevertheless some possibility of empirically testing the hypotheses.

Adequate tests would require much more extensive data than have hitherto been employed. At the very least, we would need more and better data on the pre- and post-war values of the variables which, according to the hypotheses noted, are being regulated.

For dealing with the functions of civilized war, extensive statistical data and other documentation are sometimes available (see, for example, Wright 1965), but it must be conceded that some of the needed data on primitive war would be difficult to obtain. For example, for testing the hypotheses about the regulation of psychological variables, it would be useful to have motor and projective tests and measures of hormonal levels, galvanic skin response, and the like applied to primitive warriors before and after fighting, but I know of no practical way of making such tests and measurements. Moreover, the procedure of seeking support for the hypotheses by using data on the rise and fall of suicide rates or similar variables which may be regarded as indices of psychological disturbance or tension has little utility in studying primitive societies. Such a procedure can work to some extent when, as in the case of French society (Faris 1955:312 ff.), quantitative data on the pertinent variables are available from a large population for more than a century, but the data obtainable from small, primitive societies without written records can hardly be expected to be statistically adequate.

Nevertheless, useful data may still be obtained for testing some of the hypotheses about functions of primitive war, particularly the hypotheses about the regulation of economic, demographic, and socio-political variables. Thus, native informants in New Guinea, the Amazon, and similar regions where primitive warfare was being practiced until recently can still provide not only war histories but also the following: accounts of recent boundary changes or other land transfers; accounts of births and deaths in a group and of migrations into or out of it; and accounts of all the offenses committed by particular groups against one another during at least the last forty or fifty years. Furthermore, the ecological investigations necessary for defining pressure upon the land may still be undertaken in these regions. In the continuing work of a number of us in New Guinea, we are doing what we can to obtain all of these kinds of data, and it is to be hoped that field workers in other regions will make similar efforts before all the informants with memories of the relevant events will have died.

WAR AND THE STATE

ALEXANDER LESSER[1]

IN MY EFFORT TO UNDERSTAND DR. VAYDA'S PAPER, I have had to translate much of it into more common English words. After translation, I am convinced that Dr. Vayda intends to make a useful contribution toward the understanding of war, its causes and its possible prevention. Unfortunately, he has confined his thinking within the framework of the newer ecology and the older equilibrium theory, and the conceptual trappings of these interfere with if they do not destroy the intelligibility and the usefulness of his discussion.

To illustrate what I have in mind: The "functions" of war, according to Vayda usage, are what it does to restore an equilibrium which has been disturbed, and the "causes" of war are the disturbances in the equilibrium. To prevent war we can either try to eliminate these disturbances (read "causes") *or* find some alternative to war "as a counteracting response to the disturbances," namely, some alternative that will resolve the causes of conflict. After translation, it appears that whether or not we agree with Dr. Vayda's theoretical framework is of little importance. From any empirical or theoretical framework we would all be in agreement that we want to discover and define the causes of war, we want to prevent or eliminate them, and we want to find ways other than war for resolving human conflicts; that is after all what Dr. Vayda is talking about. In short, we do not need the newer ecology or equilibrium theory to agree on the job facing us today—the overwhelming problem of human survival in our time—nor, I suggest, do we need them to get on with the job.

Dr. Vayda's discussion is by his own choice focused on "primi-

---

[1] Titled by the Editors; presented as "Comments on Vayda's Hypotheses About Functions of War."

tive war"—war in primitive or "stateless" societies. He makes this choice despite a later admission that some aspects of primitive war are unrelated to the study of what he calls "civilized war," which (to avoid such a ridiculous use of value-weighted words for the opposite of their ordinary meaning) I shall call modern war. Why this emphasis in view of its possible irrelevancy to the problems of war with which we as anthropologists and civilized men must be primarily concerned? I submit that it is a direct result of the use of an ecological-equilibrium framework. In an abstract exercise of this kind it is easier to work with the so-called "simpler" data of the primitives than with the complexity of modern situations. For example, I have heard an anthropologist of the newer ecological school, when pressed, assert that World War II was "an ecological problem." This of course is easily said and discussed in broad abstraction, but it adds nothing to the understanding of World War II that cannot be gained from the usual kind of historical, political, and economic analysis.

But this notion, that anthropologists study and should study primitives because the situations and structures are simpler, is obsolete and futile; inevitably it means that we study less, and therefore learn and understand less about the complex and modern. Historically, the reason for a great deal of the earlier emphasis upon the study of primitives—apart from the historical interest itself—was and is the comparative point of view of anthropology. It is essential that we study *other* cultures—by which we generally mean non-European, non-Western—it is essential that we are prepared and able to compare our cultural situation and its emphases with those of others—in an elementary sense, in order to avoid or overcome the fallacies of ethnocentrism; in a deeper scientific sense, in order to better determine constants and independent, dependent, or interdependent variables.

This comparative point of view is relevant to the study of war as it is to any and all problems taken up by anthropology. The study of warfare among primitives *is* useful then, along with the study of warfare among non-primitives, because taken together these studies provide knowledge of a wider range of forms and conditions of military conflict—or its absence—than we could acquire in any other way.

Unfortunately, Dr. Vayda's discussion of primitive war, because of its exclusive concern with abstract hypotheses about its functions from the standpoint of equilibrium theory, offers little that is concrete about what actually happens in armed conflict among primitives. We must remedy that defect, however summarily and briefly, if we are to be able to consider the relevance of primitive warfare to the problems of war in the world today. To do so, I propose to draw your attention back to some well-known, virtually classic, facts reported about features of warfare among primitives, and, in so doing, to certain contrasts between primitive and modern patterns of warfare. If what I present is now to be considered obsolete and old-fashioned, to be discarded because of newer theoretical designs, I submit that it must be discussed, disproved as faulty, or shown to be irrelevant to present problems. It cannot simply be put aside unmentioned while disembodied fantasies of theory are put in its place.

To begin then, it has long been held that war is non-existent in some primitive societies—stateless societies in Dr. Vayda's definition—and that the forms of armed conflict which may occur in these or other primitive societies differ in goals, in involvement, and of course in military technology, from modern war.

Warfare is reported absent for example among the Andaman Islanders, the Arunta, the Eskimos, the Mission Indians, the Semang, the Todas, the Western Shoshoni, and the Yahgan (Service 1963; Murdock 1934; Beals & Hoijer 1965; Benedict 1934). Benedict (1934) remarked, of the Eskimos and Mission Indians, that they could not conceive of organized battle of tribe against tribe or village against village. In an almost-forgotten classic, *The Tribe and Intertribal Relations in Australia,* G. C. Wheeler (1910) showed many years ago that war in the modern sense—group against group, conquest and exploitation—did not occur among aboriginal Australians.

Fighting does occur among these and other primitive peoples, and we find, as manifestations of armed aggression, homicide, vengeance, and feud. Among the Eskimos, a son may have the obligation to avenge the killing of his father, and Weyer (1932) also describes outbreaks of fighting which led to multiple homicides. Among the Arunta of Australia, vengeance is carried out by a small party of kinsmen of the deceased against individuals considered responsible for their relative's death (Spencer and Gillen 1927). In both the Eskimo and Arunta cases, and among some other primitives, it is the individual guilty of the alleged murder who is killed in vengeance; there is no collective responsibility. Vengeance involving kinship based collective responsibility is found for example among the Ifugao of the Philippines, where feuds between kin groups may be of long duration (Lowie 1920). Vengeance and countervengeance may lead to feuds among many primitive peoples.

Offensive military action in the American Indian Plains took the form of vengeance parties and horse-raiding parties. Both of these were small groups; the vengeance party composed of relatives of the deceased, based on collective responsibility, sought to kill a member of the killer's tribe; the horse-raiding party, structured somewhat differently in different tribes, was a small group of eight to ten men with a specific mission, often vision-sanctioned, to run off horses from an enemy group: it had no sanction to kill and if a killing occurred the mission was usually interpreted as a failure (Lowie 1954). Raiding for horses had nothing to do with equalizing the distribution of horses in the Plains—one of Vayda's hypotheses. Individuals raided for horses because the horse had become the most valuable commodity in a Plains economy deeply interwoven through trade and trading posts with the commercial life of an expanding America. A horse was the only trade item with which a man could acquire a gun. Individuals, not tribes, gained prestige as they became wealthy in horses. Nor is the Vayda thesis that raiding among pastoral peoples functions to reduce inequalities in ownership true of the Ruwala Badawin camel breeders of Africa. There, raiders from strong tribes preyed on weaker tribes, not the reverse (Forde 1934).

In this hurried survey it must be emphasized that what is found characteristic of primitive, stateless societies are forms of armed aggression—fighting, homicide, feud—in which involvement and motivation is deeply personal, and what is not found in such societies is organized offensive warfare to conquer people or territory, with its essentially impersonal involvement and lack of personal motivation. This difference is stated bluntly as a fact in our most widely used textbook (Beals & Hoijer 1965).

Evidently, conquest warfare and its modern development of war to advance national interests is not an inherent, inevitable feature of human social life—too many societies have existed in human history without it. The widespread occurrence of offensive warfare for conquest in societies organized as states, however, is another question. Is modern war inherent and inevitable in the modern form of state political organization? This is a question with which we are today profoundly concerned. The United Nations is an organization of "sovereign states," each of which can claim that the right to make war is inherent in its sovereignty. If we are to eliminate war, if the United Nations is to succeed as a world peace-keeping machinery, the comparative study of forms of armed aggression in human societies suggests that the state as we know it must be changed and some part of its claim to armed sovereignty given up in the common interests of mankind.

HARVEY SARLES (*University of Minnesota*): It seems that Dr. Vayda has implicitly given us only a single model to consider, an equilibrium or homeostasis model much like that of physiology. This model is useful for and generally leads to the study of pathology—in this case, war as pathology. It tends to assume that there are no particular rules governing societal behavior when things are going right, but when it somehow goes wrong it is pathological. However, the equilibrium model leads away from a more useful task; that is, war is part of the nature of things, as is the rest of behavior, and perhaps we are better off looking now at the regulations of the nonwar parts—whatever it is that stops war from happening—rather than worrying only about the supposed pathological nature of war.

DAVID F. ABERLE (*University of British Columbia*): My criticisms of Professor Vayda's paper center on two points, the issue of relevance and the scientific quality of his presentation. The symposium on war, of which Professor Vayda's paper is a part, was proposed by petition at the Annual Meetings of the Association in 1966, for a specific purpose. Some Fellows of the Association thought on the one hand that resolutions opposed to American activities in Vietnam, such as I attempted to present in 1966, were not the proper business of the Association (I disagree), but on the other hand that in a situation of growing world crisis at least some members of the Association should bend their intellectual efforts toward seeing what anthropologists could say in scientific perspective about crucial issues of our day. They therefore selected the topic of war as appropriate for such an effort. Thus the symposium was not to be merely another panel of speakers dealing with concerns internal to the discipline—say one on northern Athapaskans or alliance and descent group theory. As the introductory statement in Natural History (December 1, 1967) says, "an effort was made to have the 1967 sessions deal with contemporary issues of critical importance." Consequently it is legitimate to ask whether any given paper in this symposium did deal with warfare in such a way as to bear on warfare as a contemporary issue. If Professor Vayda was not in-

structed to point his paper in this direction, then the fault lies
with those who instructed him; if he was so instructed, then his
paper falls short of meeting the symposium's goals.

One can conceive of a paper that would deal with primitive
and modern warfare in comparative, evolutionary perspective—
one that would try to account for the evolution of war and would
try to look into the future, whether of war or of a world without
war. One could conceive of a paper that would present an anthropologist's perspective on modern warfare, or hypotheses about
modern warfare. But Professor Vayda's remarks about modern
warfare were made in passing. They pointed out differences between modern and primitive warfare, but, I would say, more with
the aim of showing that the framework adopted by Professor
Vayda for hypothesizing about primitive warfare would not be
adequate for modern warfare. Indeed, it turns out that the purpose of his paper is to develop an approach for empirical research on primitive war, by which he apparently means warfare
in egalitarian societies. (One is never sure whether he divides the
world into primitive, stateless, and civilized—state—societies, or
into primitive, intermediate, and civilized. At any rate one comes
only very late to the realization that for Professor Vayda the
chiefdom is not primitive—but since civilized war is war at the
state level, the chiefdom seems to be in limbo.) I submit that a
paper whose primary purpose is to develop a set of hypotheses
for work in the hinterlands of New Guinea, however interesting
anthropologically, does not meet the criterion of relevance originally established as a guideline for this symposium. I am particularly sorry to bring this criticism against Professor Vayda's paper,
because he is one of the few anthropologists who has tried for
some time to deal with war as a topic for systematic anthropological study.

As to the scientific quality of his presentation, my central ob-
jection is to his use of equilibrium, homeostasis (a term he employed during the discussion period), and function as guiding
concepts. In his reply to me at the symposium, Professor Vayda
asserted, correctly, that he had a right to choose any concepts or
models he wished to. But a critic has a right also—the right to say
that the approach does not seem fruitful, and this is my claim. It
is difficult to develop an appropriate polemic in opposition to
Professor Vayda's approach, because of the way he has used his
terms. He says that examination of primitive war may "help pro-

vide a basis for assessing the more general hypotheses about whether war is, in some significant way, functional." I do not see how one can assess whether war is functional without saying for what system it may be functional, or "non-functional" and "pathological," and without saying what the setting of that system is.

Professor Vayda has not mentioned the question of setting, and in his comments on function during the discussion period, he said that function refers to the maintaining or restoring of something within a range of values, and that the system within which equilibrium of homeostasis was being maintained is not necessarily a society, a community or a social structure, but can be any collection of variables chosen by the investigator. It can indeed, but unless one knows what the system that Professor Vayda is investigating is, it is exceedingly difficult to confront him head on on such issues as the utility of equilibrium, homeostasis, or function as tools for the analysis of warfare, or for that matter to endorse his views. Thus the presentation is faulty.

In addition, equilibrium models have led us into endless difficulties, for which we have been criticized by a variety of philosophers of science. It seems too bad to attempt to tackle the problem of war with tools whose utility is gravely questioned.

With respect to the topic at hand—warfare—it seems to me, as a starting point, valuable to assume that the aim of much warfare (I abandon the word "function" because I no longer know what it means) is not to equalize inequalities, as is suggested in one of Professor Vayda's hypotheses, but to increase them. Conceivably an equilibrium model might have some possibilities for application when the warfare under consideration occurs between groups at a similar level of organization and with similar technologies in similar environments—groups that are adjusting to random fluctuations of population and/or resources. But when war occurs between groups with different technologies (military, productive, or both) or different levels of organization, or both, it is typically an expansive operation for one of the systems in question; it aims at a continuous disturbance of inter-societal equilibrium. And with state societies, even when they are similar in technology and level of organization, the same thing seems often to be true. Conceivably all disequilibrating relationships between two social organizations can be shown to be equilibrating devices for one of the two parties in the conflict, but it seems doubtful that they can be seen to be equilibrating for both parties.

Since Professor Vayda has not defined his system, it is always possible that there is some mode of defining it that will show that *any* war is equilibrating for *some* system, in which case we are probably dealing with a non-falsifiable hypothesis.

In several parts of the globe we find very large continuous areas occupied by language families whose members have diverged from one another relatively recently in human history. This would be true, for example, for Bantu, Semitic, Indo-European and Sinitic. Many of these linguistic expansions can be shown to have swallowed up, shoved aside, or pushed into refuge areas groups of different linguistic background that earlier occupied the area. These distributions suggest that expansion of peoples "on the prod" is not a product of modern times or even of the historic period. Quite aside from the imperialistic expansions of the west, then, inter-societally disequilibrating warfare seems to be a widespread phenomenon.

I suggest, then, that in terms of scientific yield we are likely to get further, faster with concepts like competition, expansion, and domination, than with concepts like function, equilibrium, homeostasis, and reduction of inequalities. And if, for a given symposium, the mandate is relevance to the world crisis, these or other concepts must be applied to the examination of modern warfare, whether or not primitive warfare is considered.

JACK LEVINE (*Long Island University*): I would like to address Dr. Vayda. Under the topic of "Social and Political Variables" would he consider a function of war to be the social and political cohesion of the group resulting in a greater solidarity for the period of mobilization leading up to the war, the period of war, and the short period after the war?

ANTHONY LEEDS (*University of Texas*): I am very much bothered by today's entire symposium discussion, as Aberle has been, largely because, it seems to me, many of the main features of warfare have been completely omitted. Among other things, warfare takes place in an institutional context, is itself a complex institution, intricately linked with the contextual institutions, and occurs within the context of a power structure involving at least two sides. As Lesser said, we have had no consideration of what the phenomenon war is and what it is not. What sort of an institutional complex is war generically? What kind of evolutionary developments are there in the institutional complex in which war as an institution is embedded? How is the war complex related to the other institutions of society, e.g. to the economy in general, or to feudal, capitalist, or other types of economies, specifically; or to the polity, generically, or in particular to archaic, feudal or "modern" states, or any other classification of polities one wants to use?

What are the intra- and inter-polity triggering conditions of warfare? These should always be examined together. What are the states or conditions of the individual institutions or their complex interrelations which generate conditions of warfare? The type of systems analysis, accompanied by precisely the concepts of function Vayda wants to use, and so carefully defined by him— but definitely *not* the ambiguous term "aim" that Aberle chooses to use without definition—is highly appropriate to the analysis of such relations, the institutions and their interrelations being treated as variables operating through ranges and producing both negative and positive feedback (cf. Leeds 1961; Vayda and Leeds 1961; Leeds and Vayda, eds. 1965, especially the articles by Knight, Hickerson, Leeds, and Sweet).

Any consideration of the condition of war seems to me to entail a consideration of the condition of peace (see Leeds 1961). The treatment of war and peace in this symposium has been as if peace is "normal" and essentially "good" even "enjoyable" (e.g. peaceful conflict was said to be enjoyable) while war is treated as "abnormal," "pathological," "evil," etc. From a subjective point of view, the condition of peace can be pretty horrifying, e.g. the McCarthy period in the United States or pre-World War II Germany for the Jews. As Ambrose Bierce (1925), with usual economy remarked: "Peace, n. In international affairs, a period of cheating between two periods of fighting." From a systems point of view, it can involve great rigidity, and virtually intolerable strains. The release of such strains may be characterized by warfare as a positive feedback function in Vayda's sense of the word.

War, too, may develop intolerable strains, its own forms of rigidity, and systemic blockage to changes of state. In short, it may be quite productive to look at war and peace as alternating systemic states in societies among which warfare occurs more or less frequently. We may then inquire as to the triggering mechanisms and the contexts of and conditions for these shifts.

I feel we must have a harshly realistic and as value-free a look at the condition of peace as at the condition of war, and in equivalent analytic, definitional, logical and proportional. This should be taken free of the nominative statements of aberrancy or pathology of war and the goodness and intrinsic desirability of peace.

Finally, warfare involves, certainly today, immense ranges and vast quantities of strategic resources: material, personnel, tools and equipment, money. In contemporary warfare, such resources involve any warring country in a world ecology, consequently, in world politics, world-wide institutions (such as aid programs, service programs, colonialism, imperialism, etc., which have been virtually unmentioned here today) and, more and more frequently, far-flung or world-wide wars. Connected with this are some very excruciating questions, e.g., since both intra-polity and inter-polity property is involved, how much is modern warfare a function of the system of property under capitalism?

Somehow, all this seems to me to have been left out in today's symposium so that I am left feeling that we are talking about some sort of spirit or *Geist* we call "War" whose material foundations have been left out almost entirely, along with the real world we live in and I think it essential that anthropologists, if they intend to have something substantive to say about warfare, turn to these matters.

DR. VAYDA: I must begin my reply by resisting the discussants' attempts to substitute other terms for "function." I said I was speaking of "functions" of war, and I meant it—even if just what I meant was not too well communicated to Professors Aberle and Lesser. I am glad to have this opportunity for a further attempt at clarification, although I may not be able to do justice to the subject in the brief space available. Elsewhere (e.g., Vayda 1968; Collins and Vayda, MS), I have treated in more detail some of the issues to be considered in what follows.

As I noted in the discussion period when our symposium was held, I regard the function of anything as the contribution that it makes to keeping or restoring some property or variable of a system within a certain range of states or values. This is, incidentally, a conception taken from philosophers of science (Brown 1963:110–11; Collins 1965; Nagel 1956:251–52), but probably from other ones than the unnamed critics of equilibrium models to whom Professor Aberle alludes.

Professor Aberle grants me the right to define in terms of variables the systems within which my hypothesized functions operate, but his reference to warring groups or societies as "systems" indicates that he does not go along with me in regarding systems as collections of variables. A warring group is not a collection of variables; what can constitute such a collection are the size of the group, whether it is fighting or not, its rate of population increase, its degree of population dispersion, its level of anxiety, its efficiency of land use, the number of offenses committed against it, and so forth. In the hypotheses that I presented, collections of these and similar variables were in fact the systems that I was talking about. Judgments about whether the occurrence of war is functional in such systems can be based simply on extensive observation or measurement of the pre-war, war, and post-war values of the systemic variables, but of course any judgments made will have to be about "functionality" in my sense of contribution to the maintenance of a systemic variable within a range of values rather than in any other sense that the discussants of my paper may have had in mind.

Professor Lesser comes closer than Professor Aberle to understanding me. Lesser's recasting of my statements in causal terms is logically permissible, but it must not be allowed to obscure the point that functional relations are only a sub-class of causal ones (Brown 1963:110). Functional relations are *causal ones within homeostatic, self-regulating, teleological, or negative feedback systems,* i.e., within systems that operate so as to maintain a given variable within a range of values despite disturbances tending to remove the variable from that range. In using the special language to which Professor Lesser objects, I am trying to focus attention on this special and important class of causal relations so that it will not be confused with other classes and so that methods of investigation and analysis appropriate to it and perhaps to it alone may be developed further in anthropology. Professor Lesser's own discussion can be used to illustrate the distinctions. When he makes a point of noting that Plains Indians traded horses for guns, I see the possibility that he too is talking about functional relations but with guns rather than horses per tribe as the variable being maintained within a range of values. This is something that I can handle within the framework of func-

tional analysis. However, when, in the face of evidence that I
have cited on the conquest and redistribution of land as a result
of primitive warfare, Professor Lesser nevertheless states that
wars to conquer territory are absent in primitive societies, it is
clear that he must be talking about other kinds of causal relations
than the ones treated in my paper and that my framework of
analysis cannot apply.

On the whole, I welcome Professor Leeds' remarks, although
I am somewhat puzzled by his reference to the omission of "material foundations." I thought that my discussion of economic and
demographic variables might have satisfied him at least as far as
primitive warfare is concerned, but perhaps it is only the analysis
of modern warfare that he is referring to.

The main value of Professor Leeds' remarks lies in the answer
that they provide to Professor Aberle and Lesser's charge that
my analytic framework is not suited for research on modern warfare. (I believe that an answer does need to be made to the charge
even though I was not instructed by the symposium organizers
to make my paper bear upon warfare as a contemporary issue and
would not have taken part in the symposium had I been so instructed.) Professor Leeds is, I think, saying that war in the world
today may well form part of some exceedingly complex systems
involving feedbacks among variables on a global scale and that
the same basic concepts as I have been using are appropriate for
the analysis of such systems. I am pleased to agree with this.
There would, it might be noted, probably be agreement too both
from researchers in "think-tanks" supported by contracts with
agencies of the United States military-industrial complex and
from the Marxist scholars who see modern warfare as functioning to maintain the growth rate of capitalist economies. If I have
been discussing relatively simple systems involving primitive societies, it is because these are the systems that I, as an anthropologist, have studied professionally and have been able to begin
to analyze without either massive research assistance or the aid
of computer technology for processing vast amounts of data, and,
accordingly, these are the systems that I can most readily speak
about. It must be said, however, that even with regard to such
systems, Professor Aberle fails to give functional analysis its due,
for he seems to have no conception that the systemic variable
maintained within a range of values might be a rate of change
(cf. Cancian 1960:823)—for example, a rate of expansion, this

being a variable whose systemic regulation I myself have been concerned with in studying primitive warfare (Vayda 1961 and in press). In view of Professor Aberle's circumscribed understanding of what functional or equilibrium analysis is about, it is not surprising that he cannot see its utility in a world of expanding polities and growing economies.

One further point may be worth making explicit, and this is that "functionality" in my sense is not to be equated with adaptiveness or with utility in terms of any criteria other than the maintenance of a specific variable within a specific range of values in a specific system. Because they may be presumed to be the products of processes of evolutionary selection, persisting functional or negative feedback systems (e.g., those described in Leeds and Vayda 1965) no doubt mostly are, or at least have been, adaptive systems. This, however, does not mean that they are necessarily adaptive or meet other criteria of general utility at any given point in time, for we know that traits or systems formerly favored by evolutionary selection may persist, at least temporarily, even after a change in environmental conditions has made them nonadaptive or maladaptive. If war today is indeed part of some exceedingly complex functional systems involving feedbacks among variables on a global scale and if these systems may have become maladaptive because of the advent of nuclear weapons and other changes in the environment, then I should think that the study of these systems with a view to seeing how they can be altered might be assigned a high priority by Professor Aberle and other social scientists who want to relate their work to crucial issues of the day.

Part *V* | THE EFFECTS OF WAR ON
SOCIAL STRUCTURE

YANOMAMÖ SOCIAL ORGANIZATION
AND WARFARE[1]

NAPOLEON A. CHAGNON

INTRODUCTION

"Assertions with respect to war have emanated from philosophers, clergymen, journalists, publicists, sentimentalists, peace advocates, apologists of war, and a host of others. Their views as to the causes of war, the history of conflict, and the outlook for the future are usually dogmatically stated. When placed side by side they appear inconsistent and contradictory. They have one thing in common: they lack the basis of fact. It is so much easier and more alluring to speculate as to the how and why of war than to grub for the facts."

MAURICE R. DAVIE, *The Evolution of War*

PROBABLY NO SINGLE ACADEMIC DISCIPLINE has more facts bearing on the nature and social effects of war than anthropology. Yet it is true that anthropologists have devoted relatively little effort in attempts to make these facts intelligible, a state of affairs somewhat out of proportion to the profound effects this phenomenon has had in the evolution of culture. There have been a number of important exceptions; still, our comparative silence up to this point has resulted in a state of affairs of such incredible di-

[1] The field research on which this section is based was supported by a USPHS Fellowship F1 MH-25, 052 and attached grand MH 10575-01 BEH RO4, and an AEC Area Grant AT(11-1)-1552. I am also indebted to the Instituto Venezolano de Investigaciones Científicas (IVIC) for its support. I should also like to express my thanks to the following people for criticizing an earlier version of the chapter: Robert L. Carneiro, Gertrude Dole, William Irons, Rodney Needham, David Schneider and Terence Turner. I apologize to them for not having included many of the suggestions they made with respect to some aspects of social structure but hope to incorporate them in a separate treatment of the topic.

mensions that playwrights, ethologists, generals, and politicians
are presently among the leading spokesmen on the causes, nature, and effects of warfare.

This paper, to paraphrase Davie, grubs for the relevant facts of
one important kind of primitive warfare. While it specifically
deals with the social effects of warfare in one tribe of South American Indians, the Yanomamö of southern Venezuela, this paper
purports to have a more general significance. Yanomamö warfare represents a type commonly found in the pristine primitive
world, the essential features of which were outlined by Vayda
(1960:1–2). These features include: smallness of scale in military operations, short duration of active hostilities, poor development of command and discipline, great reliance on stealth and
surprise attacks, and the great significance of village community
or local group in organizing and conducting war parties. In short,
Yanomamö warfare is a particular expression of a more general
type.

But Yanomamö warfare also represents an important sub-
variety within this general category: *the conflicts are not initiated
or perpetuated with territorial gain as an objective or consequence.* It therefore has an important bearing on theories of aggression based on territoriality, specifically, those developed in
the recently published books by Ardrey (1966) and Lorenz
(1966). One objective of this paper, then, is to present ethnographic data that contests explanations of warfare based exclusively on genetically determined behavioral patterns.

Another reason non-territorial warfare is significant is that
adaptive explanations of it require a broader definition of cultural
ecology. The Yanomamö practice swidden agriculture and are expanding geographically and numerically (Chagnon ms.; Neel and
Chagnon in press); they should therefore be easily explained
with one of the two models developed by Vayda in a more recent
publication (1961). But they do not fit either model because their
warfare cannot be shown to be a consequence of competition for
land. For the Iban and Maori, the critical feature of the environment within which they operate and to which they must adapt is
the shortage of land, warfare being the means by which adaptation is effected through acquisition of either occupied territory or
access to trade routes. The Yanomamö, by contrast, are obliged
to adapt to a socio-political milieu in which the members of independent villages attempt to steal each other's women. A mili-

tant ideology in this situation is adaptive in the sense that each group enhances its position in the alliance networks by convincing others that it will defend its sovereignty with force and constantly threatens to do so.

The position adopted here is that the social relationships between Yanomamö villages are as important as the relationships of societies to land in so far as adaptive explanations of warfare are concerned. The model I propose combines the definition of cultural ecology given by Harding (1960) with the specific theory of cultural evolution in Carneiro's analysis of South American cultures (1961). The model makes use of Harding's argument that in specific historical and environmental circumstances, sociopolitical systems must adjust to both nature and other, neighboring socio-political systems:

> "The character of its habitat will influence a culture's technology, and through technology its social and ideological components. But nearby cultures and the relations effected with them also affect a culture's sociopolitical and ideological subsystems. Moreover, the latter may in turn, in the attempt to cope with the outside world, channel the direction of technological development." (1960:47)

Carneiro's analysis of cultural evolution in South America makes use of the relationship between demography, ecological zones that are circumscribed by geographical barriers, and the relationship between level of cultural development and the practice of intensive, as opposed to extensive, agriculture. Carneiro argues that cultural developments consistently took place in areas that were geographically circumscribed because increases in population density led to a shift from extensive to intensive cultivation as the available land was used up. Political developments, based on conquest, led to confederacies, alliances and, ultimately, political empires. In the Tropical Forest, where extensive, unbroken agricultural land was abundant, local population increases resulted in migration. Consequently, there was no pressure on the carrying capacity of the land and no impetus existed to change extensive cultivation into intensive agriculture.

The facts of ethnology relating to the Tropical Forest cultures support Carneiro's analysis: contests over land were notably absent, although warfare was common and intense; population density appears to have been very low, even at the time of Conquest (Steward 1946–48); and village fission followed by migration was a common phenomenon; finally, the tribes of the Tropical Forest had uniformly underdeveloped political institutions when compared with the Circum-Caribbean or Andean peoples.

The hypothesis I put forward here is that a militant ideology and the warfare it entails function to preserve the sovereignty of independent villages in a milieu of chronic warfare. The origin of such a political milieu seems to be the result of the failure of Yanomamö political institutions to govern effectively the conflicts arising within villages, conflicts that give rise to internal fighting and village fission with the ultimate establishment of mutually hostile, independent villages. Contributing to the generally hostile relationships between villages is the suspicion that unexpected deaths are the result of harmful magic practiced by members of other groups. To maximize their chances for independent political existence in this milieu, members of sovereign villages protect their autonomy by adopting an agonistic stance toward neighboring groups. I submit that such an ideology, with its attendant expressions of violence, is adaptive. That is, I agree with Professor Vayda that wherever it exists, warfare serves a cultural-adaptive purpose in that it results in a more advantageous relationship between people and their cultural ecology. Where I think I disagree is in his implied argument that an *expanding* group of slash-and-burn horticulturists inevitably conducts warfare over territory. The facts of South American ethnology do not lend themselves to this argument. In this connection it is noteworthy that Professor Vayda developed his models in response to statements made by Julian Steward and Robert Murphy concerning the nature of warfare among the Tupinambá and Mundurucú, two South American Tropical Forest tribes whose warfare does not appear to have been stimulated by motives of territorial acquisition (Vayda 1961:346).

Perhaps the tendency to dismiss non-territorial warfare with psychological explanations such as "release from pent-up emotions" or "expressing anger on outsiders to contribute to internal solidarity" have resulted from too few accurate descriptions of aboriginal patterns of warfare, as well as to inadequate theoretical premises. While it is true that a military engagement may have the salubrious effect of releasing the pent-up emotions of the contestants and therefore results in emotional tranquillity, one cannot account for the engagement itself by citing psychological variables such as anxiety or in terms of innate aggression. To do so is to confuse effects with functions and reduce cultural phenomena to bio-psychological variables.

If warfare does have the psychological effect of releasing the pent-up emotions of the combatants, how do we account for their frustrations in the first place? Why were the tribes of the Tropical Forest more frustrated and warlike than the shellfish gatherers of Tierra del Fuego? Psychology and ethology offer us no meaningful answers to these questions. At best, they draw attention to certain behavioral facts and phrase them in the special language of their respective disciplines. While it is true that human beings have the capacity for rage and aggression and that a strong case can be made for the ethnographic universality of warfare, it is equally true that cultural systems define and regulate the circumstances under which expressions of aggression are permitted, what form they take, against what or whom they are directed and the legitimate means of such expressions. In some cultures overt expressions of aggression are regarded as detrimental to the social order and are suppressed and contained, while in others, such behavior is applauded and encouraged. The stimuli evoking these responses are culturally determined and extremely varied, defense of territory being only one such stimulus and not a universal one at that.

The Yanomamö exemplify a type of society in which aggressiveness and warfare are admired, but their commitment to this way of life cannot be explained in terms of land shortages. The critical aspect of the cultural ecology is neighboring, hostile villages. It is the adaptation to this, rather than to the availability of land, that gives Yanomamö society its aggressive character. However, there are many variations in the intensity of warfare as one moves from the tribal periphery to the tribal center. Simply stated, warfare is more intense and frequent at the center, resulting in a different kind of cultural adaptation there.

Briefly, villages at the center, because of the relative proximity of neighbors, are not free to migrate into new areas at will. Instead, they must confront each other politically and militarily. Villages at the center are larger, palisaded, nucleated, and enmeshed in alliances with neighbors. Population density is higher and warfare more intense. Distances between villages at the center are much smaller than at the periphery, although they are well spaced. The adaptation here takes the form of extreme militancy and hostility toward neighbors.

Villages at the periphery, on the other hand, are more widely spaced and isolated. Conflicts with neighbors are less frequent and are easily resolved by migration. Inter-village alliances are not so common and the intensity of warfare is greatly reduced, compared to the situation at the center. Villages are much smaller and are not nucleated: sixty people in a village at the tribal center would occupy a single, palisaded dwelling, whereas the same group at the periphery would probably occupy three or four well-spaced, unpalisaded structures. Displays of aggression and violence are greatly reduced in frequency and limited in form,[2] and the entire complex of alliances based on formal, reciprocal trading, and feasting is either greatly diminished in scale or, in some areas, non-existent. One conspicuous way in which this diminished emphasis on feasting and alliance is evidenced is in the size of both the gardens and the village structure itself. As we shall see, feasting and alliance call forth a considerable amount of agricultural over-production, and village structure reflects the importance of the feast in the life of the people. A structure that sixty people would build in an area where feasting is an important component in alliance would be significantly larger than that required where feasting is not important in maintaining inter-village ties. In other words, villages at the tribal center are larger *physically* than those at the periphery, the difference in size reflecting the importance of regularized visiting, feasting, and dancing.

The description that follows is based on field work conducted among the Yanomamö at both the center of the tribal territory and at the periphery. It specifically refers, however, to the nature of the warfare pattern and social organization at the tribal center.[3]

---

[2] Club fights, for example, do not occur in this area of the tribe.

[3] Thirteen of my sixteen months with the Yanomamö were spent in villages at the tribal center and three months in villages at the periphery. The field work was initiated in November 1964, and is presently continuing in conjunction with a medical-anthropological project sponsored by the Department of Human Genetics at the University of Michigan and Instituto Venezolano de Investigaciones Científicas in Caracas. A considerable amount of additional field work is scheduled in conjunction with this project.

THE YANOMAMÖ POPULATION[4]

There are about 10,000 Yanomamö occupying the area shown in Map A.[5] This zone comprises roughly 110,000 square kilometers,

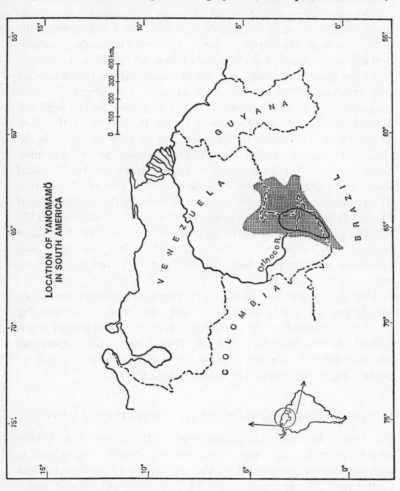

LOCATION OF YANOMAMÖ IN SOUTH AMERICA

---

[4] The Yanomamö are also described in the literature as Waika, Sanema, Xiriana, and Guaharibo.

[5] The center of the tribe is the area circled in Map A.

giving an overall population density of ten people per 100 square kilometers,[6] putting them at the lower end of the range of densities characteristic of Tropical Forest tribes (Steward 1949:675 gives the population densities for the various culture types in South America).

The population is distributed in about a hundred widely scattered villages of sizes ranging from 40 to 250 inhabitants at the center, those at the periphery being smaller. The median population size at the center is of the order of 70 to 85 inhabitants.

At the present time about a dozen villages are in direct contact with missionaries on the Orinoco, Mucajai, Uraricoera, Demeni, Cauaburi, and Marauia rivers. The first sustained contact with the Yanomamö began in 1950 when James P. Barker of the New Tribes Mission ascended the Orinoco and took up residence in the village of Mahe-kodo-teri. In 1954, a Silesian priest, Antonion Goiaz, contacted a Yanomamö village in Brazil on the Cauaburi River and initiated sustained contact on that side of the border. The remainder of the contacts, many of them by the Unevangelized Fields Mission, were made more recently, most of them in 1957–58. The greater number of Yanomamö villages have not had direct contact with outsiders even yet, although a few steel tools and aluminum cooking pots have probably reached even the most remote village by now.

The Yanomamö are divided into five major dialect areas, the two largest of which are the Central and Western, comprising roughly 75 percent of the population. With the exception of a few individuals who have learned Carib (Makiritare), the Yanomamö are monolingual. The presence of missionaries, however, will no doubt change this situation in the immediate future.

ECONOMIC GEOGRAPHY, TECHNOLOGY, AND SETTLEMENT PATTERN

The terrain in Yanomamö country is relatively low, humid, covered with jungle, crisscrossed by rivers and streams and subject to inundations during the peak of the wet season (June–July). Most of the land lies at an elevation of 500–700', although it varies from 450' to 3000'. Yanomamö villages are usually found at the

---

[6] Converted to miles, this gives an area of 35,000 square miles and 28 people per 100 square miles.

lower elevations, although in the Parima "mountains" a few are found as high as 2500'.

The major rivers may vary as much as 15 feet from season to season, and inundate the low-lying jungle along their courses in full flood. During the wet season inter-village travel is difficult, if not impossible, since the Yanomamö travel only by foot.[7] Under normal circumstances, the Yanomamö occupy themselves with gardening at this time of the year, but the military situation may alter their seasonal cycle.

The rivers begin falling in September and inter-village travel again increases. By February the rivers have reached their lowest levels; inter-village visiting, trading and feasting are at their peaks at this time, as is raiding. Swamps that were impassable during the months of May, June, and July are usually no more than soggy potholes and pose no hindrance to travel. Anxiety increases in the dry season, for everyone must be on the alert for raiders.

The Yanomamö take advantage of geographical barriers such as swamps, rivers, and rugged hills when they establish new villages. A new site is established so that enemy villages will be separated by these barriers; once the military considerations of the site have been weighed, the specific location is then fixed by soil factors, amount of jungle cover, drainage of the terrain, and availability of a constant supply of drinking water.

The Yanomamö attempt to establish their villages at least a day's walk from any neighbor. Inter-village friendships are so tenuous under even the best of circumstances that an individual never trusts his neighbors and allies. Most villages are therefore at a considerable distance from their closest neighbors, but in some circumstances villages will be found just a few hours apart. In many of these cases the size of the village has more to do with the proximity of location than lack of suitable terrain: small, militarily vulnerable villages tend to be located close to their stanchest ally, to which they turn for refuge in case of war.

Mutually hostile villages are separated by at least two or three days' march: if they are separated by a distance of less than two days and intensify their hostilities, one of the two will move to a new, more distant location, abandoning its old garden.

[7] They do, however, make bark canoes when they must cross a large river. The canoes are usually abandoned after one use.

Nearly every major village move[8] is the result of intensified hostilities; raiding becomes so intense and exacts such a heavy toll that the members of a beleaguered village are forced to abandon their gardens and establish a new one elsewhere. A study of two clusters of villages, Namowei-Tedi and Paruritawa-Tedi, showed that all but two of the numerous moves between 1875 and 1966 had been stimulated by warfare.[9] Clearly village mobility is marked, a reflection of the intensity of warfare in this area. A brief account of the historical factors relating to the moves will also be given to show the relationship between settlement pattern and warfare. Some of the villages moved subsequent to the study, an indication of the continuing nature of warfare.

Despite the frequency of village movements brought about by warfare, the Yanomamö have a relatively stable, sedentary village life characteristic of most slash-and-burn cultivators. Were it not for their wars, the Yanomamö could remain almost indefinitely in the same general area. By way of illustration, the Patanowä-teri has occupied its site more or less continuously for over forty years.[10] But regardless of the frequency of village movement, the Yanomamö must have access to cultivated foods in order to maintain coresidential groups of 40–250 people: the jungle is simply not sufficiently productive to support groups of that size for more than brief periods. Their dependence on cultivated foods therefore makes their whereabouts predictable by enemies. A group that is forced from its garden by intensive raids cannot remain away from it for very long without returning for fresh supplies of food unless, of course, it takes refuge in the village of an ally and subsists on the latter's produce. Thus raiders, knowing the current political relationships between all the villages, can usually find their enemies: if they are not in their village, they have either taken refuge

---

[8] By major move I mean abandoning a given area and migrating to a new area. This is distinct from the minor garden movements associated with swidden agriculture.

[9] The two moves not stimulated by warfare resulted, in one case, from undesirable soil conditions, and in the other the arrival of foreigners: the group in question moved closer to the foreigners (a government malaria control team) in order to gain access to a source of steel tools.

[10] Although warfare has forced the Patanowä-teri to temporarily abandon its garden on a number of occasions, it continues to return when the intensity of raiding diminishes.

with a friendly group or are hiding in a temporary camp nearby. An examination of the trails around the garden will usually decide the issue: if they are still in use, the group is hiding out in a temporary camp and returns for food as it is needed; if the trails show no indication of recent use, then the group has taken refuge with an ally.

The Yanomamö attempt to avoid situations that oblige them to take refuge with a neighbor, for such aid is never tendered without gain in mind. The protecting hosts inevitably demand access to their visitors' women, by either temporary rights or permanent acquisition by marriage. A group expecting a period of intensive raiding will therefore begin clearing a new garden in a more remote area. One group with which I lived initiated a war with a larger village in 1965; in anticipation of this war, they began clearing a new garden across a large river and broad swamp from their old one, putting two additional geographical obstacles in the path of their enemies. However, they miscalculated the rate at which the raiding would intensify and the fury of their opponents at having lost a kinsman; they were forced to abandon their garden before the new one began producing and had no alternative but to seek refuge in the villages of their allies. For the better part of a year they moved from one ally to another, leaving each one when demands for women became outrageous. They would carry food from their allies' gardens and camp at their new location to work in the garden, moving to another ally's village when they ran out of food. Fortunately, they had several allies, but they nevertheless had to give away several young women whom they might not otherwise have relinquished. When the wet season came and travel became difficult, they could return at last to their producing garden and transplant cuttings to the new location. If the water level dropped conspicuously, they repaired to their new garden with provisions from the old one and waited for new rains to raise the river. They spent most of 1965 moving from one ally to another, then to their producing garden, and back to their unproductive new site to work. All during this time they remained intact as a group and continued to subsist on cultivated foods, most of which were provided by allies. Their new garden began producing at the end of this year, but since most of the crops were planted simultaneously, they matured more or less at the same time, resulting in windfalls that were interrupted by periods of little. They still had to rely on allies for food, but to a much lesser extent. They had achieved self-sufficiency in 1967 when I returned to continue my field work; by that time they had planted cuttings in such a way that the garden produced a continuous supply of food.

TRADING, FEASTING, AND ALLIANCES

The example just given shows one of the major implications of alliance: allied villages are expected to give refuge to each other in times of need, extending the resources of gardens to the members of a beleaguered group. A second obligation in inter-village alliance is the offer of military aid during periods of active raiding. While this cannot prevent one village from raiding another, it appears to reduce the possibility of raiding: if village A plans to raid village B, its ultimate decision may be based on the relationships B has with groups C, D, E, etc. In the case of revenge, such considerations are negligible: A will raid B regardless of B's alliances. But should group A consider initiating war with group B for any other reason, B's political commitments become of great significance to A.

The members of every village, therefore, attempt to cultivate friendly ties with neighbors, but mutual suspicion is so intense and village sovereignty so crucial that the alliances are never established with the obligations spelled out by the principals involved. For example, the village in which I began my field work in 1964 had friendly ties with several neighboring villages. All the men left on a raid and were gone nearly two weeks; their women appeared every day at my hut and refused to leave it until nightfall. They incessantly asked me to show them my shotgun, a demand that began to annoy me after a number of repetitions. I finally discovered that they stayed in or around my hut because, in effect, I was protecting them from raiders! I also discovered that the few remaining men stood guard all night long, watching the trails most likely to be taken by raiders from the allied villages! As a matter of fact, a raiding party from one of these villages did set out with the apparent intention of abducting some of the poorly defended women, but the men returned before this group of raiders arrived.[11]

Hence allies confront each other somewhat boastfully and attempt to demonstrate that they do not require assistance and prob-

----

[11] I describe this particular event in some detail in Chapter 4 of *Yanomamö: The Fierce People* (in press).

ably never will, for the obverse implication is that they are weak and can be exploited by a stronger group. Were it not for the fact, recognized by all Yanomamö but rarely discussed, that no village can exist indefinitely without friendly allies, the Yanomamö would probably have very little inter-village contact. This paradoxical set of attitudes—allies need each other but refuse to acknowledge it overtly—has given rise to a peculiar relationship between economic specialization, trade, and alliance.

Each group seems to create shortages of particular items, such as bows, clay pots, arrows, baskets, arrow points, hammocks, cotton, dogs, drugs, arrow point cases, and other manufactured articles, and relies on one or more of its allies for these goods. In turn, the group provides its allies with the goods the latter request. These shortages cannot be explained in terms of the distribution of resources or a specialization in production due to esoteric knowledge. Rather, a sociological explanation is required. For example, village A may be a hammock-taker from village B but a hammock-giver to village C. A more dramatic example is the production of clay pots. In one case village A gave pots to village B but obtained them from village C. The middlemen claimed to be ignorant of the art of pottery, reinforcing their story with the assertion that the clay in their area was not the proper kind for pot-making. They acknowledged, however, that they used to know how to make pots, but had long since forgotten. When they entered unexpectedly into a war with the group that provided them with pots, they promptly "remembered" how pots were made and "discovered" that the clay in their area was indeed suitable. They therefore managed to provide their partners with an uninterrupted supply of pots.

Inter-village friendship and solidarity depends to a large extent on the frequency of visiting that takes place, and the trading techniques themselves, in addition to the specialized production, stimulate visiting. An individual will give a particular item, a dog, for example, to a friend in an allied village saying: "I give you this dog *no mraiha.*" Superficially, the *no mraiha* looks like a "free" gift, since the recipient does not give anything in return at that time. But *no mraiha* "gifts" are not free presentations: each object given must be repaid at a later time with a different kind of article, i.e., it is reciprocating trade of the kind described by Mauss in *The Gift* (1954). Thus, each trade calls forth another, a type of deficit spending that insures peaceful, frequent inter-village visiting.

(See Chagnon, in press b, for further discussion of trading practices.)

Trade reduces the possibility that one group will attack the other without serious, overt provocation. In effect, it reduces the chance that one group will attribute otherwise unaccountable deaths to the harmful magic of a trading partner. But trade does not eliminate the possibility of limited fighting or diminish suspicion: members of villages that stand in trading relationship with each other occasionally have duels with either fists or clubs, and suspect the other group of plotting to abduct women.

Trade is important in another way; it is the first step in a possibly more intimate social relationship: inter-village feasting. While trading itself constitutes a kind of inter-village alliance, it is an unstable, tenuous alliance and easily broken. When reciprocal feasting eventually results from a long period of trading relations, trade still functions to keep the two groups bound to each other and provides, in many cases, the stimulus to feast. That is, village A may owe village B a number of woven hammocks; when these are manufactured, group A will inform group B that its hammocks are completed and a feast will be arranged to provide the social matrix within which the exchange takes place.

A feasting alliance carries with it more obligations and therefore implies a greater degree of solidarity. Enormous quantities of food must be harvested and prepared; dances and chants are invented, practiced, and recited; and the trade goods promised to the visitors must be finished. The work for a feast is considerable, promotes a good deal of cooperation within the host group itself, and generates a high-level of enthusiasm and excitement that is carried over to the feast.

The visitors at a feast are presented with large quantities of food, are given a chance to display their decorations, dances, and songs, chat intimately with men from the host group, and exchange trade goods. Particularly close allies will occasionally participate in a joint endo-cannibalistic rite and consume the charred, pulverized bones of a recently deceased friend or kinsman, an act that is the supreme form of intimacy to the Yanomamö.

The obligations implied in feasting alliances involve the offering of refuge in times of need, as, for example, when one of the groups is driven from its garden by a powerful enemy. This form of alliance also carries with it an informal but weak obligation to aid the partner in his raids against an enemy.

Finally, autonomous villages may ultimately exchange women with each other and add yet another bond to their friendship. Once this phase has been reached, the two groups have achieved the greatest possible degree of solidarity. But, and this must be emphasized, even alliances based on reciprocity of women are fickle, tenuous, and easily broken. Still, compared to the two less stable forms of alliance, trading and feasting, marital exchange obligations are relatively firm and carry more binding mutual commitments.

The reasons that the marriage alliances fall apart have to do with the reluctance that each group displays in ceding women to others and the aggressiveness with which the demands for women are made. Should one of the principals in the alliance be stronger than the other, he will press his demands for women from a position of strength and hope to derive an advantage in the women exchanges that follow. Over a long term the exchanges are usually balanced, but a stronger group, especially in the initial stages of exchange, will have an advantage. One commonly employed method used to secure an early advantage is to demand nubile women and promise immature, juvenile ones in return, or even an unborn female. Another way of taking advantage of a weaker group is to press the men from that group into prolonged bride service, say three or four years, and demand exceptionally short periods of bride service for their young men, less than a year. In rare cases they may even have the bride service waived, especially in the case of headmen.

A group that is pressured by enemies will find this situation distasteful, but preferable to migrating to a new area, establishing a new garden and taking a chance on confronting neighbors that are even more exorbitant in their demands. But since the political situation is always changing, villages having a temporary advantage at one point in time will find the tables reversed at a latter point. In the long run, marriage exchanges tend to balance out.

One economic consequence resulting from the obligation to entertain allies in feasts is that gardens tend to be significantly larger at the tribal center than at the periphery. Thus, if sixty people in a village at the periphery require a garden of size X, the same sixty people at the tribal center, because of the relatively greater feasting activity brought about by alliance commitments, will require a garden of size X plus b, the additional production having been stimulated by the requirements of feasts. The surplus "b" it should be said, appears to originate because of the feast, but it is the primary reason villages are in an economic position to offer refuge to the entire group of an allied village at almost any point in time. The surplus is there, but if the village takes in refugees, it must curtail its feasting schedule.

One further effect of the enlarged gardens is that they necessitate a greater commitment to alliances rather than migration as a means for coping with chronic warfare. Since any garden entails a considerable amount of labor in clearing and planting the site, a powerful incentive is provided to attempt to cope with neighbors rather than flee and begin a new garden elsewhere. Thus it appears that by adapting to the cultural ecology by means of alliance and feasting, a stronger commitment to that adaptation leads to greater specialization. At the very least, it reduces the probability that the alternative, migration, will occur. Nevertheless, the entire adaptation is such that migration is always a last resort, thereby making a militant stance toward outsiders more possible.

THE WAITERI COMPLEX

The motif of Yanomamö ideology is contained in their notion of *waiteri* (ferocity). Members of autonomous villages gain certain advantages by presenting an agonistic stance to their neighbors in the interest of preserving their sovereignty. The primary advantage lies in the more exclusive control a village thereby maintains over its own women in a milieu where acquisition of females is a major preoccupation.

The advantages derived by adopting an agonistic stance can best be seen in the context of political behavior. Given that acquisition of females is a major goal in inter-village politics and that differences in military potential are translated into advantage in the woman-exchange practices, a good reaction for a political group is to display and imply its military potential, i.e., its ferocity: *waiteri*. In this way a village can maintain its sovereignty to a much greater extent. The closest approximation to absolute sovereignty would be when a group (a) disposed of 100 percent of its females in marriages within the village, (b) never had to take refuge in the village of an ally, and (c) never had to rely on support from allies in its raids on enemies. No village is ever completely sovereign in these respects, nor can it afford to be: remaining aloof from allies or potential allies in peaceful times is a hazardous course, for political relationships change.

Lack of sovereignty, on the other hand, reaches the extreme when a faction of a large village leaves the group and must take refuge with a friendly group. This occasionally takes place when a violent fight erupts within a village and results in the killing of one or more people, usually in a club fight. Tempers will be so hot that one of the factions must leave, usually the smaller one, before more killing takes place. If the faction is smaller than forty people, it cannot exist as a vulnerable village and must seek refuge with a larger group (a point which will be further discussed below). One of the consequences for the small faction is that it will inevitably lose women to the protectors and cease to exist as a residential, autonomous entity.

A less extreme form of dependency is found when a larger village fissions to produce two semi-viable populations of about forty people each. They may elect to fission before in-fighting becomes so intense that bloodshed cannot be avoided; by fissioning and locating their respective villages close to each other, they therefore reduce the probability of further internal fighting while at the same time are on friendly enough terms to reunite if raids threaten either's security. As their populations grow, they become increasingly independent and may eventually separate completely and lead independent political lives.

Generally, however, differences in military potential are not so obvious. When groups of roughly the same size become allies, each attempts to convince the other that it is superior and expects to gain the upper hand in the exchange of women. A difference in size, and therefore in capacity for sovereignty, results in a more conspicuous attempt on the part of the smaller group to display ferocity. In practical terms, a field worker notices that the members of smaller villages are much more aggressive, pushy, intimidating, and unpleasant to work with.[12] By behaving in this way they imply to their ambitious, larger neighbors that any attempt to coerce them will result in immediate violence. To the extent that a very

---

[12] A number of missionaries working with the Yanomamö have also noticed this and, like me, were a little uneasy and reluctant to spend much time with these groups. In a number of villages in Brazil, on the other hand, the Yanomamö were very pleasant and charming and do not show many of the attributes found where the warfare pattern is more intense.

small village can inflict numerous casualties on a very large village
should war between them erupt, the behavior of the smaller group
is adaptive in so far as it sets limits on the demands a larger group
will make on it.

An ideological syndrome of this order deserves to have a name;
I suggest that *waiteri complex* is suitable in that it is descriptive
and emphasizes the most important single element: ferocity. Other
notions and beliefs held by the Yanomamö complement and reinforce their attitudes on political behavior, and I will describe and
enumerate a few of them at this point. In as much as I have asserted that their ideology is the basis of their adaptation to a milieu
of chronic warfare, this complex is necessary.

The *waiteri complex* is not universal in the Yanomamö tribe,
although aspects of it occur everywhere in various degrees of intensity. It exists in its most extreme, purest form within the area
of the tribe where warfare is most intense, i.e., that area bounded
by the circle shown on Map A. And even within this area some
variations and nuances occur.

The Yanomamö recognize that some groups are more aggressive
and fierce than others. Their explanation for this variation is
mythological, but fits the facts of the ethnographic distribution
very accurately. According to the myth, the first creatures on earth
were the *no badabö* (literally, "those who are no longer with us,
our dead ancestors), part spirit and part Yanomamö. The origin of
the *no badabö* is unaccounted for, but most of them functioned in
the creation of specific plants, animals, and other useful things
presently possessed by the Yanomamö. One of the first beings was
Peribo (Periboriwä in some dialects), Moon. He habitually descended to earth and ate the soul portions (*noreshi*) of children
between pieces of cassava bread.[13] Two of the first beings took
offense at this despicable action and decided to shoot Peribo with
their arrows. The first was a poor shot and missed, although he
made many attempts as Peribo ascended to his zenith. The second,
his brother, was a good shot and hit Peribo in the abdomen on the
first shot. The blood that flowed from the wound fell to earth in
the vicinity of Maiyo Käkö, a mountain near the headwaters of

---

[13] The fact that cassava bread is mentioned in the myth suggests that the
Yanomamö may have relied more heavily on this cultivated food in the past.
Now, however, plantains are the major staple in most areas, a post-Columbian
introduction.

the Orinoco River, approximately at the center of the tribe. The blood changed into Yanomamö, all of whom were males. The people born in blood had one distinctive feature: they were all exceedingly fierce and waged constant war on each other. Warfare was most intense in the area where Peribo's blood fell directly on earth; as it thinned out and mixed with water, it created Yanomamö at the periphery who were not so fierce as those generated from pure blood. The groups around the periphery did not fight as much as those at the center. Thus, the myth explains why it is the nature of man (Yanomamö) to wage war and why some groups are more warlike than others.[14]

The hostility that obtains between men is also reflected in the nature of man's relationship to the spirit world. The cosmos is thought to be comprised of four parallel layers as shown in Figure 1. According to one myth, a piece of layer 2, *hedu kä misi,* fell through layer 3, *hei kä misi* (i.e., earth), carrying a village of Yanomamö with it to *hei tä bebi,* the bottommost layer. The people of this village, the Amahiri-teri, ascend to the earth layer as spirits, or send their evil demons in their stead, to eat the souls of children, the loss of soul ultimately leading to death. The reason they do so is that their neighborhood (*urihi*) was not carried down to the bottom layer and they therefore have no game and must satisfy their hunger for meat (*naiki*) by eating the souls of children. To combat the *Amahiri-teri* spirits, men on earth send their own spirits (*hekura*) to fight and ward off the evils threatening them. This same spiritual contention, moreover, is constantly waged by village shamans, who combat the evil *hekura* sent against them by other Yanomamö on this layer of the cosmos. Thus, every day in every village the shamans gather, take hallucinogenic drugs, become intoxicated, contact their *hekura* and wage spiritual war with the spirits sent by their human enemies. Some shamans also assert that they actually leave their bodies while under the influence of the drug and travel to enemy villages to kill people by eating their souls.

---

[14] This myth is from informants who lived in the center of the tribal area and I have not found it elsewhere. A complementary myth explains the origin of women and cowards (Chagnon, 1968a) from the pregnant legs of a mythological figure. The current population resulted from miscegenation of the groups created in these two origins. My informants asserted that most of the men of pure blood origin died in the intensive fighting that developed after the blood of Moon spilled to earth.

Shamans also practice other forms of malevolent magic and cause deaths in enemy villages. One common practice in some areas is to blow charms through hollow tubes at the enemy and thereby cause sickness and death. In this connection, many groups cultivate numerous species of magical plants that are employed to this end, but the use of these involves physical contact with the individual against whom the evil intent is directed. A common tactic is to touch someone with the leaves of a special kind of plant. The net effect of these practices and notions is that unexplained deaths and sickness are usually attributed to the practice of harmful magic by shamans in other villages, a phenomenon that can and does lead to war. As we shall see below, the military history of one cluster of villages has been the result of an accusation of magic that led to the death of a number of people.

Hunting is also invested with magic and associated with notions of inflicting harm on enemy groups. The Yanomamö believe that each individual has an animal counterpart, an alter-ego, whose life is coexistent and coterminous with that person. When one dies, so does the other. The person and his *noreshi* are always in complementary distribution, so that the two never meet; should they see each other, both would die instantly. When a hunter kills certain kinds of animals, he in effect causes the death of the human being, an enemy, to whom that animal corresponds.

Ethnocentrism at both the tribal and village level contribute to the *waiteri complex*. The Yanomamö believe that they were the first, finest, and most refined form of man to inhabit the earth. All other peoples are inferior because they developed later by a process of degeneration from a pure Yanomamö stock, explaining their strange customs and peculiar languages. Yanomamö, in fact, means "humanity," or at least the most important segment of humanity. All other peoples are known by the term *nabä*,[15] a concept that implies an invidious distinction between "true" man and "subhuman" man. This distinction is reinforced linguistically in some dialects by the use of honorific pronouns.[16] Common pronouns are good enough for foreigners. The term *nabä,* moreover, seems to be related to the notion of enemy: the word for enemy is *wano nabä,* and the verb for becoming an enemy is *nowä nabä.*

---

[15] In some areas of Brazil a third term, *Kreiwä,* is used to distinguish nationals from the Carib-speaking Makiritare.

[16] These pronouns are reserved for important spirits, in reference to headmen and for Yanomamö.

The Yanomamö have a low opinion of *nabäs* and discriminate against them. A foreigner is usually tolerated if he is able to provide the Yanomamö with useful items such as steel tools, but apart from this he is usually held in some contempt. I have been invited to leave some villages, as have missionaries, because I did not bring enough presents to go around, and since that was the only possible use I could serve, I was therefore unwelcome and urged not to return until I had more gifts.

Where the Yanomamö have bordered the territory of other peoples they have fought with them and consistently pushed them out. They are presently forcing the Carib-speaking Makiritare Indians farther north and have virtually exterminated the Makú Indians.[17] Farther south, some groups of Yanomamö have expanded into areas occupied by Brazilians, who quickly withdrew and abandoned the area in fear of Yanomamö raids (Biocca 1965; Seitz 1963; Zerries 1964).

Most Yanomamö warfare, however, is confined to the tribe itself. Even here ethnocentrism is conspicuous; any difference between adjacent groups is exaggerated and ridiculed. Language differences in particular are promptly noted and criticized by the Yanomamö, and taken as evidence of degeneration. The characteristic reaction of any group to a tape recording made in another area was this: "They speak crooked; we speak straight, the right way!" And the differences need not be great to evoke this response. One young man had married into the group I lived with, and spoke almost the identical dialect, but a few differences in pronunciation. He confidentially told me that I ought to be more careful about my language—I was picking up poor pronunciation habits and ought to go live in his village to learn the proper way to speak Yanomamö.

Although ethnocentrism cannot be cited as a primary reason for the intensity of hostilities, it nevertheless adds to or justifies them and therefore is a component in the *waiteri complex*.[18]

---

[17] Migliazza 1965. I am also indebted to Sue Albright of the Unevangelized Fields Mission for a detailed communication regarding the life history of the last Makú woman in the Yanomamö area and a description of the warfare between these two tribes. Albright and I interviewed this woman in 1967 and obtained only a sketchy account of the intertribal hostilities.

[18] Some sentiment between groups of common origin does appear to exist despite the fact that they may be at war with each other. It is not likely that treacherous feasts would be held for a group having a common origin, although in one case this did take place.

The socialization process selects for and encourages ferocity. Masculinity and aggressiveness are instilled in small children from an early age. It is common to see parents tease a small boy to strike at his tormentors, rewarding his anger with approving laughter. Girls, on the other hand, are taught to acquiesce timidly to the punishment they receive from their brothers, so that by the time children are six or seven years old, the boys have already learned that it is appropriate to bully the girls and spend a great deal of time at mischievous pranks calculated to intimidate them.

Boys are pampered and indulged to a much greater extent than girls and are given more freedom to play. By the time a girl is ten years old, she spends much of her time babysitting, hauling water and firewood, and helping her mother cook. Boys of the same age have no domestic responsibilities whatever, and spend their time playing at club-fights, archery, or whatever they want. Girls are usually given in marriage as soon as they go through their puberty rites, and assume the onerous tasks of keeping their own house shortly thereafter. Boys are permitted to extend their child-hood into their late teens, but are encouraged to be fierce fighters. They have numerous opportunities to participate in fights, as there are always a few chest-pounding or club-fighting duels every year. They are pressed into the fighting by their adult superiors, but are given privileged positions in raiding parties until they acquire the necessary skills and experience. The youngest raider I saw was only twelve years old, but he was an exception, as he was recruited into a raiding party because the man being avenged was his father. Usually a boy does not take an active role in raiding until he is sev-enteen years old, and even then he may be so frightened that he will fake illness and return home before the enemy village has been reached.

Yanomamö boys, like all boys, fear pain and personal danger. They must be forced to tolerate it and learn to accept ferocity as a way of life. During one feast the adult men of two allied villages agreed to satisfy their grievances in a chest-pounding duel. They also took this opportunity to educate their small sons in the art of fighting and forced all the young boys from eight to fifteen years old to duck-waddle around the village periphery and fight each other. The boys were reluctant and tried to run away, afraid they would be hurt. Their parents dragged them back by force and in-sisted that they hit each other. The first few blows brought tears to their eyes, but as the fight progressed, fears turned to anger and rage, and they ended up enthusiastically pounding each other

as hard as they could, bawling, screaming, and rolling in the dirt
while their fathers cheered them on and admired their ferocity.

Young men are competitive and attempt to show their capacity
for rage, usually by temper tantrums that are ostentatious and
faked. A commonly used excuse for outbursts of anger is the mention of their name in public, for when people no longer use a young
man's name, it is assumed that he commands respect and is to be
feared. As they grow older and acquire wives, they vent their
anger on the hapless women by beating them, burning them with
glowing firebrands, or even shooting them in the buttocks with a
barbed arrow. One of the implications of this behavior is that the
man will be equally fierce with male opponents, and so they acquire
a reputation for ferocity without much potential harm to their own
persons. The amount of punishment a man can mete out to his
wife depends on the seriousness of the provocation and on the
number of brothers the wife has in the village who will protect her
from a brutal husband. Men constantly attempt to seduce the wives
of their village mates and take extreme offense when their own
wives, in turn, are seduced. Agnatically related males in particular
are competitors in this regard, since they all are constrained by
incest prohibitions to focus their amorous intentions on the same
category of women. Thus a considerable amount of fighting takes
place between them. One young man was given a wife who had
been captured in a raid. His older brother, the headman of
the village, began having an affair with the woman. The older
brother was a particularly aggressive and fierce man, and his
brother feared him. He therefore satisfied his rage by shooting
and killing his wife, an action that was considered appropriate
under the circumstances.

But the social effects of this agnatic competition are as significant as the hostility existing between men related in this fashion.
Such men display their personal autonomy by refusing to comply
with suggestions and requests made by their agnates, for complicity
implies that the command is given from a superior to an inferior.
This decreases cooperation among agnates and increases the solidarity between affines, a phenomenon dramatically illustrated in
the structure of village fissioning, to which we will turn shortly.

Another example of the degree to which warfare and aggression
are influential in the socialization process is the practice of memo-
rizing "death speeches." Young men invent and commit to memory the words they will say in the event that they are mortally

wounded. The speeches extol the courage of the warrior and heap contempt on his assassins. Some young men even practice the noises they will make when they are struck with arrows, a different groan being associated with wounds to different parts of the body! They seem to fear that they will say or do something unbecoming when they are wounded. Several young men described to me in contemptuous terms how one of their enemies wept and cried out for his mother when they mortally wounded him. This was considered bad form.

Expressions of ferocity can take various forms. There is a graded series of contests ranging from innocuous chest-pounding duels to treacherous feasts in which the male guests are murdered and their women abducted. From an analytic standpoint, both individuals and groups seem to attempt to establish a threshold at which their bluffs and challenges dissolve into action. Inter-personal and inter-group behavior reflects the attempt each potential opponent makes to discover precisely where this threshold lies, and to adjust behavior accordingly. Ostentation and bluff are largely attempts to convince others that the flashpoint is easily reached, although men who have deserved reputations for ferocity are less compelled to behave in this fashion. Sooner or later individuals and groups must make their boasts credible and take action, the particular form of violence being determined largely by the seriousness of the grievance. Apart from wife-beating, the most common form of violence, contests can be in the form of chest-pounding duels, club fights, spear fights, raids, or treacherous feasts, the last not being a contest (Chagnon 1967). The form that a fight takes can be escalated to the next, more serious, level: the causes of a fight are soon forgotten once it starts, and it is perpetuated largely by reasons of its own being.

Chest-pounding duels are always conducted between members of different villages and arise over accusations of cowardice or in response to excessive demands for trade goods, food, or women. The implications of the demands are that if they result in the desired articles and goods, the giver is thought to be lower in status as a political group than the receiver, i.e., one group has coerced the other.

Duels of this kind are frequently associated with feasts and are prearranged. Village A entertains village B and makes ostentatious displays and presentations of food in a general spirit of solidarity and friendship. The day after the feast, both groups go

to the center of the village, take hallucinogenic drugs to put themselves in a fighting mood, and begin to fight. One man represents
each village. The first to enter the fight stands with his legs spread,
head in the air and arms held back to expose his chest. This challenges someone from the opposite group, who enters the ring, seizes
his immobile opponent, adjusts his stance so as to give himself
maximum advantage, and then delivers a tremendous, close-fisted
blow to the man's chest. The blow occasionally knocks the man
down, but more frequently, he merely shakes his head to recover
his senses, and sticks his chest out again for another wallop. Fierce
fighters will take as many as four blows before demanding to hit
the opponent. The recipient of the blows then has a chance to hit
the first man as many times as he was hit, unless he knocks him
unconscious before delivering all the blows. One can only retire
from the fight after receiving blows or because of injury. As the
fight develops, tempers grow hot and everyone is in a state of
frenzy. The fight ends if one of the contestants is seriously injured,
although it may continue as a side-slapping duel after everybody's
chests are too sore to take more punishment.

The same rules and stance are employed in the side-slapping
duel except that the blow is delivered with an open hand across
the flank just above the pelvic bone. Side-slapping never lasts very
long, as it is quite easy to knock someone's wind out, which either
ends the fight or escalates it to a club fight. Some chest-pounding
duels last three hours.

The losers always insist on escalating the fight to a more violent
level, while the winners are content to stop. This usually ends in a
stalemate, the winners being smugly aware of their victory and the
losers proud of the fact that they were so fierce that the opponents
were afraid to fight them in a more manly contest.

If the duel was prearranged in conjunction with a feast, the fighters chant to each other after the duel ends. One man will sit on
the ground with his legs spread out and his opponent will sit facing
him, spreading his own legs over the man's thighs. They hug each
other intimately around the neck and chant melodically to each
other, face to face, vowing to remain life-long friends and to give
trade goods and women to each other.

Club fights are more serious, and can take place within as well
as between villages. These usually result from adultery or suspicion of adultery, although food theft can precipitate a club fight
under some circumstances.

The offended party walks to the village clearing with a sharpened 10-foot long club and challenges his opponent by hurling insults at him. Although clubs are not intended to be used as thrusting instruments, some men sharpen them to indicate that they will escalate the club fight to a mortal contest if need be, thereby hoping to intimidate the opponent into admitting his cowardice by refusing to fight.

If the challenge is accepted, the opponent comes forward with his own club, usually a pole ripped from the house frame. The first man jams his club into the ground in a near vertical position and leans on it with his head prominently exposed. In many cases the two men just dance up and down in a frenzy, waving their clubs menacingly at each other. If the fight does take place, the opponent will strike the first man on the head with a tremendous blow. He must then expose his own head in the same fashion and let the first man hit him. Club fights rarely remain confined to the two principal fighters, for at the first sight of blood, all the able-bodied men pick sides and enter the fight with their own clubs. Thus, club fights usually end in a free-for-all, each group clubbing the other wildly, hitting whoever can be reached on whatever spot available. They are so disruptive that the village headman arms himself with his bow and arrows and threatens to shoot anybody who appears to be deliberately trying to kill his opponent or who attempts to escalate the fight to bows and arrows. In one club fight in 1966, one of the two principal contestants stabbed his opponent with the sharpened end of the club and wounded him seriously. The headman then took a sharpened club and ran the assailant completely through, killing him. The wounded man then took his deviant wife home, cut her ears off with a machete, and discarded her. The faction of the man who was killed fled to villages of their *enemies,* vowing to get revenge.[19]

Club fights are potentially mortal contests. Should someone die in the fight, a war will follow. If the death takes place in an internal village dispute, one of the groups in the fight will flee to a different village for refuge. If the death occurs in an inter-village fight, war will follow after the two groups separate.

Spear fights are very rare. Only one took place during my field work, and informants rarely mention them when discussing past

---

[19] Small factions, even from enemy groups are allowed to join the village when it is likely they will aid in the war against that village's enemies.

hostilities. This spear fight was precipitated when the headman of a large village took his sister away from her husband in a neighboring, small village. The husband had been too brutal in his treatment of the woman. The incident resulted in an immediate club fight between the two groups, but the smaller one was thoroughly beaten. It then announced that it was going to recruit help from its allies and would return with spears. The grievance was important enough to demand a contest more serious than a club fight, but not of sufficient moment to call for an outright war. The woman over whom the fight started ran away from her brother and rejoined her husband, but the die had been cast and it was now a matter of honor and sovereignty that the fight should take place. Within a week the smaller group, its ranks swelled with men from allied villages, attacked the larger one and drove it from the village in a hail of spears. Several people were seriously wounded, and one later died of his wounds. The large group reformed and chased its assailants until it caught them, several miles from the village. Another brief skirmish with spears took place, but the two groups retired after nearly losing their tempers. One of them wanted to escalate the fight; they subsequently raided each other (see Chagnon, ms. for further details).

The next and penultimate form of violence is the raid. With this we arrive at the level of warfare proper, the previous kinds of fighting being different kinds of contests. In fact, they might even be considered as alternatives to war.

Raiding takes place between villages whose members are: (a) unrelated and unknown to each other, a situation arising when a group moves into a new but occupied area, (b) unrelated but known to each other, an outcome of a situation like the above, but after the groups have developed alliances with each other, and (c) kinsmen and have a common history. The last type of warfare is relatively common in the center of the Yanomamö tribe: it results when large villages divide into mutually hostile new groups. Hence, kinship ties are not used to define the units which are permitted to conduct war, a commonly used criterion in other parts of the world.

Warfare between related groups is peculiar and deserves further discussion, for it throws light on the relationship between the size of village at the time it fissions, the possibility of warfare developing between the resulting groups, and the general intensity of warfare in a given area.

Villages usually fission after the population reaches 80–90 people, but intensive raiding may inhibit this. If, however, it does fission and produce two groups of forty-five people, the relationship between these groups will tend to be amicable. The authority mechanisms in Yanomamö society are confined to kinship obligations, age differential, and the abilities of the headman to gain compliance with his wishes. The ability of the headman to enforce his wishes increases during times of intensive warfare, resulting in the additional authority required to govern the internal affairs of a group that exceeds a hundred people in size, the apparent limit of village growth in periods of peace. But as villages grow, internal fighting increases sharply, so that when the fission ultimately does take place, the relationships between the resulting groups tend to be hostile. Thus, feedback to the causes of inter-village hostilities results: new villages are created with a pre-existing conflict and enter into immediate hostilities. Some of the bitterest wars are waged between groups of closely related kinsmen due to the nature of the circumstances leading to their separation.

The raid has a structure, ceremony, and specific set of tactics. It is normally organized to coincide with a feast, but if the group mounting the raid does not plan to have members of allied villages participate, the feast is not held. The day before the raid a mock war is conducted: a dummy made of grass or a log is set up and decorated to represent the enemy. The raiders circle the village with their weapons and approach the target with great stealth. At the signal of the raid leader, they shoot the dummy full of arrows and retreat quickly, their hammocks dangling from their backs. Others in the village pretend they are the enemy, examine the footprints, and give chase. Occasionally the raiders will "abduct" a female as they make their escape, the entire ceremony being conducted in a spirit of merriment and horseplay. It is as much a spectacle for the non-combatants who remain at home as it is a method of training for war.

If the raiders are avenging the death of a kinsman, they will consume his calcined, powdered bones mixed with a soup of boiled, ripe plantains. They mourn for him on the eve of the raid by weeping and sobbing aloud, chanting their sorrow in a formal mournful song.

In the early evening on the day before the raid the participants sing their war song, "I Am a Meat-Hungry Buzzard." Each raider marches to the village clearing mimicking the noise of some carnivorous animal, bird, or insect, clacking his arrows against his bow as he slowly takes his place facing the enemy's village. The line-up is dramatic and full of suspense, often taking as long as twenty minutes. When the last man takes his place, the song is sung by one of the fierce men and repeated in unison by the others. Several stanzas are repeated, after which the line breaks and the men group together to shout in the direction of the enemy village. After each shout they listen for the echo to return, a good omen and reassurance that the enemy is indeed where they think he is. Then the raiders run back to their respective houses and simulate vomiting, passing out of their bodies the rotten flesh they have symbolically eaten during the line-up and singing.

At dawn the warriors line up shoulder to shoulder again, facing the direction of the enemy. Each man has painted himself with masticated charcoal, a common design being the legs and upper torso completely blackened with the intervening space undecorated. Their wives have prepared quantities of food for them, which is stored outside the village with their hammocks. This allows the raiders to leave with dignity, unencumbered with unwarlike bundles of bananas on their backs. They shout in the direction of the enemy again, and when the echo returns, they leave the village in single file, marching quickly and with great determination.

If there are novices on the raid, the older men conduct additional mock raids en route to the enemy. The most inexperienced raiders are positioned near the center of the line of marching men, the fierce ones leading the column and bringing up the rear.

Raiders travel slowly at first, since they are burdened with their provisions. They pace themselves to arrive at the enemy's village at dawn, sleeping the night before the attack without the benefit of fire for warmth. By this time they have formulated a strategy, as well as contingency plans in case they are detected and must retreat individually. Some distant spot is decided on for a meeting place should this happen. They usually split into two groups and approach the village under cover of darkness. Ideally, they hope to catch someone alone outside the village, kill him and retreat before being detected. Most raid victims are shot while bathing, fetching drinking water, or relieving themselves.

If the enemy expects a raid, the headman forbids anyone to leave the village without his permission. Nobody is allowed to leave the village alone in these circumstances, for the headman must go out and find him, a dangerous and frightening task. The raiders may lie in wait for hours before they catch someone alone. If this does not appear to be possible, they may shoot several volleys of arrows over the palisade and make a hasty retreat.

As soon as they shoot someone, or are detected, they retreat rapidly, frequently traveling all night. The retreat is well planned: two men lie in ambush while the others retreat a specified distance. The first two men then retreat past them, their flight covered by a new pair of men, etc. Thus, a raiding party separated into two groups involves the participation of at least eight or ten men; I have not seen a raiding party of fewer than ten men. The tactics of raiding, therefore, require a minimum village size of about 40–45 people, for the population must be at least that large to field a raiding party of ten men and still permit a few men to remain at home to protect the women.[20]

If their victim is some distance from the village and has a woman with him, they may abduct her and any small children with her. The decision is determined by the probability of being overtaken by pursuers, for women and children hinder the speed at which the raiders can travel, and therefore jeopardize their safety. Women are rarely killed in warfare, but in a few circumstances the animosity between enemy groups will be so great that no holds are barred and both women and children are considered fair game.

The ultimate form of violence is the *nomohoni,* or "trick." It involves the collaboration of two or more allied villages, one of which invites a different group to a feast. The unsuspecting guests are treacherously murdered and their women abducted and distributed among the confederates in the incident. For example, if village A and B are at war, one of the groups may persuade the members of a third village to hold a feast and invite the other to it. The third village must be on visiting terms with the victims. The feast is conducted, the guests fallen upon at some point during the festivities and brutally killed with clubs and staves. Those

---

[20] Yanomamö sex and age distribution is such that about ⅓ of the population is comprised by males of the warrior age. Thus, if a few men must always remain at home to protect the women, the demographic parameters, coupled with tactics of warfare, require a village of approximately 45 people. If a village fissions in such a way that one of the factions is smaller than this, it must take refuge in other villages and is not likely to continue to exist as a sovereign, political entity.

who manage to escape the slaughter inside the village are shot
from ambush by the other principal in the treachery.

The *nomohoni* is a drastic and somewhat rare form of violence, but it occurs with sufficient regularity that allies can never
completely trust each other. When it does occur, the victims are
usually from a group having no kinship ties to their treacherous
hosts, so that in one respect kinship does define the community
within which at least one form of violence is not likely to occur
(although another treacherous feast, described below, did involve groups that had a common origin and kinship ties between
them).

WARFARE AND DEMOGRAPHY

One expression of the emphasis on masculinity is the preference
of the Yanomamö to have a son as the oldest child. In many
cases a woman will kill a newborn female in order to keep her
husband pleased. Males are desired because they will grow up to
become warriors and will contribute to the group's defense and
sovereignty. Females, by contrast, are not considered to be as
useful and often are lost to the group because of marriages with
men in other villages.

Male babies are also killed, but only when the mother has a
nursing child whose health would be jeopardized if it had to compete with a younger sibling for milk and maternal attention. They
are aware that infancy is the most critical period in life because
of children's susceptibility to diseases, and if a child has survived
the first two or three years, his chances for further survival should
not be compromised by permitting a new baby to compete for
milk.[21]

But despite the practice of killing both males and females, the
bias in selecting for males as the eldest child in the family has
resulted in a sex-ratio favoring males. In some villages there may
be as many as 30 percent more males than females,[22] the discrepancy being most pronounced in younger age categories. As

---

[21] Babies are nursed until they are three years old. A fascinating demographic consequence of this is that the Yanomamö space their children and
show unexpected similarities to industrialized populations. See Neel and
Chagnon, in press a for the demographic data bearing on this.

[22] Chagnon, ms.; Neel and Chagnon, in press a. I hope to present more
demographic data after the completion of the projected 1968 field work.

middle age is approached the high male mortality due to warfare evens out the sex-ratio, and among the older people there are more women than men.

The component of mortality due to warfare is surprisingly high by comparison to our own demographic standards (see Livingstone, this symposium). The following table summarizes the causes of death, diagnosed by my informants, of 240 adult ancestors. As is apparent, violent death in warfare (including club fights) is second in importance only to epidemics (mostly malarial), and accounts for 24 percent of all male mortality (cf. Table 1).[23]

TABLE 1: Causes of death among 240 (adult) ancestors of three related groups.

STATED CAUSE OF DEATH[1]	MALES	FEMALES	TOTAL	PERCENTAGE
Malaria & Epidemics	58	72	130	54.2
Dysentery, Diarrhea	16	5	21	8.8
Warfare	31	6	37	15.4
Club fights	2	0	2	0.8
Snakebite	2	3	5	2.1
Sorcery[2]	15	10	25	10.4
Tigers	1	0	1	0.4
Chest infections	3	1	4	1.7
Hayaheri[3]	1	2	3	1.2
"Old age"	4	0	4	1.7
Pains in groin	3	0	3	1.2
Childbirth	0	3	3	1.2
Other	2	0	2	0.8
Totals:	138	102	240	99.9

[1] These diagnoses were made by the Yanomamö.

[2] These deaths were probably due to such pathological causes as malaria. When malaria first reached epidemic proportions in some of the Yanomamö villages in the middle 1950's most of the deaths were attributed to the practice of harmful magic on the part of enemies.

[3] This is a peculiar sickness associated with intense pains in the upper abdominal region; the pains may last several days. In most cases the Indians recover.

---

[23] This is probably an underestimate. The Yanomamö have very strong proscriptions on discussing the dead by name, and statistically adequate data requires complete genealogical information which is particularly difficult to obtain with respect to individuals killed in warfare. Their anguish at the mention of killed kinsmen precludes intensive questioning on this topic.

Another measure of the significance of warfare in shaping the demographic pattern is the fact that one village of two hundred people was raided approximately twenty-five times during a period of fifteen months (November 1964–February 1966) and lost 10 people, i.e., 5 percent of its population in slightly over a year. A more dramatic example is the outcome of a treacherous feast to which the groups I studied fell victim in 1950: fifteen people out of a population of roughly 115 were killed in a single day!

The shortage of women, indirectly a consequence of an attitude that admires masculinity, ultimately leads to keener competition for the available females and thus reinforces the entire *waiteri complex* by resulting in more fighting and aggression. In practical terms, nearly every village fissioning I investigated resulted from chronic internal feuding over women, and in many cases the groups ultimately entered into hostilities after they separated.

YANOMAMÖ SOCIAL ORGANIZATION

The Yanomamö kinship terminology is of the bifurcate merging type with Iroquois cousin terms. A number of interesting features of Yanomamö kinship include a paucity of terms in general, a lack of terms that specifically differentiate affinal from consanguineal kin,[24] the merging of some lineal kinsmen with collaterals of a different generation, and the equation of wife's mother's mother with wife. Perhaps the most important single feature of the terminology is the fact that a male ego's female bilateral cross-cousins are referred to as "wife" whether or not he is married to them, reflecting the prescriptive marriage rule. Men are obliged to marry women whom they address by the term *suaböya*, two genealogical specifications of which are MoBrDa and FaSiDa, i.e., their bilateral cross-cousins. Corroborating this prescriptive rule is the fact that of the six primary kinship categories into which men classify all their female relatives, five are prohibited marriage categories because of incest regulations.

The kinship system is extended to all Yanomamö with whom

---

[24] There is one exception: men who marry into the village from other groups are called by a term that does not embrace consanguines, although they are frequently incorporated into the kinship system by using the appropriate primary term interchangeably.

one is personally acquainted and/or demonstrably related. Kinship terms are extended to members of unrelated groups and are therefore not isomorphic with biological relationship. Within the village, however, there is a good correlation between kinship usage and biological relationships, but enough incestuous marriages take place to cause genealogical manipulations and changes in kinship usage that the kinship system cannot be relied upon as an invariable, faithful reflection of genealogy. Nevertheless, the important point is that all interpersonal relationships, even between members of autonomous villages, are defined by the kinship system, and regulated to a great degree by the obligations implied in the terms used.

Extensions of kinship terms to outsiders follows a pattern that reflects the Yanomamö preoccupation with marriage exchanges and the obligations deriving from them. Village headmen call each other *shoriwä*,[25] a term that at once implies friendship and mutual obligations. In brief, it relates the two men as brothers-in-law and they stand in wife-giver/wife-receiver relationship to each other. Moreover, their children stand in the same relationship and, in turn, theirs, etc. *ad infinitum*. Thus, by adopting this specific kinship usage, the headmen maximize their own and their children's advantages in terms of woman exchange possibilities and confront each other on a friendly basis: mutual obligations are structured into their interpersonal relationships. Since headmen usually represent significant factions of the villages they lead, the widest possible network of kinsmen, by a simple adoption of one kinship usage by the village headmen, confront each other as affines and friends.

Descent is patrilineal, although the agnatic ideology is very weak by comparison to, for example, the Nuer (Evans-Pritchard 1951). Genealogical relationships are always demonstrated, i.e., the Yanomamö have lineages rather than clans. Members of the same lineage have a feeling of oneness that is frequently expressed in such sayings as "We are of the same species"[26] or "We are truly one and the same." While this feeling is acknowl-

---

[25] Unless there is a demonstrable actual relationship of a different kind. Evans-Pritchard 1951.

[26] The word used for "species" in a kinship context, *mashi*, defines the lineage.

edged wherever a demonstrable kinship link through males exists, the degree of solidarity between agnates varies tremendously, the principal axes being closeness of genealogical tie, co-residence, and age difference (Chagnon ms.:106 ff).

Yanomamö lineages have a genealogical depth of only three or four generations, an indication of the weakness of the agnatic ideology and a measure of the lack of corporateness of the lineage members. Village fission and population growth are such that third or fourth generation descendants of a man are scattered in several widely separated villages that frequently have no contacts with each other. Unless direct contacts are maintained, members of the same lineage forget their agnatic links and pursue independent political lives. Again, village politics are such that notions of agnatic solidarity count for very little compared to the opportunism characterizing inter-village relationships, particularly with regard to obligations arising when neighboring groups enter into alliance with each other. Thus two groups linked by agnatic ties may be on neutral terms with each other, and one of the groups may be actively conducting a war against a group allied with the other. Yet the one group will not be compelled to side with its agnates in the struggle, and might even take sides with the strangers, especially if marriage obligations exist between them. In brief, one cannot predict hostilities exclusively on the basis of kin-non-kin data.

At the local village level, segments of the lineages are corporate groups. Their estate consists of women and the rights to dispose of these women in marriage. In large villages, there may be two or three local descent groups of the same lineage, each making its own marriage arrangements with other lineages in the village. These agnatic groups are, in effect, the corporate lineal descent groups described by Leach (1951). Their functions consist mainly of making marriage arrangements for the female members; they are corporate in the sense that membership hinges on agnatic descent and co-residence and have an existence independent of the lives of particular members.

Yanomamö villages are usually dominated in composition by two lineages. But while dual organization exists in a *de facto* sense, there is no overt ideology of dual organization. That is, the village does not have named halves, rules stipulating that half of the village should be the domain of one lineage and the other half the domain of the second, etc. One might argue that this dualism is implied in the bifurcate merging kinship system, lineal descent with lineage exogamy and a symmetrical marriage prescription, but this is not commonly taken to be the form of ideology to which we apply the definition dual organization.[27] This situation parallels the Melanesian and Polynesian cases analyzed by Sahlins (1963, 1965) and illustrates again the argument that group composition need not be enforced by the existing ideology, nor can the ideology be predicted only from a knowledge of the group composition (Needham 1967).

The fact that villages have marked dual composition seems best explained in terms of the marriage arrangements that the local descent groups establish. Members of local descent groups enter into protracted marriage exchanges with other groups of a different lineage and exchange women back and forth over several generations. The advantage derived from this is that males stand a better chance of obtaining a wife if they give their sisters consistently to the same group, for by giving women one can therefore demand them in return. The reciprocal obligations emerging from this are strong enough to keep the two local descent groups bound to each other when a larger village fissions, and the result will be a new village containing a pair of local descent groups representing two different lineages.

Figure 1 represents a model of Yanomamö social structure based on the kinship system, marriage rules, and method of incorporating new lineages into the village. The sibships might be taken to be portions of local descent groups, the entire group being represented by three generations of sibships. In generation I, the village is comprised of two lineages (actually, two corporate local descent groups of lineages X and Y). Members of lineage X seek their spouses in Y and vice versa. There are still only two lineages in generation 2, and reciprocal marriage exchange also continues as in the previous generation. But the marriages here are examples of the prescriptive marriage rule: each male has married his MoBrDa or FaSiDa. A new lineage, W, appears in generation 3 and is incorporated into the village by marriage exchanges with members of lineage X. It is at this point that two local descent groups of the same lineage begin to emerge, dis-

---

[27] Chagnon, ms., Appendix A, contains the group composition data on which this statement is made. Field work conducted after the thesis was written indicates that the dualism is even more striking in other villages.

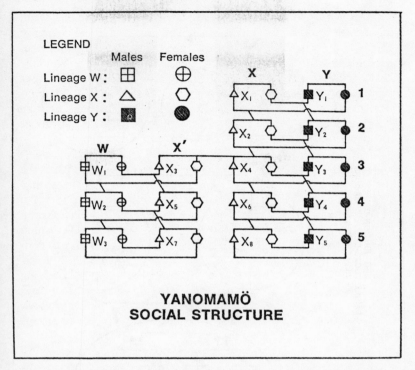

**YANOMAMÖ
SOCIAL STRUCTURE**

tinguishable only on the basis of the marriage exchange obligations they have created. Generation 4 shows more clearly the
structural implications of reciprocal exchanges contracted by the
respective descent groups. At this point the individuality of the
two descent groups in lineage X begins to show itself in the attitudes and behavior of the agnatically related men of lineage X:
individual X_5 would feel more closely related to his actual brothers than to X_6, although nominally all males of this generation
and lineage would be brothers. If the village were to fission in
generation 5, the paired local descent groups would comprise the
newly-formed villages: W and X' would separate from X and Y.
The new groups would again show the dual composition, and
lineage X would be represented in both groups (as X' in one of
them). Hence, affinal obligations are strong enough to overcome
agnatic ties, and the latter break when new villages emerge from
a larger one in the fissioning process.

Figure 2 represents the same phenomenon in another way.

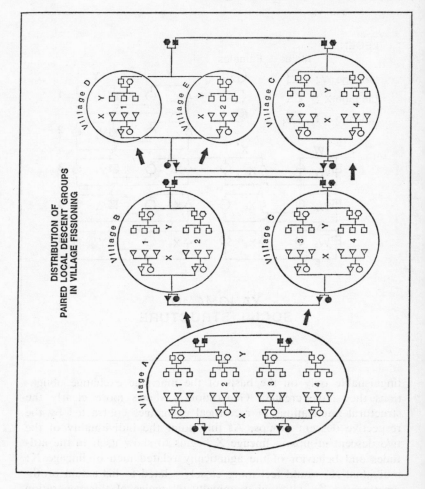

Each circle represents a village. Village A has four paired local descent groups of lineages X and Y. Members of lineage X live together on one side of the village while those of Y occupy the other. When village A fissions, the agnatic links break as shown, resulting in villages B and C, each having two paired descent groups. If the fission resulted from a club fight over a woman and someone died in the fighting, members of village B would raid village C and vice versa. The genealogical connections between members of the same lineage are sufficiently remote that the agnates, although they would call each other "brother," would have no qualms about shooting each other. If village B fissioned to produce villages D and E and the circumstances were not extremely hostile, the members of the two new villages would remain on good terms with each other. Depending on their size, they might even reunite in the face of raids from village C'. It should be noted that lineages X and Y are still represented in all three villages and that all three maintain a dual organization. Villages D and E, assuming that they represent militarily viable groups, are more constrained to enter into alliances with neighbors; compared with village C', they are numerically inferior and more vulnerable.

One thing that cannot be specified in a diagram such as this is the role of the headman. Each of the local descent groups will have one spokesman, so that in village A there would be eight men with some authority (the oldest men, those in the 2nd generation). In a village as large as A in Figure 2 there may be several men who are very prominent, and in fact there might be two acknowledged headmen, one representing lineage X and one lineage Y; they would be related to each other as brothers-in-law. In times of peace, it would be difficult for the headmen to control the feuding that would develop in the village, since many agnates are related so remotely that they would succumb to the temptation of conducting affairs with each other's wives. A comparison of the structures of village A and village D on Figure 2 shows that many kinds of potential problems are eliminated in the smaller village: incest prohibitions are sufficiently strong to reduce one category of sexual affair, and agnatic solidarity sufficiently great that men would not be tempted to provoke a brother's ire by trysting with his wife. The same degree of internal harmony can only be achieved in village A if the headman has increased authority, but the limits on authority in Yanomamö society are such that a considerable amount of in-fighting would take place in village A. If village A was being raided frequently, the authority of the headman would increase but still would not be sufficient to control all the fighting. Once the war diminishes in intensity, his authority likewise diminishes and he becomes largely a *primus inter pares*.

The similarity of the ideal pattern represented in Figure 2 to the actual pattern is illustrated in Figure 3 and Map B. Figure 3 gives the genealogical relationships of the adult males of three

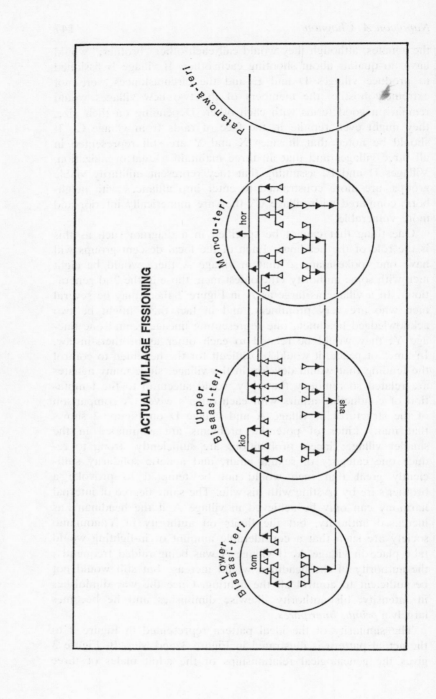

ACTUAL VILLAGE FISSIONING

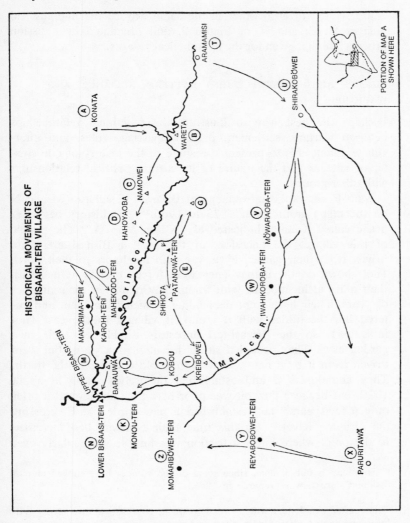

related groups and shows how the lineages extend into the fourth related village. Map B shows the historical moves of these same villages, representing graphically how they fissioned. The history of these moves will be discussed below to show how the warfare pattern fits into the picture and how it specifically resulted in the pattern shown in Map B and Figure 3 (for complete genealogies see Chagnon ms. Appendix A). The three villages given in Figure

3 are related to each other in the same way as the hypothetical villages D, E, and C′ of Figure 2, and originated by a fission process like that given for the hypothetical villages.

VILLAGE HISTORY, SETTLEMENT PATTERN, ALLIANCE, AND WARFARE

Perhaps the best way to illustrate the functional relationships between warfare, settlement pattern, marriage rules, and inter-village alliances is to present a résumé of the history of one cluster of villages and the nature of its current political relationships with other groups.

Map B shows the movements of Bisaasi-teri village (M and N on the map) from about 1875 to 1966.[28] The history begins at a site called Konata, indicated as "A" on Map D.[29] The people of this village, the ancestors of the present Bisaasi-teri, were driven from their garden by a war with neighbors to their north (not shown on the map). They were forced to take refuge with their allies at location B, with whom they remained for a number of years. Their hosts kept demanding women from them and entered into hostilities with a group of villages to the east (not indicated), so the Bisaasi-teri ancestors established their own garden at C. They occupied site C for about ten years, but were driven from it by a new war with their old enemies to the north. They abandoned C and established themselves at D in about 1920, but because the soil was poor here they abandoned it after only a few years[30] and established a new garden at E, crossing the Orinoco River.[31] By this time their numbers had increased to the point where internal friction was intense, particularly over

---

[28] This map is out of date, since some of the villages have moved and/or fissioned since it was prepared in 1966.

[29] Hereafter just letters will be used to avoid confusing native terms. Villages are named after garden sites, and the people take the name of their gardens. Thus, the present Bisaasi-teri were known as the Konata-teri when they lived at Konata, etc.

[30] This may have been an excuse to rationalize their move; the true cause of the move may have been their fear of the groups to the north.

[31] The groups north of the Orinoco call most of the people south of the Orinoco "Shamatari." See Chagnon, ms.:27 ff for a discussion of this term.

sexual liaisons. The group fissioned at this site about 1940 and two gardens were established.

Before they became fissioned, village E had entered into trading relationships with village V to their south. An epidemic broke out shortly after the two groups began visiting, and a number of deaths in village E were attributed to sorcery on the part of members of village V. An unsuspecting visitor from village V arrived to visit and trade and was summarily murdered, initiating a war between groups E and V.

The two groups at E gradually became independent of each other and ultimately entered into hostilities. The group at E abandoned its garden and established a new one at H. The war continued between H and G, and about 1949 H was abandoned and site I established.

The group at site I then entered into friendly relationships with village W, a group related to their old enemies, V. The people of W were persuaded by those of V to invite the group from I to a feast. The plan was to massacre the men and abduct the women, thereby permitting the members of V to get revenge. The feast was held early in 1950[32] at a site then occupied by the members of W, and resulted in the killing of approximately fifteen men from village I. The treacherous hosts descended on them while they reclined in their hammocks and killed them with sharpened staves and axes.[33] Those who escaped the slaughter inside the village were shot at from ambush by the members of village V, who were secluded outside the village. A more complete slaughter was averted when the hosts began fighting over the victims' women,[34] a number of whom were captured.

The survivors fled to site J, a garden they had begun clearing

---

[32] This data is based on the arrival of James P. Barker, the first non-Indian to make sustained contact with the Yanomamö, at the village of Mahekodoteri in 1950.

[33] The source of the axes was ultimately the Makiritare according to my informants; the trading network linking the villages appears to have distributed steel tools throughout Yanomamö territory at an early date. The Makiritare are known to have traveled as far east as Georgetown to acquire steel tools, and at the present, glass beads from Guyana still reach the Makiritare via a long trading network involving several tribes.

[34] My informants also said that a few people among the hosts did not participate in the killing and actually aided the victims in their escape.

before the fateful treacherous feast, perhaps in anticipation of hostilities from that area. But the new garden had not yet begun producing, so the people were obliged to return to I for food. They remained at J long enough to recover from their wounds, subsisting on food obtained from the garden at I. Shortly after they returned to I they were visited by the headman of village F (on the Orinoco River), who had heard of the massacre. He invited them to take refuge in his village, an offer that was accepted with some reluctance. The men raided their treacherous hosts once before taking refuge in village F, managing to kill the headman and recapture some of their own women. They also took the headman's son, a boy of about 8 years, but later killed him.[35] They raided their enemies persistently from village F, being aided by their hosts. The return raids took no toll on their own population, but two men from village F were killed.

The refugees continued to work on their garden at J, hauling food from the gardens of their hosts. They also began clearing sites K and L, as they had agreed to split into two groups because of internal fighting. They also suspected their hosts of plotting a second massacre against them in order to capture their women, a fear that was later substantiated.[36] They worked assiduously at finishing their site at J, remaining with their hosts for brief periods to rest from their gardening activities. They managed to take permanent leave of their hosts within a year and moved into site J, from which they finished their gardens at K and L. As soon as they finished these new gardens, they fissioned and abandoned J. The group that occupied site L subsequently moved to M, fissioned again to produce N, two inter-dependent groups now known as Upper and Lower Bisaasi-teri. Their last move took place about 1959.

In 1960 the Bisaasi-teri, along with their congeners of site K, began visiting the group X to their south. The people of site X had fissioned from W and V many years earlier, but were still

[35] The man who killed the boy explained to me that the children were tormenting the boy, so he shot him with an arrow while he played in the river to put him out of his misery.

[36] After village F fissioned in the mid-'50s, one man in the disgruntled faction exposed the details of the plot long after it had failed to materialize. Group F had gotten into two new wars and required the aid of their visitors in the raiding.

on visiting terms with them. The people of X were persuaded to invite group V to a treacherous feast. Village X was in the process of fissioning, again a result of feuds over women, so they established two new gardens at Y and Z in anticipation of the raids that they knew would follow the treacherous feast. The feast was held in 1960, but only a few people from village V actually came: a malaria epidemic was raging in this area, so most of the people were too sick to travel and remained at home. Three of the four men who came to the feast were summarily killed and their women captured. Village X then fissioned and occupied sites Y and Z. They sustained the entire brunt of the revenge raids mounted by the members of V, and had to rely on support from the Bisaasi-teri and the members of K.

But the Bisaasi-teri were not satisfied with the degree to which their revenge desires were alleviated. Village Y had, in the meantime, established peaceful contacts with V and intermittent visiting took place between the two groups. The Bisaasi-teri pressured the members of Y into staging a second treacherous feast in February 1965. The invitation was accepted by the members of group V, who began traveling toward village Y. They had gotten nearly half-way to the village before being warned by a friend in group Y of the disaster that awaited them.

The current alliance pattern of the several groups can now be interpreted against the background of this historical data. Villages Y and Z are the westernmost groups in this area; the land to their west is uninhabited, to their south are several villages with which they have hostile relationships, and to their east lie the groups they have been inviting to the treacherous feasts. Hence their only allies are the Bisaasi-teri and the group at K. When I began my field work in 1964 the relationship between the two clusters of villages was such that the Bisaasi-teri and group K had a conspicuous hegemony over villages Y and Z and were systematically stealing their women. The political relationships were so much to the advantage of the northern group that a Bisaasi-teri man forcibly took a woman who was promised to him away from her family in village Y and nobody attempted to stop him. This incident in a different set of circumstances would have resulted in a bloody club fight, or even a shooting war; but the members of group Y were so dependent on the Bisaasi-teri that they had to tolerate this behavior—if they had taken extreme offense at this they might have lost their most important ally.

The political relationships altered appreciably during the course of my field work. Group G, old enemies to the Bisaasi-teri and the members of K—but kinsmen, had gotten into a war with several villages to their north and east. They had fissioned into three distinct groups prior to the war but reunited to form a large village of over two hundred people. They had just one ally, a large village to their south (not shown), and were interested in patching up their differences with their kinsmen. They indicated their desire to make peace and were eventually invited to Bisaasi-teri for a feast in November 1964.[37] Both Lower and Upper Bisaasi-teri participated in the preparations; the members of K refrained from any involvement, but did send a delegation of men to Bisaasi-teri on the day of the feast: these men discovered a group of seven unprotected women outside the village and abducted them. Five of the women were recovered in a bloody club fight the following day, but the two groups parted on hostile terms and vowed to raid each other.

The members of village K raided first, about a month after the club fight, and killed one man. Before they raided, however, they began clearing a new garden west of their village in anticipation of the war they knew would follow. The Bisaasi-teri had elected to remain neutral in any hostilities that might develop, but when a raiding party from group G killed the headman of village K to avenge the death of one of their kinsmen, the Bisaasi-teri were infuriated and decided to aid the members of K.

Thus the Bisaasi-teri and the members of village K became actively hostile to village G, and their alliance with villages Y and Z suddenly took on a different significance: they needed the support of these two groups and lost their authority over them in the marriage exchange practice at that point. Six raids against village G were initiated by the Bisaasi-teri, members of group K, and their allies in Y and Z, and they participated in a number of raids against group G initiated by other villages.

The members of village G were harassed by no fewer than ten villages, but they confined their revenge raids to just two of their enemies, one of which was village K. The members of this village had to abandon their gardens and take refuge with allies in Y and Z and with the Bisaasi-teri.

An important consequence was that the members of village K

---

[37] The feast was in progress when I initiated my field work; see Chagnon in press, for a brief account of the details.

had to cede women to men in village Z; although these women had initially been promised to village Z, village K, in a superior position until this time, had withheld payment.

COMPARISON OF MARRIAGE BEHAVIOR IN TWO VILLAGES

A comparison of the marriage practices in Lower Bisaasi-teri and village G, Patanowä-teri, reveals that the smaller of the two villages has deviated from the ideal marriage pattern because it has been obliged to enter into alliances with its neighbors. The Patanowä-teri, a much larger group, has managed to confine most of its marriages to within the group and has not had to rely on support from allies in maintaining its autonomy; its population numbers over two hundred, compared to fifty-one in Lower Bisaasi-teri.

Table II gives the distribution of marriage types in the two villages. (The sample consists of all married males under 35 years of age.) The "prescriptive" marriages are those taking place between men and females standing in the proper kinship category, i.e., the women were *suaböya* to their husbands. Incestuous marriages involve individuals standing in any other kind of categorical relationship to each other when they are married, although their respective kinship categories were afterwards adjusted to fit the facts. Alliance marriages refer to those between members of different villages to establish political ties between the groups and cement their mutual friendship.[38] Finally, the unexplained marriages are those between individuals whose descent groups have only recently begun exchanging women and who therefore stand in ambiguous relationships to each other: the marriages between their descent groups have not been consistently between individuals of the same generation, a phenomenon that takes place when a new lineage is being incorporated into the village.

TABLE II: Marriage types in two related villages.

	PATANOWÄ-TERI	LOWER BISAASI-TERI
Prescriptive	37	7
Incestuous	4	1
Alliance/Abduction	8	9
Unexplained	3	0

[38] These include a few abductions in each village. Their removal would not alter the point of the argument.

One interesting theoretical conclusion is implied by the marriage data in Table II; it hinges on the interpretation of the term "prescriptive" marriage. One school of thought maintains that a marriage alliance system can be called prescriptive only if men are obliged to marry women of a specific, single kinship category (Needham 1962; Leach 1965; Maybury Lewis 1965). I have adopted this point of view in presenting the data. One of the arguments marshalled by proponents of this view is that there would be no systematic entailments to a marriage rule that were non-prescriptive (Maybury Lewis 1965:225) and therefore the analysis of such systems would presumably require different concepts and procedures. Another, less defensible, argument would be that a model of the social structure of the type shown in Figure 1 could not properly be used to represent the marriage system. However, the model rests largely on precise genealogical specifications of the prescribed category and therefore weakens the argument made by proponents of the prescriptive definition given here: that a sharp distinction between genealogy and category is essential in an analysis of systems of this kind.

Applying the definition of prescriptive marriage just given, the data in Table II does not reveal any difference in kind of social structure between the two groups. Both villages are identical in their kinship and marriage rules, and the discrepancy between them in marriage behavior represents no more than the outcome of the functional interrelationships between alliance formation, economic dependence on cultivated foods, intensity of warfare, demographic parameters, and attitudes about sovereignty and ferocity.

An alternate school of thought (Coult and Hammel 1963; Ackerman 1964; Mark 1967) maintains that a marriage system can be described as "prescriptive" only if a high percentage of the marriages, close to 100 percent, actually follow the rule (Coult and Hammel 1963). If the marriage behavior of the Patanowä-teri is sufficiently like their stated rules to characterize them as having a prescriptive marriage system, then we are led to the logical, but perhaps absurd, conclusion that this village has a social structure[39] different from that of their closely related

---

[39] This assumes that social structure is largely the consequence of the kinship terminology, descent rule, and marriage rule, a contestable point of view, to say the least.

cogeners in Bisaasi-teri, whose frequency of prescriptive marriage behavior is significantly less than 100 percent.

But these are academic arguments; the important point is that the effects of warfare on inter-village alliance patterns, village size and composition, ideology and attitudes about neighbors, demography, and the overall social organization are clear and understandable. Perhaps a more basic issue is the utility of identifying social organization or structure with the kinship terminology, descent rule, and marriage rules. As I have attempted to show, the intensity of warfare in Yanomamö culture has important direct and indirect effects on many features of their social system. While it is possible to isolate the effects of warfare on marriage behavior for purposes of refuting or defending particular notions relating to the analysis of marriage systems, a general understanding of the relationship of warfare to social organization and adaptation can be gained only by considering many other aspects of culture in the analysis of the whole adaptive system. In an analysis of Yanomamö adaptation, one must emphasize the immense significance of the belligerent ideology in accounting for the nature of the adaptation.

The political milieu within which marriages take place emphasizes the immense significance of marriage *as alliance*. It would be my guess that labile political conditions such as those found among the Yanomamö are probably more representative of the kinds of conditions under which primitive kinship systems and marriage practices were evolved than the more stable political situations under which most field work is conducted. Tylor's dictum on exogamy, "marry out or die out," has a somewhat hollow ring to it when applied to tribal peoples for whom warfare is no longer a dominant influence in their marriage practices. I hope I have amply demonstrated that Tylor's dictum applies very convincingly to the Yanomamö; it has a universal application because these situations probably obtained to a much greater extent in the past than most of us are willing to concede.

In this connection the work of Rose (1960) among the Groote Eylandt Aborigines takes on a different kind of significance than that which he intended it to have. Apart from playing down the significance of kinship as a system of categories and overemphasizing the close genealogical specifications characterizing these categories, his work raises an important question: why are some kinds of marriage rules maintained in social systems that make use of them either infrequently or not at all? I believe that we must seek the answer to this question in ecological situations such as that to which the Yanomamö must adapt—political environments that call upon the full potential of all aspects of the marriage rules—for it is largely by marriage alliances that tribal peoples of this general cultural level come to grips with the world about them. And, in the case of the Yanomamö, the major threat to security and survival is represented by the social aspects of the cultural ecology—their neighbors.

Studies of marriage as systems of alliance have paid relatively little attention to the implications alliance has for survival. While we have learned a great deal from the analyses of social systems that emphasize exchange obligations (the communication of ideas, women, and goods, as Professor Lévi-Strauss puts it), the ethnographic frequency of warfare would seem to suggest that the origin and perpetuation of these systems took place under conditions that gave alliance a more profound meaning, one that might have been measured in terms of positive selection. The ethnographic distribution of the bifurcate merging kinship system in general, the Iroquois sub-type in particular, and the bilateral cross-cousin marriage systems might be investigated from this perspective. It would seem that a social system that coupled these features would have an adaptive advantage in situations where it is important to relate whole groups to each other in terms of alliance, a process that is more readily accomplished in a short period of time by symmetrical marriage practices.

A final point can be made regarding Yanomamö warfare. Sovereignty and autonomy, rather than acquisition of land, are the goals in the alliance system. A model that could analyze these alliances might also be applicable in the analysis of the political behavior of modern nation states: the basic parameters of the phenomena appear to be the same. Some of these are:

1. non-territorial motives for warfare;

2. enforcement of sovereignty by displays of force and aggressiveness;

3. alliance commitments that are reluctantly honored after the political conditions under which they originated alter;

4. shifts and flux in the alliance system;

5. a greater compulsion for smaller groups to enter alliances and to suffer most of the disadvantages; and

6. attempts to maximize or improve chances of political survival as sovereign groups by entering alliances or emphasizing military capacity, or both.

WAR AND OUR CONTEMPORARY
ANCESTORS

ELMAN R. SERVICE

D R. CHAGNON'S PAPER is exciting to me because it generates
some thoughts of theoretical and methodological significance
for cultural evolutionism. Nearly all of our modern ethnographies
describe only "former savages"—that is, either proletarianized
peasants, or at best, peasantized primitives—but in any case they
are adapted to modern civilizations in a complication of direct
and indirect ties. The Yanomamö, however, seem more like pristine savages, our contemporary ancestors, acting out their un-
trammeled Hobbesian destiny. I have been reading early accounts
of relatively untouched savages and this impression is sustained,
particularly with respect to the nature of the fighting and to its
causes.

The Yanomamö are "fierce fighters," but much of the fighting
is between individuals, though it often escalates into greater action. People do get hurt and killed, but these battles are so individualized, so unorganized, and so limited in many ways that it
seems advisable to call them fights rather than wars.

The sources of the troubles, as well, serve to distinguish this
fighting from true warfare. The causes are personal and familistic:
usually the Ynomamö fight over women, sometimes over an insult, sometimes simply as bullying—to intimidate and prevent.
When our teen-aged kids get in a fight for reasons like these we
do not confuse it with organized warfare, nor do we counter it
with the same means.

The direct relation of fighting to the forms of social organization and particularly to the size of Yanomamö villages is of special interest. The smaller villages of around forty people are
cohesive and able to regulate themselves with the rudimentary political machinery available to an egalitarian, unstratified society.

But when villages become as large as 150–200 people they tend to split into feuding factions. On the other hand, when an exterior threat is present the larger village is likely to compose its internal differences.

This waxing and waning of the size of a socio-political unit in response to changes in perceived external *vs.* internal threats is a universal process and has been commented on many times. But it should now be emphasized that the changes among the societies that experienced the worldwide increase in warfare caused by the spread of the Western nations were vastly more drastic responses. The increase in true warfare, as opposed to Yanomamö-style fighting, was so great that even among egalitarian tribal and band societies the political-military consequences ranged from the formation of unprecedentedly great confederacies to refugeeism and downright extinction. The modern ethnographic record that we use in comparative studies is wildly skewed for these reasons (and for others as well, of course, especially because of depopulation due to European diseases). The following illustrations are not supplied merely to remind us of the devastation but also to suggest that a revision of evolutionary classification seems in order. Particular attention is paid to adaptive political-military responses that were both early and *indirectly* attributable to European expansion. Many of these showed so few signs of acculturation that we often treat them as though they were pristinely aboriginal, although the social organization had in fact been drastically altered.

The wars of the Iroquoian Confederacy are well known and make an instructive illustration to begin with. The legendary date for the founding of the confederacy is about 1570, not long after first contact with Europeans. It is entirely possible that the proposal of alliance among the five tribes was aboriginal—the idea of alliance is commonplace, after all—but the later full-scale and long term acceptance of it and the development of its rather elaborate machinery were clearly contingent upon Dutch and later English influence and to the strategic position of the Iroquois in the new kinds of wars. As early as 1614 the Dutch at the Albany trading post armed the local Iroquois against the Algonkians. Later, when beaver became scarce in New York State the Iroquois became middlemen in the trade from the northwest. Their old enemies the Huron were directly in the way and in 1649 the Iroquois mustered about a thousand warriors and destroyed the

Huron. This is a good example of the tremendous change in the character of American Indian warfare—from primitive hit-and-run raids and ambuscades to a truly organized army (Hunt 1940).

The demise of the Huron left the Chippewa of the Georgian Bay region exposed to the Iroquois. These people had been allies of the Huron and the French and were, according to Jenness (1967: 193), subdivided into independent territorial groups of about 300–400 persons each, but connected by intermarriage and crosscut by exogamous totemic clans. As Hickerson has shown (1966), their tactical response to avoid the Iroquois resulted in the "atomized, individualized" northern Chippewa, who adapted to a hunting-gathering-fishing economy in discrete family units, which by no means resembled their aboriginal socio-political structure.

Thus the explosion of European-catalyzed warfare resulted in these hide-and-seek polarities: the breakdown of social organization as a tactical consequence of military weakness, the Northern Chippewa; in grand contrast to the enormously extended socio-political body as a tactic of successful war, the Iroquoian League.

Much later and therefore more immediately known to us, were the great changes that warfare wrought on the societies of Basin-Plateau Shoshone. On the basis of recent documentary researches, Steward and Voeglin (ms. p. 52) said:

> "Among the Great Basin Shoshoneans, there seems to have been no native forms of national or group warfare. Conditions necessary for such warfare were absent; there were no organized groups which could carry out unified military action, and there were no motives for concentrated effort, such as defense of economically important territories. . . . It was not, in fact, until a radically new pattern of life was created by the introduction of the horse, by the encroachment of the white man upon natural resources, and by new mobility and organization around chiefs who had recently acquired power that group warfare developed among these people."

The turmoil caused by variations in the acquisition of the horse and then the gun in the Western states (cf. Secoy 1953) caused the same hide-and-seek tactics as in the East earlier and resulted in the same polarity of fragmentation *vs.* confederation. In the northern, or Plateau, part of the Shoshonean area the first to acquire the horse and to confederate into large war-making bodies were those known generically to the trappers and explorers as

Snakes, while their victims were usually called Diggers (and also variously as Bannock, Ban-a-tee, and Sheepeaters). The Snakes and later the intruding Blackfoot and Piegan were clearly the cause of the Diggers' poverty and fragmentation. As reported by Alexander Ross in 1824, a Ban-a-tee said: "We can never venture into the open plains for fear of the Blackfoot and Piegans, and for that reason never keep horses (1956: 176)." In 1825 another Ban-a-tee explained to Ross that his people had to live scattered and in hiding because "were we to live in large bands we should easily be discovered (1956: 277–78)."

In 1833 Bonneville referred to the Mountain Diggers ("Sheepeaters") as "a kind of hermit race, scanty in number, that inhabit the highest and most inaccessible fastnesses. . . . Miserable poor, own no horses. . . . They are to be found scattered about the countries of the Shoshone, Flathead, Crow, and Blackfeet tribes; but their residences are always in lonely places, and the clefts of rocks (Murphy and Murphy 1960: 309)."

Hiram Chittenden said of the Sheepeaters that they were "veritable hermits of the mountains, utterly unfit for warlike contention, and seem to have sought immunity from their dangerous neighbors by dwelling among the inaccessible fastnesses of the mountains (Murphy and Murphy 1960: 309)."

A similar instance occurred in the Great Basin farther south. The Shoshone now known as Utes became mounted hunters and predators early in the eighteenth century and eventually drove the other Indians into inhospitable refuge areas. According to Farnham (Steward 1938: 9): "These poor creatures [the Diggers] are hunted in the spring of the year, when weak and helpless . . . and when taken, are fattened, carried to Santa Fe and sold as slaves . . ."

In South America the shock waves of Iberian conquest caused many complicated military responses. Strikingly parallel to the later North American Plains and Great Basin response of the Indians to the introduction of the horse was the situation in Argentina where very large predatory bands also arose. Meanwhile the peopling of the Gran Chaco by broken groups of refugees occurred, although some parts of this region eventually became dominated by mounted predators such as the Mbayá, Abipón, Guaycurú, and others as well. In modern times we have ethnological knowledge of well-known groups of hunter-gatherers like the Sirionó of Bolivia, the Guayakí of Paraguay, and many others.

Richard Lee (ms.) has pointed out how badly skewed our ethnographic sample of hunting-gathering societies is, simply because so many, such as his Kalahari Bushmen, are simple cases of "marginal isolates," whose present condition is not at all typical of their aboriginal status. Furthermore, he states, Bushmen, Central Australians, Shoshone and others actually have a more substantial food base than they are usually credited with having. I agree wholeheartedly with this point, and add that the examples mentioned so far suggest that so very often the low level of social organization is a defeated, non-belligerent level. And then we should add that the other pole, the great belligerent confederacies are likewise not simply consequences of a superior food supply. More relevant was the military superiority and the tactical organization that produced societies of greater size.

Similar cautions should be made for the more complex hierarchical societies. The smallish chiefdoms of southeastern United States got caught in the early struggles between the Spanish and English and later in the French and Indian War. This resulted in the rise of the great Creek Confederacy, on the one hand, and the destruction of the Yamasee, Apalachee, Natchez, on the other, with refugees retreating into the Florida swamps.

In the Circum-Caribbean area the native chiefdoms simply disintegrated shortly after the arrival of the Spaniards and the surviving inhabitants fled to the interior forests. The Miskito-Sumo case is instructive. Once these were numerous villages of horticultural-fishing chiefdoms located in favorable areas along the Gulf coast of Nicaragua. In the late 1600s those now called Miskito received guns in trade with the buccaneers and began raiding for slaves. The defeated Indians retreated in small groups into the interior. By 1700 the Miskito had formed their famous Kingdom while the scattered victims became the "Sumo," which is simply a collective name for such refugees. These extremes in forms of society were made out of identical aboriginal material.

In Tahiti, Tonga, and Hawaii the small and numerous aboriginal chiefdoms were made into large kingdoms by means of European weapons and increased militarism, and in some cases with direct European tutelage.

In Africa the increase in warfare caused by the penetration of Europeans was at once more devastating and more complex than elsewhere because of the slave trade. By the nineteenth century the African continent was in chaos because of slaving operations

penetrating inland from both coasts (Bohannan 1964: 109).
Wiedner (1964: III) says of the eastern penetration:

"The Arabs had remained near the coast for a thousand years until
1840. Within eighteen years their caravans, armed posts and agents
advanced as far as the Upper Congo, halfway across Africa. The
Zenj traders carried Swahili into the interior, making it the lingua
franca of East and Central Africa, but they also generated an unprecedented series of ferocious tribal wars. Settled agriculture was
disrupted. Bantu villages were enslaved or massacred, and the population declined sharply."

Much earlier, Southwest Africa had been ruined by the
Portuguese-Brazilian slave trade. According to Duffy (1961:
138) ". . . by 1600 the Congo kingdom was a shambles; the
(slave) trade through the mouth of the river had probably aver-
aged over five thousand slaves a year throughout the century."

In Southeastern Africa the indirect effects of the disruptions in
central Africa were striking. This area was once filled with small
chiefdoms, and during the eighteenth century warfare among them
was desultory, indecisive, and largely ceremonial in nature. But
by the beginning of the nineteenth century the shock waves of
migrations from central Africa resulted in intensified warfare and
new tactics of annihilation (Otterbein 1967). The socio-political
consequences were enormous: refugeeism increased, of course,
but also several unprecedented, huge military conquest states
like the Zulu, Ngoni, and Swazi resulted (Bryant 1929).

Considering the continent-wide disruption in Africa, one won-
ders what was the purpose of the comparison of modern state
and stateless societies in Fortes and Evans-Pritchard's *African
Political Systems* (1940). "States" in their sample such as the
Zulu, Ngwato, and Bemba were, before the European-engendered
disruption, a series of small simple "segmentary" chiefdoms, with
only a system of ranks rather than stratification. On the other
hand, their classic "acephalous" society, the Tallensi, had actually
been a dependent part of the Mamprusi kingdom, but were defeated and dispersed by the British at the turn of the century and
lost their organization at that time. (See the interesting critique
of *African Political Systems* by James Stevenson, in press.)

Fortes and Evans-Pritchard have here misapplied the comparative method, mostly by trying to compare incommensurables—
societies simply in different states of breakdown or readjustment
to colonialism and imperialism. So, to get back to the Yanomamö:

here is one of the rare cases in modern ethnography where the people described are apparently in an aboriginal enough state to be truly useful in the comparative method.

Originally, the comparative method was a product of evolutionary thought, by which contemporary accounts of primitive peoples were used in thinking about past ages. This method has a long, honorable, and classic history. Aristotle did it in his *Politics,* as did Thucydides in *The Peloponnesian War,* and later such greats as Hobbes, Locke, Ferguson, Lafitau, Rousseau, Turgot, and many others (Bock 1966).

Of course there are methodological dangers in the comparative method (Boas 1940). The most usual criticism of the 19th century evolutionists was by American ethnologists who spoke disparagingly of the earlier "anecdotal period," referring, that is, to the naivete of untrained missionaries' or explorers' accounts. (But, as E. B. Tylor answered [1871: Vol. I, 7–8], there are tests of reasonableness to apply, just as in historiography.)

But there is no point whatsoever in using the comparative method for evolutionary or "laboratory" purposes when we are including modern so-called "scientific" ethnographies that are mostly reports on the surviving remnants of the devastation caused by the European colonial and imperial expansions. To be sure, it is good to have that record, but its usefulness for the comparative method is nil. It can even be dangerous, as in the astonishing and erroneous conclusion of *African Political Systems: viz.,* that the more complex stages of society, the states, do not have higher population densities than the simpler acephalous, or tribal, societies (Stevenson, in press).

In concluding, I offer two related recommendations. First, for evolutionary purposes of the comparative method, travelers' and missionaries' accounts are still useful, whereas our modern dissertations by trained anthropologists are not, except for such rare cases as Chagnon's study of the savage Yanomamö.

My second point is a criticism of my own work. Elsewhere (1962), I warned about the effects of European penetration, especially its diseases, on our sample of hunting-gathering bands. I particularly recommended abolishing the so-called Composite Band as an aboriginal type. But now, continuing the line of argument presented here, I would warn that the stages Band, Tribe, Chiefdom, and Primitive State are not true to the aboriginal state of affairs. They may be useful for a classification of modern ethnography but not useful if they are to be used in extrapolating from extant stages to extinct ages.

Morton Fried (1966) recently criticized my formulation of the band-tribe dichotomy by arguing against the concept Tribe. I accept that, but go further and also abolish Band. If such extremes of tribal confederation as that of the Iroquois do not represent anything aboriginal, then neither does the fragmentation of their victims, the northern Chippewa. If the large mounted tribes of Snakes and Utes are not an aboriginal form of organization, then neither are *their* victims, the poor scattered Diggers. The true egalitarian, acephalous, stage of society was probably somewhere between these two poles—varying, to be sure, but not nearly so greatly before the enormous disturbances caused by European expansion. I think, therefore, that the safest way out is to abolish both Tribe and Band in favor of the single type, the *Egalitarian Society*.

Similarly, the distinction between Chiefdom and Primitive State is worrisome. The Chiefdom, a hierarchical, or ranked, society was clearly widespread in aboriginal times. But the despotic military states that were so characteristic of Africa seem to be definitely products of slaving, new weapons, population removals, and outright colonialism. The only safe way, until further documentary research suggests something more plausible, is to think of only three aboriginal types which might represent evolutionary stages: (1) the Egalitarian Society, out of which grew (2) the Hierarchical Society, which became replaced in only a few instances in the world by the empire-state that led to the next stage (3) the Archaic Civilization or classical empire.

CAROLYN HECKERT (*Walt Whitman High School, Bethesda*): If women are such an important commodity, why is there infanticide for girls?

DR. CHAGNON: The Yanomamö place a great deal of emphasis on masculinity and one expression of this is a strong preference for a male as the first born child. Frequently a couple will have their hopes set on having a male and instead a female child is born. Occasionally, she is killed by the mother shortly after birth so that the husband will not be unduly disappointed. The Yanomamö also practice male infanticide, but the bias introduced by their desire to have males as the first born has resulted in a highly disproportionate number of males in the population.

The intensity of infanticide might be mentioned at this point. There is a 30 percent excess of males in some villages so the degree to which they practice infanticide must be incredible considering the fact that 24 percent of all adult males who die, die in warfare. This suggests to me that the degree, or intensity of infanticide is much, much greater than what the sex ratio would at first indicate.

MALCOLM WEBB (*Louisiana State University in New Orleans*): I'd like to address a comment to the paper given by Dr. Service, which I found very interesting. Judging from the effects war has had in shaping social geography in the ethnographic present— an effect that we can assume was also associated with the development of the great ancient empires—it would seem that we are all to some extent beneficiaries of past warfare although we don't like to admit it. I'm not at all in favor of this activity (being against war is as safe as being against sin and I'm certainly heartily opposed to both). I would like to suggest, however, that the institution of war is so deeply ingrained in the state structure —the structure of state-societies—that our task of eliminating it is going to be considerably more difficult than any of the participants in this discussion have indicated so far. War is not an external nuisance but a very basic part of our way of life.

I fear—in fact I fully expect—that if we were not fighting in

Vietnam, we would be doing so somewhere else, and, if we were not to wage war ourselves, that other nations would still do so, as has happened in the past. The 5000 year history of the "state" suggests that aggression is inherent in this type of organization. I therefore think that our efforts as scientists in understanding war are more important in the long run than our attitudes as citizens toward any particular war. What we must do is find a way to continue enjoying the benefits of state organization (all the nice things we call "civilization") without having to endure the unfortunate aggressive aspect of the system.

DR. SERVICE: I very much agree with you that we haven't paid enough attention to war as a feature of cultural evolution. In fact, we seem to have acted as though war would go away if we ignore it. I think this is irrational. I also agree with you that the great watershed of human history, the organization of the state and subsequent archaic empires, was an adaptive process that closely involved predation, conquest, assimilation, and so on— in short, new and intensified forms of warfare that came about as a new aspect of governance.

PSYCHOLOGICAL PREPARATIONS
FOR WAR

ANTHONY F. C. WALLACE

WAR IS THE SANCTIONED USE of lethal weapons by members of one society against members of another. It is carried out by trained persons working in teams that are directed by a separate policy-making group and supported in various ways by the non-combatant population. Generally, but not necessarily, war is reciprocal. There are few, if any, societies that have not engaged in at least one war in the course of their known history, and some have been known to wage wars continuously for generations at a stretch.

Because war is apparently perverse, being both painful and sought after, people frequently give psychological explanations for it. Those who think about it with resignation, or with favor, conclude that making war is part of human nature, like making love; others are equally convinced that nothing so evil can be explained except as the result of social- or psychopathology. In this discussion, however, we shall not be concerned to answer the ultimate question, but a more limited one: What, if any, psychological preparation is required for a society to enter *a* war?

THE STATE OF MOBILIZATION

The principal psychological preparation for war is the training of all members of the society to participate efficiently in a social process that I shall call mobilization. I do not refer here simply to military mobilization in the modern sense of calling up reservists and drafting hitherto uncommitted men and resources to a war, although that is one instance of the larger phenomenon. Rather, I refer to the fact that all human societies, and the societies of many of the higher primates below man, are observed to exist alternately in two states. In one of these, lone individuals and a variety of subgroups occupy themselves in resting and in diversified and complexly co-ordinated economic, sexual, educational, and other activities. In the other state, the population arranges itself precisely into three well-defined groups—the policymakers, the young males, and the females and children—and the entire society co-ordinates its activities under the leadership of recognized authority toward the achievement of a single task. The former state I shall call the relaxed state; the latter, the mobilized state; and mobilization is the process of transformation from the relaxed to the mobilized state.

Among the lower primates, the baboon troops described by DeVore (1965), and DeVore and Washburn (1963), and others are the most obvious example of this alternation of states. In the relaxed state, the troop is dispersed: an aggregate of individuals and small groups engaged in feeding, grooming, sleeping, sex, and play. In the mobilized state—which is assumed while the troop is traveling—there is an exact partition of the troop into three groups, which occupy different and traditional positions in the line of march: the lesser males are at the front and rear, where they can confront challenges from predators; the dominant males and females carrying infants are in the center; and the other females and juveniles surround the central group. Similar formal traveling, hunting, and defensive dispositions have been described for a number of other social species. The capacity to mobilize is a widespread feature of animal behavior.

In man, the mobilized state, and its contrast to the relaxed state, has also been described in detail for many societies, although the large size and complexity of human groups often obscure the generality of the distinction. Gearing (1958) clearly conceptualized the difference in Cherokee culture between what he called the structural pose of peace and the structural pose of war and described the institutional arrangements associated with each. These two structural poses for peace and war, in similar institutional form, are assumed by a number of North American Indian tribes. One thinks also of the elegant and rigid arrangements of camp circle and police developed by the Plains Indians when they were hunting buffalo. In band and tribal societies generally, travel, hunting, and war require the state of mobilization. But in modern societies, characterized by urbanism, the nation-state, and complex and powerful technology, the alternation between the relaxed state and the mobilized state in matters of transportation, food getting, civil defense, and so on must proceed on different schedules for different institutions and localities. The whole nation still mobilizes only for a revitalization movement (a movement whose aim is to reform and reinvigorate a culture) and for war.

THE PROCESS OF MOBILIZATION

In order for a society to shift from the relaxed to the mobilized state, the population must receive a releasing stimulus, in response to which everyone promptly disposes himself according to a plan. Obviously the stimulus must be broadcast in order that all members of the population receive it quickly, correctly, and simultaneously. For a small band, most of whose members are always within earshot of one another, this is relatively easy. But the larger the group, the more difficult it is to prevent the communication from being distorted in transmission, from reaching individuals at different times, and from being seriously delayed in reaching some. Hence, as a society increases in size and as its territorial boundaries enlarge, cultural innovations are required that will ensure speed and reliability in communication of the releasing stimulus and any associated instructions. This requirement has probably prompted many tribal and early urban societies to invent special language codes, systems of graphic symbols, broadcast devices, and roads and other transportation methods, and to train men in the arts of precise memorization of messages and of rapid and careful travel.

It is also obviously desirable, although not necessary, that the releasing stimulus not merely elicit a disciplined response but evoke a motivational system appropriate to the action to be taken. Here the society enters into a kind of conspiracy with itself to combine the alerting signal with symbolic content that, given a certain distribution of modal personality variables, will arouse maximum desirable emotion. The releasing stimulus is therefore apt to be—particularly in the case of mobilization for war—a report that a certain kind of event has occurred to which people with that character type will respond with anger, determination, fear, or whatever affective state is desired by the communicating group. For Iroquois Indians, this symbolically arousing stimulus was always a report that a kinsman had been killed and that a survivor demanded revenge. For twentieth-century Americans, the symbolically arousing stimulus is apt to be the report that helpless Americans or their allies are being held prisoner or are under attack, and must be rescued.

It is important to note, however, that this embellishment of the releasing stimulus is not, and cannot be, necessary to ensure mobilization. A population is composed of persons with a variety of character structures and personal motives, many with limited intelligence and others suffering from greater or lesser degrees of psychopathology, and mobilization must proceed independent of private motive. Hence, atrocity stories, scare reports, and the like are never adequate to ensure mobilization; indeed, in some situations, such as medical emergencies, they appear to interfere with it. Thus the intensity of the emotion aroused must not be so high as to preoccupy the person being mobilized; the symbol must function more as a rationalization for personal sacrifice than as a stimulus toward unrestrained violence or flight.

TRAINING FOR MOBILIZATION

It is apparent that the shift from the relaxed to the mobilized state must be taken by people who have already learned what to do in response to the releasing stimulus. In all societies this learning probably occurs very early in life, and very largely without didactic instruction, in the course of the child's living through the alternating states of relaxation and mobilization. He learns, while acquiring the language, and by constant observation and participation, the difference between the two states and the nature of the three main status groups characteristic of the mobilized state. And as he grows older, he is trained more and more explicitly to recognize the releasing stimulus, to take orders, and to play specific roles in one of the groups.

One critically necessary feature of this learning is the development of a readiness to move from a situation characterized by considerable personal freedom and democratic, consensual decision making to a hierarchical and authoritarian structural pose. In many band and tribal cultures there is little in the way of coercive authority exercised in the making of decisions during the relaxed state but a very high degree of it in states of mobilization. Thus, among the Iroquois daily life in the village was largely managed by tradition, supplemented by consensual decision when alternative policies had to be chosen, and children were generally given a great deal of freedom. The Iroquois were famous, at least among European observers, for their intolerance of personal constraint. But when a war party mobilized, the participants suddenly assumed a posture of rigorous discipline under the command of a captain who had unquestioned and absolute authority during the military mission. At the end of the expedition, however, this authority terminated, and the captain's influence after that depended entirely on the willingness of other citizens to take his advice in council.

How the early Iroquois trained their children to be able to switch structural pose is not clear from the records available to us now. But a great deal of information is at hand to reveal how our own children are trained to switch poses. A classic example is the school fire drill, which, in addition to improving the chances of evacuating a school quickly in case of fire, provides a general model of how to mobilize in an emergency. At the sound of the alarm, the physical disposition and social relationships of the children abruptly change from the relaxed order characteristic of class or play group to the exact discipline of the fire drill line of march. Similar training in mobilization is given in athletic activities and in popular literature and film, where the training takes the form of play and spectator sport. The principle that is communicated in such exercises, apart from their specific utility, is that when the mobilization signal is heard, automatic obedience to recognized authority is required and assumes priority over other motives.

THE IMPERSONALITY OF WAR

So far, we have discussed the phenomenon of mobilization as the central theme in psychological preparation for war. But what of the fear, suspicion, and hatred of "the enemy," traditionally believed to be prerequisites for war, that are often invoked by the releasing signal? It is my contention that far from being necessary, these attitudes are almost irrelevant to war except as rationalizations. Human beings generally reserve their settled fears, suspicions, and hatreds for those closest to them: kinsmen, neighbors, and colleagues. Today's enemy in war is yesterday's stranger and tomorrow's ally. The psychological target of lethal weapons in war is an abstraction rather than a person (as the saying goes,

"I have nothing against you personally"); hence any member of a society that at the moment happens to be classified as an enemy is apt, in one way or another, to be fair game (with "no hard feelings," of course). Few soldiers ever personally kill anybody; those who kill often do not actually see what they hit; and most never push a button, pull a trigger, or throw a grenade in combat.

War is never really total; its aim is never the absolute annihilation of the enemy and all his works; death and destruction are limited by more or less arbitrary restraints concerning the weapons to be used, the treatment of prisoners, civilians, and nonmilitary targets, and the goals of military action. Thus, being removed from hate, war is also relatively free of guilt. This is not to say that some persons may not displace domestic hate upon foreign enemies by psychiatrically familiar mechanisms of defense, nor that bereaved persons, or those who have suffered personal threat or injury, do not experience, at least for a time, a very personal hatred. But such feelings are not a reliable indicator of efficiency in combat, where an ability to maintain cognitive orientation and a commitment to task-completion in noisy, fatiguing, and dangerous surroundings may be much more important than a high level of primitive urges to fight-or-flight.

Nor can war usefully be regarded as essentially an outgrowth of mass hysteria or mass movements, although some wars, and some events in most wars, are affected by such contagious enthusiasms. A religiously dedicated population, for instance, is likely to be easy to mobilize and difficult to defeat. But the action of a mob in sacking a building or in lynching a neighbor is almost the opposite of war, for it is directed toward the matériel and persons of one's own community, and by definition is carried out without communication of the releasing signal by authority.

Thus, in our own technologically sophisticated society, it is readily apparent that it is possible for half of the national budget and a substantial proportion of our young men to be mobilized to fight an enemy seen by few and rarely recognized even when seen. Lethal weapons are employed by technicians who never set eyes on their human targets. Nor can the other side claim a much more personal focus of their military activities. War is an extremely impersonal business conducted by persons whose private motives—apart from the motive of efficient participation in the state of mobilization—are highly diversified.

THE INTERESTS SERVED BY WAR

We have, so far, discussed the psychological preparations required for a people as a whole to conduct war effectively and have argued that little more is required than a population trained to respond affirmatively to the mobilization signal and to carry out orders from recognized authority. But what determines the communication of this signal?

The signal must be given by a person or group recognized as having the responsibility to do so when the situation requires it. This, in contemporary industrial societies, is apt to include at least some of the persons who will make policy during the mobilization state, but in general it is not necessary that the body that gives the signal for war be the body that directs the conduct and arranges the termination of the war. It is obvious enough that this signal will be given when an authorized person perceives that a threat exists to the continued functioning of the system that cannot be met by the society without shifting to the mobilized state and using lethal weapons against members of another society. When the society is under physical attack itself, the danger is obvious, and war may be the only alternative to abandoning hope of maintaining, or returning to, the traditional form of relaxed state; it may even be the only alternative to destruction. But sometimes even when no serious attack is threatened, the authorized body communicates the releasing signal, the society mobilizes, begins to use lethal weapons, and initiates an extremely costly and, sometimes, fatal conflict.

I have already suggested that war is often perverse. It is well known to pacifist and soldier alike that many wars are unnecessary, disastrous, even catastrophic mistakes. They do not serve the purpose, whatever it may be, for which the society has mobilized, and they cause immense suffering and damage. The sense of moral outrage that such events arouse does not carry us far, however, in trying to understand how these disasters happen. Political witch-hunting and accusations of psychopathology and criminal conspiracy may simply obscure the facts. In one minor war whose inception is very well documented—the Black Hawk War between the United States and the Sac and Fox Indians in 1832—the record clearly shows that the responsible policy-making bodies on both sides were *not* in favor of war. An irresponsible insistence by an Indian faction on crossing the Mississippi River to join forces with a religious prophet, and lack of discipline in an Illinois militia detachment, precipitated the first firing of guns, and a sequence of events followed mechanically that resulted in the death, from disease, starvation, and bullets, of several hundred Indians and whites. The critical event was a misunderstanding. The Indians, disillusioned with their prophet, attempted to surrender to the militia before a shot was fired in order to gain free passage back across the Mississippi to their tribal territory. The militia were drunk, had no interpreter, and were unaccustomed to discipline, and fired on the peace party. In the ensuing melee the militia were defeated by the Indian warriors, who then fled with their women and children in an effort to escape across the river by a different route. But the use of lethal weapons on a militia detachment automatically set in motion a sequence of communications that resulted in the mobilization signal being given by the President of the United States. The Sac and Fox council, however, refused to broadcast *their* signal, and the fighting was restricted to the east bank of the Mississippi; the Indian territory across the river was not attacked.

Such examples could, of course, be multiplied *ad nauseam.* The point they illustrate is that unwanted wars—and most wars are now unwanted—occur as a result of a perversion of administrative process rather than as a result of popular folly. The types and sources of such perversions are complex. In some cases, the psychopathology of administrative personnel is evidently responsible (the case of Nazi Germany is the best example of this type). In other cases, responsible and intelligent administrators attempting to act in the best long-term interests of their society are precipitated by misinformation, communication failures, and a rigid, poorly designed system of decision making into unnecessarily mobilizing the society for war.

From this point of view, it would appear that the administrative structure of any society—and every society has an administrative structure at least latent during the relaxation phase and active during its mobilization phases—is extraordinarily vulnerable to perversion in regard to war decisions.

THE PREVENTION OF WAR

There are few people who take the position that *all* war is a mistake or is morally wrong, and who refuse therefore to mobilize for war on behalf of their society in any role and under any circumstance whatever. Most pacifists refuse to kill personally but support mobilization in other ways. Generally speaking, organized opposition to war is opposition to *a* war that is believed to be morally wrong or, practically, a mistake. These opponents of war are willing to fight if mobilized in what they regard as a good cause. Nonetheless, despite the rarity of true and radical pacifism, there are few persons in industrial countries today who would deny that preventing war from occurring is a task of paramount importance. It has come to be recognized as one of the principal unsolved problems of mankind.

Short of universal pacifism or the inclusion of all countries in one state, the means of preventing war would seem to lie in the invention and diffusion of more effective political and administrative processes. It is, to put it crudely, a problem of developing a number of interrelated "fail-safe" systems that will reduce the probability of mistakes (in technology, in intergroup relations, in communication, and in personality function) from precipitating a war while other means of resolving conflicts of interest are being employed. The kind of fail-safe devices to which I refer are not merely sophisticated electronic systems, which control the weapons themselves. They are also principles in human relationships that, making use of what we already know about human beings, minimize the likelihood of any society perceiving itself as being in a situation of external threat so dire that war or destruction are seen as the only alternatives. Not all such intersocietal threats are economic and military; perhaps the most dangerous threats of all are threats to self-respect and threats to interfere with local revitalization movements.

It is not very likely, in the immediate future, that universal disarmament or a single world state will come into being. Nor is it desirable, even if it were possible, to eliminate the principal psychological preparation for war—training for mobilization—for societies must be able to mobilize for other purposes, even if not for war. And it is irrelevant to propose that undeluded, non-hating, freely loving young people be raised and nourished, for they will be the best fighters of all. If the last century has taught us anything about human nature, it is that good persons can do impersonal evil and that war does not require hate.

CONCLUSION

In conclusion, my argument may be summarized briefly as the assertion that the main process of preparing a people for war is simply training them to participate obediently in mobilization for concerted action in emergencies. War does not require training a people to hate an external enemy. Since training for mobilization is unavoidable, and the elimination of intergroup hostility would be irrelevant, it is clear that the prevention of war will not be accomplished either by eliminating its basis in psychological preparation or by improving human nature. Rather, the problem of ensuring peace must be approached by the innovation of political and administrative safeguards that guarantee that alternative processes of conflict resolution are not interrupted by war-by-mistake.

WAR AND THE DISSOCIATED
PERSONALITY

STANLEY DIAMOND

I AM IN GENERAL DISAGREEMENT with Professor Wallace's presentation, elegant and logical though it appears to be. There are contradictions under the surface; more seriously, in the cause of neatness, there is a necessarily casual dismissal of several absolutely central, and rather untidy issues.

Let me say at once, because of the impossibly brief time, and many problems involved, that the notion of mobilization for war in the nuclear age is antiquated. Such ultimate wars, if waged, will be waged by technicians. So-called civil defense procedures have failed everywhere; the trick is, rather, to keep the population *immobilized,* or not much more "mobilized" than they are already, by virtue of being citizens of a highly developed State. But mobilization on the scale necessary to wage nuclear war is socially, economically, psychologically, that is, culturally, impossible. Any such serious effort would certainly lead to revolution, riot, rebellion, or civil discord on a cataclysmic scale. If we cannot unravel the traffic snarls in New York, or in this fair city, how shall we engage in the impossible venture of nuclear mobilization. If *the* war should occur, the country will simply disappear some sunny day, while most of us are going about our apathetic business. So far as less complete wars are concerned, they must be more subtly defined than they have been; it is enough to say now that we are fighting on a major scale in Vietnam with only a segment of our human and technical resources mobilized, with a bit of civil discord at home, and with a good deal of apathy abroad in this land. I do not refer to the honorable, if amorphous, rebellion of a certain segment of our youth. Mobilization for war in highly industrialized states is organic to the routine position of the citizenry—which is, ordinarily, fragmented, alienated, bureaucratized, and subject, without noticeable enthusiasm, to civil imperatives. That is to say, as State power has increased in civilization, the alternatives routinely open to the citizenry shrink, as does voluntary participation in secular, centralized undertakings. Citizens of States are, ordinarily, preadapted to mass war. It was Tylor who noted this as the origins of civilization. The State, he wrote, is originally patterned after the army. It is this structural position of the person in modern society that must be overcome, and there are signs that it is at least possible.

Having made this initial point, permit me to choose several other related issues which seem to me wrongly put. Can Professor Wallace be serious, for example, when he tells us that the case of Nazi Germany, and by implication, the Second World War, was "evidently the result of the psychopathology of administrative personnel." He is talking about a war which cost 30,000,000 lives, had its roots in the internal structures of contemporary Fascism, Capitalism, Soviet Communism—a war which was not only the precipitate of a formal nation-state system whose fail safe mechanisms had not clicked, but one which had the most complex and intricate revolutionary implications, and which probably could have been avoided only by radical surgery on the international body politic, beginning in 1918. German society since 1918 had been a laboratory for the vices of the Western world. The Nazis stole a revolution before they won the State for a war. War and revolution in the modern world are like society and culture— try separating them. Let me mention as an aside, that Karl Jaspers is worried about Germany today, about the German people, the German social structure, Germany in its interstate matrix. Germany (and not only Germany, of course) was, and is, deeply diseased. Observe, for example, the work of Jakov Lind, Gunter Grass, et al,—they are not referring to merely "administrative psychopathology."

Professor Wallace's approach, in its central theme, shares the perspective, albeit in a beneficent vein, of the deterrent strategists. This is implicit in his chalking up the Second World War to the "psychopathology of administrative personnel." He feels that war can be administered out of existence—presumably by rational politicians, properly checked and safeguarded, in command of various, politically defined populations, which are, as he puts it "composed of persons with a variety of character structures, and personal motives, many with limited intelligence, and others suffering from greater or lesser degree of psychopathology." This is a strangely non-political, but most custodial, administrative, and bureaucratic view of a human population. One does not dare to raise the question of what is meant by psychopathology here (could it be, perhaps, passivity in totalitarian situations), or of intelligence, or of presumed "cultural" goals or social roles which, after all, may be coterminous with personal motives in societies such as ours, where so many people are constantly being reduced to so limited a number of functions. That is to say, the statement about "administrative psychopathology" raises these obvious questions—if the most catastrophic war in human history can be neatly ascribed to a class generated by administrative psychopathology—then what was the basis of the psychopathology, what were its manifestations and causes, to what degree was it shared by Germans, and others, who did not have positions of immediate decision? If the psychopathology was decisive, then I would contend that it was the result, the symptom of a widespread disease in modern civilization, a pathology that cannot be outwitted or evaded but must be confronted and overcome; a people may not get the leaders it deserves, but it deserves the leaders it can endure. Moreover, once having entertained the notion of psychopathology, I do not see how Professor Wallace can fail to unite personal character and societal disease in depth.

I must hurry along in this truncated response to a systematic paper—so I shall not enlarge upon my opposition to eliding mobilization among baboons, primitive, and finally civilized war behaviors on a level of abstraction that only serves to obliterate critical distinctions. Apathy, bound anxiety, may be more important than flight or fight responses—especially in complex bureaucracies. Conscription does not exist among primitives: most wars in authentically primitive societies are, as Malinowski pointed out, highly ritualized, self-limiting, and qualitatively distinct from ours. Animals, baboons, or other higher mammals, kill protectively, or almost always for food, and do not decimate other populations; they tend to maintain inter- and intraspeciational territoriality, their social organizations are fixed, that is, not developmental in the historical sense, and, under natural, non-symbolic conditions, they seem to have minimal problems in making what I shall call love, expressing aggression, or relating appropriately if not always harmoniously to congeners of different

ages, sex, and so on. In short, they really don't have our problems, if we are to be refined and sophisticated in defining our
problems. Further, in talking of mobilization, Professor Wallace
grants a critical point, that in the contexts he carefully chooses to
describe the process, it can be multifunctional. This is true—and
leads us to question its relevance to the kind of modern war with
which he is really concerned. Any kind of systematic, cooperative
activity acutely circumscribed by time, and demanding action in
response to authority or tradition may be called mobilization. A
cooperative men's work group in Africa is a highly mobilized,
effective, traditional, peaceful force. In parts of the continent it
is coterminous with the age set structure, and the military group-
ings. An initiation rite is a form of mobilization—sometimes of
the entire society—and in rank order. The point is that war and
peace do not at all serve, in human populations, as the major
catalysts for mobilization of energies in situations defined as culturally critical. Moreover, as noted, mobilization of the specific type which serves as the organizing principal of Professor
Wallace's paper, is contraindicated in the waging of modern
nuclear war, and is unnecessary in what the Pentagon calls limited,
conventional wars.

I can barely mention, and Professor Wallace omits to mention,
that civilized wars are fought, in significant part, for class or
group interests, with which critical segments of opposing populations may identify. These special interests may be basically socio-
economic, but they are expressed in terms of ideology and power
—and the danger is that the identification may be complete enough
to cripple compromise, and make defeat intolerable for desperate
men. There is also a lack of political depth in the claim that a
World State could, theoretically, be a solution to war, although
not now feasible. However, a World State would simply convert
wars into revolutions, into the internal affairs that they have in
fact, not in law, already become. That is, the issue here is render-
ing tolerable the ills and estrangements of civilization, making
viable the lives of disinherited millions, from the bottom to the
top, by social structural, and cultural changes, not by administrative or constitutional fiat.

This leads me to the merest mention of an adjacent issue—
when is a war a war. Is our operation in Vietnam a war in Wallace's definition? It is undeclared, not between two recognized
nation states who made some kind of mistake, but between a

colonially punished, domestically exploited, and now revolutionary population—and a punitive, overarmed, confused, highly bureaucratic and collectivized modern society. Why does Professor Wallace omit all mention of this war—with its keenly trained professional cadres, the Marines, the pros in the Air Force, the Green Berets, the companies that produce napalm, defoliants, rockets, the interests at work, the geopolitical mythos, the immobilization of most of our population, the mobilization of a relative few, and the efforts made to isolate and absorb dissent. But this is a limited war, one may reply. Well, it is not limited for the Vietnamese and their ravaged land. *Our* cities burned last summer, *our* welfare programs administered from the top down don't work very well. Our power is being used genocidally—are not these situations organically linked? We worry about war by mistake while systematically ruining a whole population.

I must also indicate in passing that I do not recognize the stately, abstract wars that the speaker has described. I find it particularly ironic that he should use, as an example of a limited and apparently judicious conclusion to a "war by mistake," the special case of the Sac and Fox Indian War of 1832. But what of the relentless conquest of the North American Indians, the more general case, that began a century or so earlier and lasted about half a century later. Can one honestly believe that hate and conflicting interests did not merge here. The Whites may not have hated the Indians whose cultural and human resources they destroyed, but *they* must have hated, and still, as Professor Wallace well knows, in a certain sense, *hate* us.

However, it is true that absolutely modern, up-to-date war, lacking in ritual, lead by technicians, in a kind of rationalized madness, does not require hate, or rather, I should say, the open and direct expression of hostility. Such a war between antagonists at more or less equivalent levels of civilized development, would be, of course, obliterating, but if there were survivors, it would leave, I believe, a heritage of hate at the commission of *dissociated evil* that staggers the emotional imagination.

On this point I should like to close. Professor Wallace tells us that the last century has taught us that "good persons can do impersonal evil." No. Dissociated, not good, persons can do impersonal evil. Persons who have become *personae*, masks; persons who have permitted themselves to be reduced to social functions, alienated, bureaucratized; persons who can kill out of abstract strategy, but who are out of touch with their own capacities to express and transcend hostility, persons who obey orders in societies where the civilizing process has become hyperrationalized. Dissociated persons can do impersonal evil; good persons may do personal evil—the whole history of folk and written literature, through Euripides to Dostoyevsky is testament to this limiting confrontation and transcendence of evil. It is dissociated persons doing impersonal, and therefore potentially boundless, evil who are the threat in modern civilization—they are the irresponsibles. We recognized this in a complexly legal and not entirely candid way at the Nuremberg Trials, and twenty-four hundred years ago, Euripides, one of those poets who would have been exiled from Plato's Republic, a polity armed to the teeth in a war system, made the same point. In *Iphegenia at Aulis,* he has Achilles say—in effect—"I am a man, my sword is my own, I take responsibility for my behaviour. I shall not obey an immoral command." It is on this point, and its profound political implications, that civilization stands or falls. Not on deterrent strategies, and fail safe mechanisms, no matter what the guise.

General Discussion

DIETRICH LUTH (*Richmond Professional Institute*): I wonder whether Professor Wallace and Professor Diamond cannot come to an agreement on the question of "psychopathology." It seems a misplaced effort to me to speak of "psychopathology" when the debility in question is never specified, but rather couched in a term having very obvious value connotations. Perhaps it would be better if the whole notion of psychopathology were tossed out of the arena of war decisions and who makes them. If Professor Wallace would like to make a case for it using the Germany of the period 1933–45 as an example and, moreover, consider it "the best example" (Wallace 1967: 53), he might look into the record of all belligerents participating in the Second World War and into the Allied plans that led up to it. He will find that no one nation can claim pre-eminence in the matter of "psychopathology of administrative personnel" (Wallace 1967: 53).

By the same token, of course, the judicial farce called "The Nuremberg Trials" where the victors judged and condemned the vanquished in line with the dictum *"Vae victis"* provides no evidence of psychopathology in the German leadership but a rare insight into the mentality of the organizers of this spectacle. The same applies to the Tokyo Trials, and if we add the Treaty of Versailles to the above two events, at least one of which grew out of them, we cannot escape the conclusion that since the year 1919 it has become a crime to lose a war. This country's continued efforts to bring the Vietnam conflict to a favorable conclusion may well be grounded in the precedents set at Versailles in 1919 and re-affirmed at Nuremberg in 1946.

FATHER STEFANISZYN (*Duquesne University, Pittsburgh*): I would like to hear Professor Wallace's comments on the following remarks, as I think they may fill a gap. Any past war seems to be a psychological preparation for the next one as the heroism and sacrifice shown in the previous war is glorified and approved. This is achieved by the way history is taught, by processions or celebrations of peace-war anniversaries, by the building of monuments and war memorials, and the giving and proudly wearing of medals or decorations on festive occasions. A tomb of the Unknown Soldier becomes a national shrine, a center of a simple mystic cult where rites are performed even by visiting Heads of State ritually laying a wreath there.

Such behavior betrays social values, and thus a dormant potential of war psychology may be easily activated. By this means war almost qualifies as a quasi-institution though this may not be generally accepted. The whole idea is expressed in the ancient Roman dictum: Vis pacem, para bellum.

RICHARD GOLDBERG (*George Washington University*): Would you agree that the reason for widespread reaction against U.S. involvement in Vietnam is that the present generation, not having lived during any war—having been born after the Second World War—has not been subjected to this mobilization stimulus?

MATTHEW HALLINAN (*University of Pennsylvania*): I would like to question both speakers. I am a little confused because I felt that Dr. Diamond was criticizing Dr. Wallace insofar as Dr. Wallace's position traced wars back to psychopathology, while Dr. Diamond seemed to feel that deeper kinds of social explanations were required. Ultimately, however, Dr. Diamond's position seemed to resolve the causes of war into the operation of certain timeless, absolute categories of evil. In fact, it would appear that he merely substituted a moral for a psychopathological explanation.

I would like the speakers to consider an alternative approach. Is it not more fruitful to conceive of warfare in social terms—as the product of normal, everyday human beings, who in the course of pursuing their own interests, as these are socially and historically circumscribed, are brought naturally into conflicting situations. If we focused more on those social relationships that could prosper or maintain themselves only through the exercise of violence, we would get a much clearer picture of the causes of modern warfare. Perhaps then it would be possible to get away from explanations that lead ultimately to either the sickness or evil of certain men.

DR. DIAMOND: I had said originally that the Nuremberg Trials were not entirely candid and if I had had more time I would have gone on to explain that. What I meant was that of course, if there were to be a trial at all, many other people should have been in the dock, not only Germans. I said "Germans and others."

So far as the most recent speaker is concerned, with reference to the problem of good and evil, I raised this because Professor Wallace in his paper, of which I am only a discussant, made the statement that if we have learned anything from the past century, it is that good men can do impersonal evil. That was the note on which he concluded his paper; therefore, one must assume that he considered the statement rather important. I think his conclusion is incorrect, and I was at some pains to point out why I thought this. So far as psychopathology is concerned, I think that it is deeply involved with the character of our social structure in almost every conceivable way and I did indicate what I meant by that, e.g., the class interests involved in war, passivity under totalitarianism, etc., but I was differing from Professor Wallace on the basis of his assumption that the Second World War was the result of *administrative* psychopathology. Obviously I disagree, and obviously my own conviction is that we are dealing with a tremendous social, economic and cultural problem of the most profound dimensions.

DR. WALLACE: In amplification of my response to the questions, may I point out that the argument of my paper is not that all war is caused by the psychopathology of administrators but that going to war depends upon the mechanisms of mobilization. Administrators' psychopathology of one sort or another certainly has precipitated, or helped to precipitate some wars but it cannot, and is not, proposed as *the* cause of war. Furthermore, I see even less merit in the proposal that any war can be explained as a result of national psychopathology. As the history of national character studies in World War II shows, there is a tendency to find comfort in the conviction that those who differ with you are sick. The notion of guilt by dissociation seems to me to combine all the unfortunate features of both national character explanations of war, and explanations of war in terms of good and evil.

DR. DIAMOND: I didn't say, Tony, that the Americans in Vietnam are evil. I said that it is dissociated men who can do impersonal evil. Good men can do personal evil.

WAR AND THE DRAFT

SOL TAX

IN ADDRESSING QUESTIONS OF POLICY in our society, my task as an anthropologist is not simply to express my citizen views, however well founded in special knowledge; nor simply to serve up warmed-over expertise of colleagues in the most relevant disciplines. Rather, I begin by putting the issues in anthropological perspective, by examining the process of decision making relevant to United States manpower procurement, and thus pose new questions for laymen and experts alike.

Large questions of war and peace require the very broad perspective provided in most of this symposium. My question is relatively small. In the U.S.A. in the late 1960s, should government force some persons to become soldiers, and if so, which persons?

It is only two years since many of us began to ask this question in relation to the deferment of students and what soon came to be recognized as an unwitting collaboration of the Universities in a system of selective service that violates two basic American values: freedom and equality.

Since a democratic society requires order as well as freedom, it must sometimes sacrifice the individual interest to the common good. Thus we do forcibly deprive people of some of their property.

We call this taxation, and though it violates an individual's freedom, we try to maintain equality, by applying taxation uniformly—whether absolutely, or relative to ability to pay. Sometimes, for the common good, we force an individual to sell his property to the community, but in theory at least he is fully compensated with equivalent property.

In punishment for crimes, a democratic society also deprives some people not only of their property, but of their personal liberty and even their lives; but we do this very carefully, ideally safeguarding at every step the rights of the accused.

Given these qualifications on freedom and equality—the practices of (1) taking property from all people or from a few for presumed social necessity; and (2) taking life or liberty from persons deemed dangerous to society, after "due process of law" —the issue then becomes: should government take life and liberty from selected innocent persons for the public good?

At least when stated so categorically, most Americans would say No.

A society requires for survival not only some minimum of internal order, but surely protection from external enemies bent upon destruction. Thus in the case of an actual military attack of dangerous proportions or one which is clearly imminent, a rampant violation of our values of freedom and of equality is usually condoned without much question. In such cases so many members of the society spontaneously rise to the defense of their homes that there may in fact be no violation of their values. In any case, we can dismiss as an intellectual problem the special case of an emergency in which the prospect of destruction is immediate and visible.

The questions therefore become first, how do we react in not-so-clear-cut situations, and how do we perceive our present situation; second, whether, in any situation as we perceive it, there are any alternative means that would satisfy our needs, while violating our sacred values less than the draft does; and third, if there are such alternative means, how does it happen that we have, through our democratic process, continued to maintain a system of manpower procurement that we do not want or need.

Eighteen months ago, the faculty of my University asked me to bring to a national conference those who have most studied these problems. The papers prepared for the conference, and a full report of all the discussions, are just off the press, under the title *The Draft: A Handbook of Facts and Alternatives* (Tax, ed. 1967). The conference showed that there may indeed be feasible alternatives to our System of Selective Service which violate less the values of American society. So the third question will become critical: how is it that the draft is nevertheless our national policy?

"The draft" is a system of military manpower procurement that can be put into perspective by describing three others, which I call the "Spartan," the "warrior caste," and the "voluntary" systems. In the Spartan system, at least all male citizens are born to be warriors, trained from childhood and hopeful of getting their chance for glory. This system is characteristic of tribes in whose cultures war is important. In the traditional Navaho society, for example, all of the able-bodied population were potential warriors. After the age of seven, boys were subjected to rigorous physical-fitness training. Their diet, exercise, and sleep habits were carefully scrutinized. An indoctrination was begun that would result in a fierce pride in masculinity. To the Navaho, masculinity was almost synonymous with accomplishment in battle. This indoctrination also instilled the group paranoia necessary for continuation of the system. "If you sleep late, the enemy will come and kill you. If you are awake, you can face your enemy and die like a man." The approach of the enemy was always felt to be imminent. Dissent from the system did not exist. The big day in the life of a Navaho boy was when he was allowed to join a war party. If the boy had done well in his training, usually this occurred between the ages of seventeen and twenty.

The warrior caste system is characteristic of larger societies, in which a special geographic subdivision or else a class of society supplies the standing army. The warrior caste itself tends to have a Spartan system, with ideals of bravery and glory instilled with military training from childhood. An examination of the traditional system of the Kerala in India will serve to illustrate how this system functions. The militia is a leisure class. All retainer Nayar boys are inducted to the king's service at the age of seven. They train in gymnastics and swordsmanship for nine years. When they "graduate" they receive their arms from the king. They remain in military training until they are obliged to leave the king's service and to succeed to the head of their matrilineal property-group to manage lands.

The third alternative is a voluntary army, which in peacetime is small and "professional," and in emergencies is swelled either by sufficient increase in volunteers or by recourse to the draft.

Any discussion of means of recruiting military personnel is complicated when one makes the usual distinction between officers and soldiers and both their means of recruitment and the psychology and consequences of their service. In the Spartan type, to speak either of "volunteers" or of "conscripts" is meaningless; all non-Spartan societies, whatever their military system, might in emergency add to their strength either volunteers or conscripts, or both. There are societies, however, in which the central system is the draft. In surveying the Human Relations Area Files, one finds the draft so common in feudal-type societies that one is tempted to call it the feudal system. Although feudal societies have had military castes, generally they also have recourse to the draft. For example, in traditional Burma the standing army was furnished willingly by one geographic location; however, all citizens were eligible for the draft. When the king issued a draft call, he gave quotas to his underlords, who in turn divided up their quotas among local officials, who were then free to obtain the needed number of men in any way they chose. Usually, a local official issued the first call to the rich, who he knew would bribe their way out of it. He could then use this money to pay off his own superiors if for some reason he could not meet their demands. The men finally sent were those who could not get out of it by some means, fair or foul.

The pressing of people into service by force may be called conscription (as opposed to ascription in the Spartan and the warrior caste societies). Systems of conscription could be classified in many ways—to include everything from permanent enslavement to brief military periods of training or service in public works. For example, the Russian czars conscripted citizens for twenty years as compared with our two years; but I gather that the Russian conscript assumed that it was for life, or at least that he would find it difficult to return except as an old dependent.

The problem in our country seems to be that while on one level there are inequities in the System of Selective Service that are difficult to resolve, there is also impatience with the draft system as a whole.

The inequities—as well as the arguments in defense—of the present system are spelled out in considerable detail in the newly published book. Insofar as the recent revision of the law has changed anything, it appears to have substituted new difficulties for some of the older ones. The present situation is described in an epilog in the book, and may be pursued further in the newspapers as events of the next months unfold. I shall turn instead to the problem of our general impatience with the idea of selective service. I begin with some analysis of the current situation in the United States in light of our own evolving cultural values precisely as I would hope to do in a hitherto undiscovered culture in the New Guinea highlands.

It has been said that Vietnam is the most unpopular war in our history. If this is true, we might hypothesize that it conflicts with some traditional American values. Therefore I set up a chart to check this hypothesis.

I am neither a historian nor a political scientist, and have long since permitted my schoolboy knowledge of American history to rust away. I need not dwell on the disadvantages this ignorance entails. The advantage is that I could more than I dared hope look at the data somewhat as a stranger, and undertake an exercise as an anthropologist.

First, I looked at the data and saw that there have been basically three reasons why we have gone to war: (1) Our national security was in danger. (2) We wanted to acquire land or economic gain. (3) We were provoked to fight for some rationalized form of idealism. Second, I isolated twelve different wars: the Colonial and then the U.S. wars against American Indians; the war against Britain for independence and that of 1812; the Mexican War; the Civil War separately in the North and in the South; the Spanish-American War; the two World Wars; and Korea and Vietnam. Third, I compared these twelve wars, where I could, with respect to:

(1) how they involved the national interest, both from the point of view of our self-preservation, and from the point of view of territorial and/or economic gain;

(2) how they were rationalized or idealized, in terms of (a) the missionary spirit; such as was characterized by the World War I slogan "Let's make the world safe for Democracy"; (b) our racial or cultural superiority, which degrades an opponent to something less than human—a strong factor in our annihilation of the American Indians, who were said to live like beasts and so deserved to be treated like beasts; and (c) a feeling that our opponent is not properly handling his land or his government, and that we could do the job better—and anyway our need is greater than his; and

(3) how well they were accepted by the American people.

I sought in vain the help of a colleague in American history who told me the task of rating our wars in such a manner is impossible. He knows too much. In my innocence, with the help of an equally innocent research assistant, I put a set of answers into a neat chart which I call "American Wars: Motives, Reasons, and Popularity."

Arbitrary value judgments must be made in completing such a

TABLE III: American Wars: Motives, Reasons, and Popularity.

U.S. WARS	RATIONALIZATIONS OR IDEALS			NATIONAL INTERESTS		POPULAR ACCEPTANCE
	MISSIONARY SPIRIT: THEY NEED OUR HELP	THEY ARE INFERIOR ANYWAY	OUR NEED IS GREATER; WE CAN DO A BETTER JOB	NATIONAL SECURITY: SELF-PRESERVATION	TERRITORIAL OR ECONOMIC GAIN	
Vietnam	11–12	•	•	1	•	5
Korea	11–12	•	•	2	•	8
World War II	7	5	•	12	•	10
World War I	•	•	•	7	•	7
Spanish-American War	8	•	8–10	4	7	9
Civil War (North)	3	2	6	9	•	4
Civil War (South)	•	6	8–10	8	•	6
Mexican War	4	3	8–10	3	8	2
War of 1812	•	•	7	5	9	1
Revolutionary War	•	•	5	6	6	3
U.S. Indian wars	1	12	12	10	12	11
Colonial Indian wars	10	8	11	11	11	12

chart. Should one treat the popularity of the war at its outbreak? Its conclusion? Or in total? I chose the last. Should one treat the real rather than the purported threat to our national security? I chose the former—which of course called for a number of other judgments that might be very shaky. Where I saw no basis for judgment, the space is blank. Which brings us to the question of what the numbers represent. Rather than try to state the absolute amount of dissent over any war or the absolute amount of avarice that provoked the war, I rate the wars only relatively. Therefore, what the figures say is that the greatest threat (rated 12) to our national security occurred in World War II and the least threat (1) to our national security is occurring now in Vietnam; that the greatest national unity in favor of a war occurred during the Colonial Indian wars (12), etc. Remembering all the limitations of this chart, and admittedly there are many, what kinds of generalizations can we make from it? Three things stand out:

1. National unity is high, and the war popular, when either or both measures of interest (security, expansion or economic gain) are high. Thus the Indian wars and World War II were most fully accepted. It should be noted that the most idealistic and most popular of our wars were the Indian wars. And yet, in retrospect, these seem most immoral to many in the twentieth century, since the idealistic rationalization that the Indian needed to be turned into a European (culturicide) is no more justifiable today than the taking of the land.

The war with Spain was accepted even though national interests were not highly involved—presumably because patriotism was artificially whipped up, and the war was won before it had dissipated. The Korean war was also accepted (at least for its first year) although our security was little threatened and we had nothing economic to gain; this relatively successful excursion in idealism was accepted partly in hopes that through the United Nations (which supported the war) we might gain security.

2. Wars for territorial expansion or economic gain—when national security is not also at stake—are rationalized in the least idealistic terms and are not accepted. Thus the War of 1812 and the Mexican War. Again the Spanish-American War was a partial exception. Cuba and Puerto Rico were popular additions to our territorial sphere. Not so the Philippines, which were seen as too

difficult and expensive to govern, and were thus destined for in-dependence.

3. When there is doubt that the war serves our interest (this is seen if no high figure appears in either of the two "interest" columns), it is only partly accepted. The war in Vietnam and, in lesser degree, the Revolutionary War and World War I fall under this rule. It is now time to review our current interests in Vietnam in this light. It is said that we are fighting in Vietnam to protect our own national security against the Communist threat and that if we do not stop the enemy now, we will have to stop them later—in San Francisco. But a great many Americans evidently doubt the reality of the danger. And if the danger seems to them not real and present, this may seem rather a preventive war, putting us in the position of the policeman who justifies shooting into a group of teen-agers because statistics say that some percentage of teen-age groups turn out to be dangerous. Against this doubtful danger to our security, many Americans weigh the destruction of the homes, fields, and the women and children of our allies in South Vietnam.

When our national security does not seem to be in danger and there appear to be no economic interests, *then* idealistic rationalizations come into question. Hence, many doubt our right to interfere, as well as the virtue and sincerity of our missionary spirit, and suspicion arises abroad that we have territorial aspirations. Our sensitivity to world opinions adds to our unease as perhaps never before in our history.

However, after refreshing my memory on the history of dissent and after checking with historians, I quickly reached the conclusion that this is certainly *not* our most unpopular war. The reason this is so is that our purported reasons for fighting are entirely within our tradition. The missionary spirit that we have professed so long may indeed have trapped us. If we shun it now, we may have to admit that other wars have also been fought for the less idealistic motives (economic or territorial gain). Hence, we may have been carried on into a medium unpopular war by idealistic inertia.

If the Vietnam war is not—relatively—extraordinarily unpopular, why are we having extraordinary trouble obtaining military manpower? The answer would seem to be that this trouble is not at all extraordinary. Opposition to the draft is as old as American war itself. In some cases, it has been a result of dissent over the nature of the particular war. Those who feel that either the draft or the war itself is unfair to them have always refused to fight. Whereas we have traditionally harassed or prosecuted our pacifists, we have not always had legal means to prosecute draft dodgers.

But if the draft is so unpopular, why do we continue to use it? Why do we not consider either of the two major alternatives to the present draft discussed at the recent conference at the University of Chicago? One proposal would incorporate the present draft into a system of *national service* going well beyond military functions and including a much larger segment of the population; the other would abolish conscription and establish a purely professional *voluntary* army.

The arguments for widening national service were argued persuasively in many of the papers prepared for the conference; clearly many of us yearned to put the whole problem on a very different footing, in which military service would become incidental. If there were no war at all, and no draft, the ideas developed for the invigoration of American society through a resurgent desire to serve might alone have justified the conference. Indeed, some must have felt that the results of such a conference might even compensate for the pain of war and the draft. Many of us were exceedingly conscious of the fact that the System of Selective Service was not only drafting people for military duty but using the threat to remake society in a manner which many of us like far less.

In 1965, the Selective Service distributed to its offices a document, since withdrawn, on what it called "channeling." I quote from the very beginning and the very end. Much more of it is reprinted in the December 1967 issue of *Ramparts* magazine:

> "One of the major products of the Selective Service classification process is the channeling of manpower into many endeavors, occupations and activities that are in the national interest. . . .
> "While the best known purpose of Selective Service is to procure manpower for the armed forces, a variety of related processes take place outside delivery of manpower to the active armed forces. Many of these may be put under the heading of 'channeling manpower.' Many young men would not have pursued a higher education if there had not been a program of student deferment. Many young scientists, engineers, tool and die makers, and other possessors of

scarce skills would not remain in their jobs in the defense effort if there had not been a program of occupational deferments. Even though the salary of a teacher has historically been meager, many young men remain in that job, seeking the reward of a deferment. The process of channeling manpower by deferment is entitled to much credit for the large number of graduate students in technical fields and for the fact that there is not a greater shortage of teachers, engineers and other scientists working in activities which are essential to the national interest. . . ."

Deciding what people should do, rather than letting them do something of national importance of their own choosing, introduces many problems that are at least partially avoided when indirect methods, the kind currently invoked by the Selective Service System, are used.

Delivery of manpower for induction, the process of providing a few thousand men with transportation to a reception center, is not much of an administrative or financial challenge. It is in dealing with the other millions of registrants that the System is heavily occupied, developing more effective human beings in the national interest. If there is to be any survival after disaster, it will take people, and not machines, to restore the Nation.

Those of us at this conference who were—as it began—uncommitted to any particular solution to the problem of military manpower procurement were particularly impressed by what we learned favoring voluntary service. Two congressmen—one a Republican and the other a Democrat—attended the conference, and both came away enthusiastic for this solution. Yet the House of Representatives did not seriously consider either this alternative or the possibility of broadened national service. Two senators attended the conference and both favored reforms in the present system, many of which their chamber accepted. But even these reforms were rejected by the House. And the House view prevailed.

In the American system of representative government, it is assumed that the conclusion must represent the will of the American people; yet opinion polls and other evidence contradict this. In the anthropological tradition, it is necessary therefore to seek an answer to our questions in the "real" structure of the U.S. lawmaking system.

The United States theoretically leaves international decisions in civilian hands. The military carries out policies of the civilian

President and the people, through their representatives in Congress. Congress must do its complex work through committees; committees have administrative staffs who provide continuity through changing elected administrations. The executive branch also does its work through staffs that continue from one administration to the next. These staffs are continuing groups with lives and interests of their own. Elections come and go; Presidents and Congresses change; but the committees and staffs remain and, as experts in their fields, educate their new chiefs. We cannot assume that the military is subservient to civilian control in our system until we have examined the actual status relations among these staff people. In dealing with the American Indians for example, the congressional staff is dominant in determining policy (a worrisome fact because their tradition dates back to the days when Indian affairs were in the Department of War); but the Pentagon staff people—often in uniform—may well be dominant over congressional committee staffs.

The congressional committee staff of experts must educate the new congressmen to what they conceive to be the fixed "policy of Congress" (an often-used phrase). How much of this policy of Congress with respect to military matters comes from the tradition in the Pentagon would depend in part on how technical and bureaucratic the issue; manpower procurement could well involve a set of problems in which the congressional staff people bow to their colleagues.

Any committee chairman and House minority leader depend heavily upon, and work exceedingly closely with, the committee staff. The chairman and his counterpart (who change places when the majority changes) grow into their positions over the years, advancing through seniority and interest in this committee rather than in others of which they are members. Indirectly through their staffs, as well as directly, they co-operate with the related executive office. In many cases there is the usual horse-trading that is necessary in the arts of both politics and administration. Congressional leaders—who get their seniority through being continually re-elected—need to provide facilities for their districts; it must be that the large military budget makes co-operation especially easy between congressional committee leaders and top Pentagon personnel. Since the congressional committee is exceedingly influential—at least has virtual veto power—in making legislation, its leaders in large part are the filter through which policy passes.

The individual congressman may or may not have a "national" point of view; he must—to achieve leadership—be re-elected. It is his particular constituency that he must please. If his district for any reason favors one policy or another, he tends to follow this policy, which may not reflect either the national opinion or what others would think the national interest.

So it is not Congress but congressional committees; not only these committees, but the traditions of their staffs and the interests of their leaders and their small districts that largely determine what laws are made.

There is another influential circumstance that may bear upon any issues involving defense. Other things being equal, the election of a war veteran is easier than that of his non-veteran opponent; and support of veterans' organizations is useful. Therefore, members of Congress are disproportionately veterans; rare is the election of a conscientious objector!

Thus, while the public may disapprove of the draft system, it does not necessarily follow that their opinion will be translated into law, given the *modus operandi* of our Congress and congressional committee system, and given the influence of the "Pentagon rationale," which persuades these groups. Having thus traced the endorsement of the Selective Service System to its source, the question must therefore be asked, why does the Pentagon prefer the present Selective Service System to any alternative?

Usually three reasons are given. The first and most common has been that it is the only system financially feasible for the military. The second is that they need the mechanism for quickly swelling their manpower resources in case of emergency. The third is that the military would lose prestige, and hence, morale of its personnel would lag if the system were abandoned. Since all of these objections can be refuted (see *The Draft: A Handbook of Facts and Alternatives*) perhaps the compelling reason is structural. The military is based on hierarchy and power; indeed wars could hardly be managed without power applied within the system and, of course, to the enemy. The power to conscript is simply part of the power that any military establishment should want.

It is precisely because the military depends upon hierarchical authority and power, while a democratic society stresses values of equality and freedom, that our Constitution places the people over the military. In the case of military manpower procurement, however, the Pentagon appears to rule, and the draft persists despite the contradiction of our most sacred value that innocent people should not be arbitrarily selected and deprived of life and liberty without due process of law.

If there were no alternatives to satisfy our need for national security, this might be conceived of as a simple "necessary evil." But this is not the case! The two major alternatives discussed above need first to be explored.

The first emphasizes the value of equality in American culture. National service for all, perhaps women as well as men, attracts many adherents. If we must draft some, let us draft all; and if we must serve the military, let us also serve civilian society. The Peace Corps abroad could be extended, and our domestic problems helped at the same time that the idealism of individuals could be served and strengthened and the anomy of the large society qualified by work together.

The second alternative emphasizes the value of freedom. End conscription altogether and depend upon volunteers. Assume rather the patriotic idealism of Americans; but make it financially possible for them both to serve their country—for any period of time—and to support their families and begin to save for their children's education. The standing army would be no less civilian because it is properly paid like other civilians; the selection would be no less representative of the population because it comes from free choice rather than from force.

In time of war a nation is in a state of danger and less free than usual to discuss policies fully and rationally. At such a time the nation is particularly reluctant to dispute the military. The defense establishment is therefore at its political strongest. If the war goes well, one does not "rock the boat." If it goes badly, it seems safer to strengthen, rather than to undermine, the establishment. It is, therefore, not likely that the judgment of the military on these basic alternatives to the draft will be upset while the Vietnam war is in progress, nor surprising that Congress does not seriously discuss them. Nor will basic alternatives be fully explored in peacetime when they seem to have no relevance. Thus for twenty years of our first peacetime draft (the draft was reestablished after a brief lapse following World War II) it was not a public issue, until we became embroiled in a questionable war. Thus, the American people must choose a moment of peace—but one when a questionable war is still fresh in memory—to discuss alternatives to a policy that violates our sacred values of both freedom and equality.

THE DRAFT AND THE UNITED STATES CONGRESS

E. ADAMSON HOEBEL

IF ANTHROPOLOGY IS WHAT ANTHROPOLOGISTS DO, then Sol Tax's paper is anthropology. What is more, he assures us that it is, for he says he is "putting the issue in anthropological perspective" and that his method is "an analysis carried out precisely as I would hope to do in a hitherto undiscovered culture in the New Guinea highlands." If this were indeed the case, then I would say, "New Guineans, beware!"

The method is purportedly quantitative and realistic. It is not the method of cross-cultural quantification, to be sure. Rather, it is an internal diachronic comparative method of putative precision employing the very latest scalogram technique. This is really fun to do. The numbers represent a series of judgments which Professor Tax quite candidly acknowledges "might be very shaky." What is more, the game is a free-wheeling sport. Anybody can play it by rearranging the figures to his heart's content or even by adding some! "Which brings us," says its inventor, "to the question of what the numbers represent." That *is* a good question. What they represent is "all mixed up." I had thought that Professor Tax was going to let it rest there as a jolly spoof. But no! For all the muddle in the method, "three things stand out." From the welter of digits three generalizations are put forth about why the people of the United States go to war and how they justify their bellicose enterprises.

The method is purportedly realistic, seeking the hidden and the latent in the national legislative structure and process. By ignoring the researches of political behaviorists and focusing on one very small aspect of the complex machinery of the electoral and legislative process, it produces a simplistic conclusion:

"So it is not 'Congress' but Congressional Committees; not only these committees, but the traditions of their staffs and the interests of their leaders and their small districts that largely determine what laws are made." "Largely determine" is very different from "factors that enter into."

Now as for the draft itself. It is more than just "the pressing of people into service by force." A more apposite formulation is stated by Eldridge Colby in the Encyclopedia of the Social Sciences: . . . ." [a] deliberate levy by the state in preference to other possible means of building an army and [which] is imposed on a selected group of citizens who would otherwise have the choice of non-participation if they so desired." It involves a state or national policy requiring an officially determined number of military personnel. Conscripted service may be invoked because there are not enough volunteers or simply because it is more convenient to the state and its officers. The kind of draft we are concerned with here is a means to an end. It cannot be analyzed separately from national policy. Conflict over the draft is conflict over national policy, individual self-determination, and the relation of the United States to its total international environment, exacerbated by the division of opinions over Vietnam. It began, for the United States, with George Washington's proposal of a draft for the Continental Army in the American Revolutionary War and its actual adoption by Massachusetts and Virginia in 1777. Given a broad national policy that has changed its focus but not its character since 1939, the question is: does the policy require a draft? The draft is not to be explained by the character of the structure of congressional committees and their staffs nor by speculation about how many veterans are in Congress (a point that could readily be determined, if it is important). More relevant, perhaps, is the fact that a large proportion of the members of both houses in Congress are reserve officers, and therefore directly committed members of the military establishment: Of one hundred senators, thirty-two are reservists. Of the Senate Armed Services Committee, three are generals, five colonels, two majors, and one a lieutenant commander in the reserves. All five Republicans (including Margaret Chase Smith) and six of the twelve Democrats on the committee are reserve officers. In addition, there is the former Secretary of the Air Force, Senator Symington. In sum, eleven of the seventeen members of the Senate Armed Services Committee are reserve officers.

In the House of Representatives, where appropriations bills

must originate, 107 of 435 members are reservists. Five of the ten members of the House Appropriations Sub-committee on Defense Funds are reservists; twelve of the forty-one members of the House Armed Services Committee are also members of the military reserves.

These military lawmakers are themselves but an expression of a basic national stance that willingly supports a behemoth Department for Defense. It supports a Defense Department which spends more each year than the net annual income of all the corporations in the United States, holds 27.6 million acres of land for its own uses, has 470 major and more than 6000 minor installations in some 5300 cities and towns in every state except Vermont and West Virginia, whose spending provides jobs for nearly one in every ten Americans, and defense business for 22,000 prime contractors and 100,000 sub-contractors. It is a national policy that generates so much internal "good business" that "delegation after delegation" has visited the Pentagon to protest the shutting down of 862 non-essential bases since November 1964 (Hoffman 1964). If the same national policy is determined to require 3,380,000 men in the Armed Services (the present figure), there is little serious question but that it will get them. This is the basic fact, lamentable though it be.

If there is to be a draft, there are those, who as Professor Tax notes, so love liberty that if the liberty to choose is withheld from some, they would deny it to all. They would press all the youth of the land into a complementary civil draft euphemistically called "National Service." What a solution!

The final conclusion of Professor Tax's discussion is one with which I find myself in full agreement. Make military pay comparable to civilian pay and see whether that does not obviate the need for the draft. Army base pay, plus pay-related benefits, is well below the federal minimum wage level of $1.40 per hour. It is, as the proposal of Congressmen Stafford, Horton, *et al,* states, a difference which amounts to a tax that "should be shared by society generally and not imposed solely on the young men in service." It results from a pay scale that is "not only not an inducement to enlistment, it is an obstacle to enlistment and serves to perpetuate the draft" (Minneapolis Tribune, October 23, 1967, p. 4). That is good sense, but its authors do not present it as anthropology.

SCOTT ROBINSON (*Cornell University*): To this point, panelists have been discussing the anthropology of war rather than anthropology *and* war, which is appropriate given the original intent of the symposium. Implicit in Professor Tax's statement, however, is the question of what is to be the political role of the anthropologist *qua* anthropologist *vis à vis* war today, during the late 1960s and beyond. I refer specifically to the issue of the anthropologist doing counterinsurgency research whether wittingly or unwittingly, and contributing to a political process which I think oftentimes denies the legitimate political aspirations of the anthropologist's own constituency, for example, primitive tribesmen, peasants, even overseas nation-states—for that matter, anybody anywhere.

Some anthropologists, both members and non-members of the American Anthropological Association, insist on doing research designed to aid the government in its military operations abroad and its control of urban riots at home. I suggest this type of research taints all of us anthropologists, involving us in political acts over which we have no control. This type of research, furthermore, represents a prostitution of the discipline to the political needs of our government, allowing that government to sponsor research which is designed to ask certain questions but not others. I consider it professionally irresponsible to engage in counterinsurgency research—in short, an anthropology *for* war. I think it self-evident that such research cannot meaningfully add to our knowledge and conceptual sophistication, not to speak of the stature of the profession, especially abroad.

DR. TAX: If you ask what the position of the anthropologist is when he finds himself doing research which appears to work against the interest of the people he studies, the answer for me is that he shouldn't do it. Last year the American Anthropological Association undertook a study, following disclosures of CIA and War Department involvements in Social Science research, of the ethics involved in research, particularly abroad. The result was the so-called Beals report, which was approved almost unanimously (Ralph Beals 1967).

In normal times anthropologists can sometimes mediate between native peoples and the establishments who dominate them. When this becomes hopeless, the anthropologist can do little as an anthropologist; if he joins a revolution, it must be in his private role. The research anthropologist can operate as an educator, pressing upon anybody who will listen the relevance of his special knowledge to establishing more constructive relationships. Many of us think he not only may, but should go out of his way to use his knowledge for constructive purposes. If it is too late for words, then the anthropologist (as such) retreats to his studies. Whether then as citizen he engages in something going beyond education, or scientific neutrality, is another matter. Each of us has to work his way through the problem. Personally I find it difficult to separate myself into two halves, anthropologist one day and citizen the next. So I take as a primary value the right of people to be free and to protect their identities and cultures, and am willing to help them do so in any way that I can. This value is consonant with anthropological knowledge as I understand it, but I don't doubt it has other than scientific origins—I would do whatever I can to influence my own government or anybody with whom I have influence, in a direction that I think the data of my profession leads me and which I think my own system of ethics requires me to accept. The relation between these two is obviously difficult, but I would argue that this is necessarily personal and if somebody throws me out of my profession because of the view I take, then that's one of the things I'll have to study next time.

Part VIII | ALTERNATIVES TO WAR

ALTERNATIVES TO WAR

MARGARET MEAD

IN CONSIDERING ALTERNATIVES TO WAR, I shall consider together all forms of warfare in which defined groups engage in purposeful, organized and socially sanctioned combat involving killing each other. I will not introduce any distinctions between primitive warfare and warfare in states organized on the basis of script and other organizational devices of civilization. Nor will I, for purposes of this analysis, distinguish between warfare among sub-units of a society, such as so-called banditry, or vendetta in remote parts of modern states, guerrilla warfare within states in which revolution is being attempted, or gangland warfare between juvenile or adult gangs. Warfare exists if the conflict is organized, and socially sanctioned and the killing is not regarded as murder. The fact that imperfectly superordinate units attempt to suppress it will not be considered relevant. The figurative extension of the term warfare to forms of conflict in which the killing of persons is not sanctioned, as in tariff "wars," "battles" between labor and capital conducted without lethal physical violence to persons, psychological "warfare," etc., may be treated as one set of "alternatives to war." In these cases the hostility, desire to dominate or destroy which characterizes warfare, may be present but lethal violence directed against members of the other side is not sanctioned by both parties to the conflict. Also political activities in which those in power hunt down, and if necessary kill the individual "traitor" or "outlaw" will not be considered to be warfare if the traitor or outlaw does not belong to an organized group which regards his activities as having legitimacy within the sub-system which he represents. The criteria used will therefore be: organization for the purpose of a combat involving the intention to kill and the willingness to die, social sanction for this behavior, which distinguishes it from murder of members of its own group, and the agreement between the groups involved on the legitimacy of the fighting with intent to kill. Socially sanctioned revenge to the point of inflicting physical injury, or death itself, by one member of a group towards another, as in the case of Eskimo individual murders, cases of men who shoot their wives' lovers and are acquitted under "the unwritten law," fighting which inflicts small injuries but in which killing is interdicted—Iatmul fighting with sticks but not with spears within the language groups and between friendly villages, (Mead, n.d.[1]) clashes between fraternal groups, freshmen and sophomores, representing town and gown—will also be excluded.

Warfare will be regarded as a cultural invention consequent upon group identification, the existence of shared taboos against intra-group killing [comparable to and to some degree related to cultural taboos on incest (Mead 1968; Durkheim 1963)] and the equally culturally defined social sanctioning of killing members of the opposing group. If a people have, as part of their cultural repertoire of behavior, a set of articulated rules which distinguish intra-group killing from organized extra-group killing, they will be said to have the institution of warfare, whether it occurs frequently or infrequently in practice. Further distinctions may be made between peoples who put a positive or negative value on warfare, as for example when membership in a military caste confers high distinction, or participation in organized killing is a necessary validation of manhood—as in headhunting societies, etc. The development of societies in which resort to warfare is regarded as legitimate only in the face of invasion, while it may be seen as one of the conditions that may lead to the suspension of warfare for long periods in a particular region of the world, will be regarded as part of a warfare system, however infrequently invoked.

In terms of these definitions, the Eskimo (Boas 1888; Thalbitzer 1914, 1923) did not have the institution of warfare; peoples like the Arapesh did have the institution although they avoided invoking it regularly and treated killing, either within or without the group, as ceremonially dangerous (Mead, 1963a).

---

[1] Mead, Margaret, unpublished fieldwork under National Science Foundation Grant No. GS-642, to the American Museum of Natural History, entitled "The Cultural Structure of Perceptual Communication, 1965–69."

The Andamanese had warfare (Radcliffe-Brown 1964), New Guinea headhunting societies, like the Iatmul (Bateson 1958), the Mundugumor (Mead 1963a) and the Orokaiva (Williams 1930) were actively warlike societies with rewards for the sanctioned killing of enemies. In such headhunting societies killing of a single member of the other group, by lucky accident, and not on a battlefield, can be counted simply as part of a *permanent* state of warfare. The existence of other relationships between groups, such as intermarriage and trade will not be considered grounds for distinguishing between headhunting, vendetta, ceremonial revenge, and other forms of warfare, but different kinds of hostile relationships between identified groups which may constitute more or less self-perpetuating warfare. From this point of view, the Manus, who had no built-in institutions that required killing a member of another group, and no adequate sanctions against intra-group conflict between localized clans or intra-village entrepreneurial clusters, were characterized at different periods in their history by periods of purposeful rapine and attempts to drive out or exterminate other groups (Schwartz, n.d.[2]). The Dane (Matthiessen 1962; Gardner 1964; Mead 1964a), on the other hand, would have to be described as a people for whom warfare was so institutionalized that it was self-perpetuating. Many such warfare forms lack such objectives of destruction of property and crops, conquest, extinction, dispersal, or incorporation which have made warfare a device for the spacing out of populations, and for the establishment of larger units within which other forms of domination, paying tribute, slavery, and modified allegiance or actual incorporation as full citizens have been successor conditions.

I also assume that warfare, as defined here, and the distinction between intra-group and inter-group killing itself are social inventions without a specific biological basis. I assume that we must take into account man's capacity to use symbolic means to define who is and who is not a member of his own group, and that in man—in contradistinction to members of other mammalian species—there are no built-in, culturally independent devices for ritualizing intra-group fighting. Instead, the capacity to symbolize makes it possible for men to socially define other men either as

---

[2] Schwartz, Theodore, unpublished fieldwork in the Admiralty Islands under National Institute of Health Grant No. MH-07675-05, 1963–67.

comparable to con-specifics, and so inappropriate objects for killing (although often appropriate objects for physical combat
especially between rivalrous males) or as, effectively, non-
conspecifics, and either prey, predator, or rival.

The ethological literature on aggression and territoriality
seems to me to lack clear discussion of the conditions within
which other creatures, non-conspecifics, are neither prey nor
predator, but coincidental rivals for the same prey, or the same
hunting, nesting, territory or even highway. The occasionally reported "battles" between troops of apes or monkeys, and the
controversy between those who claim that there are yearly "battles" between eagles and storks, during the joint migrations over
Turkey (*Times,* 1967) would be cases in point. Territoriality
which reduces conflict among con-specifics, would, under conditions of temporary or periodic crowding, result in something that
looks very like the least organized form of human group conflict
and that might be theoretically regarded as the precursor of warfare. There is still a strong case to be made against identifying
the social institution of taboos on murder, with any built-in instinctual equipment for the recognition of con-specifics or any
built-in aggressive tendency to kill other human beings, or members of other human groups who carry physical indicators or
social indicators of belonging to another human group. I would
simply argue, as Gorer does (1966a), that man lacks instinctual
controls, and not, as Lorenz and Ardrey do, that warfare is
an extension of built-in aggression towards rivals for mates,
territory or food (Lorenz 1966; Ardrey 1966; Gorer 1967). But
I would add to Gorer's argument the factor of symbolization in
man, and argue that the identification of an enemy suitable for
warfare, is socially analogous to the non-human biologically based
identification of prey or predator, in which other human beings are
seen as non-human. I would further argue that those forms of
warfare that are sometimes identified as play—tournaments, conflicts between individual "champions" of rivalrous groups, American Plains Indians' warfare with death low on the list of counting
coup (Benedict 1959), can be seen as analogies to those con-
specific rivalries that do not have as their aim, but may have as
their by-product, the death of one or the other of the two involved
in ritual aggression, and which under conditions of crowding
(Mead 1963b), may lead to murder (Calhoun 1948).

The resolution of this argument, which is still being pursued with inadequate knowledge of culture by the ethologists, very preliminary experimentation by the experimental ethologists, and the invocation of selected ethological examples by anthropologists, is essential if alternatives to war are to be scientifically considered. If the claim of built-in biological aggression as made by Lorenz (1966), and adumbrated journalistically by Ardrey (1966), and as assumed in many psychoanalytic discussions (Masserman 1963 passim), were to be substantiated, then the social measures necessary for the prevention of warfare might include ways of modifying the gene pool or radical changes in diet, which might, as Lorenz believes, have serious consequences for the exercise of other valuable human characteristics. In the present state of the evidence there remains the possibility that certain types of aggression may be "built-in" to some individuals —which would leave open the possibility of differential distribution of relevant genes in different populations, especially in very small populations. There is also the accompanying possibility that such behavior can therefore be "read-in" to or programmed culturally into many other human constitutional types, as well as the possibility that there may be constitutional types endowed with built-in controls against lethal aggression where not only con-specifics but also living prey or predators are concerned. It may be that the production of a social environment in which there were no living creatures used as food or pets or work assistants might be sufficient to extinguish the human capacity to kill living things, or, alternatively, might make it socially impossible to modulate and teach the difference between permitted and impermissible killing either of other living things or of other human beings (Mead 1964b).

If we regard warfare as a cultural artifact (a sociofact in Bidney's terminology), which can be used by any human group, but is not specifically biologically underwritten, it may then be described as a social invention, in the same way that the wheel is a social invention, with the probability that it was invented many times by early man in the course of the development of language, tools and social organization (Mead 1940, 1965a). Here one further historical peculiarity must be mentioned: the distinction between the sexes in the use of tools and weapons. Tools are extensions of the manual abilities of both sexes, although they may be restricted in some special forms to one sex or the other. Weapons, designed for hunting, defense, and combat, have been almost completely restricted to males. With a very few brief exceptions, social sanction has never been given to the habitual use of weapons by women, and women have been left to fight, when they fought, with only their natural equipment of fingernails and teeth, or temporarily adapted tools, the rolling pin, distaff, digging stick, etc. This circumstance has not been sufficiently integrated into the ethological discussion. It is notable that all consideration of females disappears when Lorenz (1966) reaches his discussion of human aggression, and that one of the most insightful treatises on the possibilities of innate aggression, *Lord of the Flies* (Golding 1959) creates an artificial society of boys in which females are lacking. It is important to take into consideration the possibility that the biological bases of aggression in the two sexes—in human beings as in other mammals—may differ significantly. The female characteristically fights only for food or in defense of her young, and then fights to kill, and may be without the built-in checks on con-specific murder that are either socially or biologically present in males. Arming women, as has been done in this century in Israel, the USSR, Indonesia and Vietnam, may be a suicidal course.

If war is an invention, we can then examine the functions that it has served in the past. In any discussion of alternatives to war, as in any discussion of sequences of inventions, it is necessary to investigate whether the functions fulfilled by warfare in the past are functions necessary in modern society, and if so what other inventions can fulfill them better. Recognizing the extent of cultural lag in many cases, we may, I think, insist that a functioning invention will be used at least until rendered obsolete by another invention or set of inventions, by the disappearance of the function it performed, or by becoming itself dysfunctional. It may therefore be argued that unless a better invention is found, a previous invention will continue to be used as long as it does fulfill some social function. We must also reckon with the continuation of earlier inventions even under conditions of long obsolescence, as when human labor is invoked in the absence of machines, or during warfare and revolution when people return to earlier technologies. (This was the case in the use of candle nuts for light and a return to bark cloth making in the south seas during World War II, after both had been abandoned.) It is unlikely at present that the possibility of warfare —as an invention—could disappear from human knowledge.

Therefore, this knowledge has to be reckoned with as one of the conditions in any discussion of the hopes for a warless world. Correspondingly, the knowledge of methods of nuclear warfare has to be regarded as a component of modern culture in the foreseeable future, however much we may succeed in banning nuclear tests or eliminating stockpiles of bombs.

A further question thus becomes: given warfare as a known functional response to a variety of identifiable conditions, what are the necessary conditions under which this invention will *not* be used? Warfare may be used to repel attack, add territory or subjects to one's own territory, establish autonomy or freedom from subordination, provide targets outside the country when the maintenance of power is threatened from within, provide sources of food or minerals, and even, in some cases, provide a market for munition makers or an excuse for the maintenance of a wartime, heated-up economy which serves a group in power. Such a discussion leads to a consideration of what are essentially other forms of warfare: economic and psychological warfare, and the destruction of weapons, buildings or crops rather than persons, without attempting to alter forms of social organization of large groups so that hostile conflict is no longer functional.

One condition which might leave the existing types of hostilities otherwise uncorrected, is the recognition, by all relevant groups, that scientific warfare would result in the complete elimination of the own group as well, and consequently of the values which its members have been educated to defend. We have in some respects approached this condition today, as far as some of the leadership of the industrialized blocs are concerned. Most of the world's citizens, however, are still willing to go to war under nuclear threat, including the citizens of those states whose leaders are best informed about the consequences of nuclear warfare, suggests that the task of convincing people that it is useless to die for something which will no longer be embodied in other human beings, is still very difficult. This can be attributed to the same capacity to symbolize, that has made warfare possible by defining other human beings as non-human, and so preserving side by side the socially cultivated sentiments of cooperation, protection of group members, and the ruthless extermination of members of other groups.

The last ten years have demonstrated that the threat of nuclear warfare, and the accompanying relative immobilization of

the great powers, vis-à-vis each other, does not, as the world is
currently organized, prevent the proliferation of other forms of
warfare, or the decrease of violence which may turn to civil war,
within national states. It is therefore necessary to distinguish
between the recognition that warfare, on a world scale, is not
only no longer functional, as it has often been in the past, but
actually endangers the entire population of the planet and the
recognition of the importance of the development of values that
may in time contribute to a climate of opinion that will make it
easier to discard war as a political tool. However, these recog-
nitions need not prevent the active propagation of an understanding of the consequences of scientific warfare as part of the
preparation of world opinion for the outlawing of war as obsolescent and destructive to *all* participants alike. We may also
argue that the failure of the efforts to use the invention of nuclear
warfare as a sufficient condition for the establishment of international order after World War II, was due to the absence of
other necessary inventions, and alternatives to the political-
economic arrangements in this interconnected world.

It is these other arrangements with which the remainder of
this paper is concerned. Warfare depends upon the establishment
of unequivocal and mutually exclusive identities and loyalties,
today represented by national boundaries. As long as there exists
a permanent definition of the own group, within which to kill is
murder, and others, whom it may be or is virtuous to risk one's
life to kill, warfare or the threat of warfare with its accompani-
ments of uncontrolled violence among smaller nations, or sub-
national groups, can be easily invoked.

Various modifications of our present conceptions of the nation state are possible. The present definition predicates the state
upon its absolute right and continuing ability to make war on
other states. This definition, supported by properly developed
sanctions and accepted definitions, could be changed to an emphasis on nationhood, in which the identity and power of each
state was a function of the identity and power of all other nations. This is the case where federations succeed in binding internal warfare and strengthening the security, well-being and
identity of each group as a function of its membership in the
larger group. It is frequently argued that federations have been
dependent upon external enemies and therefore are impractical
forms to use as models for a single world order. But internal

order has been attained by societies without the need of invoking external enemies, once the social forms made it possible to identify all members as equally human and exempt from treatment as non-human. Slaves have been freed, children released from the brutal domination of parents and teachers, women given rights, and minorities given full citizenship, as the social identifications have been altered, in belief and in practice. The definition of nations as owing their status to the existence and prosperity of other nations, their security to the security of other nations, and emphasis upon interdependence rather than independence, could result in concepts of nationhood replacing concepts of nationalism (Deutsch 1964). Such changes in our present world organization would require altering the present appeal of nation-states. We would have to find ways to perform those organizational and identity bestowing functions now met by nation-states. Substituting multilateral responsibilities for bilateral agreements is one way in which this change can be promoted. A second structural device is the development of multinationality, but it seems unlikely that this would be adequate without further changes in international structures. As long as nation-states are the building blocks of international structures, regional organization, and non-localized power blocks must represent the weakness inherent in their component parts. Any component in an over-arching structure designed to eliminate war must, by definition, not be defined in a way that permits warfare and the definition of members of another group as non-human and suitable for killing. International organizations built of nation-states, in whatever combination, retain this liability of return to warfare. The simple federation model is, for this reason, not a feasible alternative.

Furthermore, if the model of a single hierarchical state is used to represent a possible future world community, we then have to reckon, not with the traditional view of warfare in which the enemy are defined as non-human, but with the cultural acceptance of the less ancient, but equally well-supported social belief in the rights of local, geographically based groups vis-à-vis superordinate groups governing larger territories. This belief, which those who think that territoriality is important trace to animal societies, is, however, also subject to man's capacity to symbolize. The intrinsic right to self-determination and autonomy of a localized group can easily be extended to non-localized groups that consider themselves human—as opposed to the less human or the non-human other. Religious groups have this capacity, and most of them have exercised it; divisions along lines of racial identity, language, custom and political ideologies have also proved as potent rallying points as geographical continuity. It is true that since the invention of the autonomous nation-state such groups have had to capture the state mechanism in order to actually make efficient and socially sanctioned war, so that the cultural appeal of mutually exclusive geographical and ideological identities reinforce each other. But at present, scrutiny of history suggests that the elimination of one without the other will not be sufficient. The current demand for a theology of revolution (World Conference on Church and Society, 1966) is only another form of the old demand for a theology of the divine right of kings and the legitimacy of wars between nation-states in which the priesthoods of the same religion could each pray for victory. Any form of world state within which the components can rearrange their loyalties so that members of other identifiable groups can be defined as legitimate prey cannot be regarded as a social invention that can actually prevent war. Ideas of revolution and holy wars would continue to threaten its stability, just as geographical loyalties would continue to threaten the federation model.

Our organizational task may then be defined as reducing the strength of all mutually exclusive loyalties, whether of nation, race, class, religion or ideology, and constructing some quite different form of organization in which the memory of these loyalties and the organizational residues of these former exclusive loyalties cannot threaten the total structure. The difficulty of arriving at such a conception only attests to the dangerous hold of past models on our imaginations. Even our most imaginative science fiction writers continue to deal either in the fantasies of other planets, against whom the inhabitants of Earth can unite; or superordinate and unbearable forms of world organization against which human beings must finally rebel; or totally superordinate angelic beings—in twentieth-century flying saucers—who because they are super-human, can keep order among us.

One of the principal contributions of anthropology should be to distill from our available treasure house of small and unusual social models—many of them outside the single narrow and steadily converging mainstream of "civilization"—new combinations and new forms that will release us from our historically limited imaginations (Mead and Metraux 1965).

The proposals which I am going to make stem from a series of anthropological contributions to the subject of alternatives to war, in the specification of necessary conditions and the prefiguration of new forms (Benedict 1948; Malinowski 1948; Mead 1948). Ruth Benedict (1948) insisted upon the importance of institutional arrangements rather than human motives as the essential and modifiable elements in the consideration of warfare. Gregory Bateson brought warfare within the formulations of cybernetics, self-perpetuating systems and positive feedback runaways (Bateson 1946), by combining Richardson's neglected theory of an armaments race (Richardson 1939, 1960), with the emerging cross disciplinary language of cybernetics (Von Foerster 1950–1956; Bateson 1947). Geoffrey Gorer (1966b) has concentrated on the importance of developing smaller, and cross-cutting forms of group identification, and the relationships between ethology and discussions of warfare. Finally, Alvin Wolfe (1963) drew upon his anthropological training in identifying an emerging form of acephalous control, against which rebellion or revolt are structurally impossible.

As a prelude to more specific suggestions which utilize all of these, I should like to discuss Alvin Wolfe's model in some detail. In his original paper, called "From Cape to Kantanga," he identified a new form of control over minerals in Africa. This involved overlapping membership of Boards, each with different geographical centers of influence, with memberships reaching from Brussels to San Francisco, and with international agreements (including Moscow) on the subject of the controlled production of industrial diamonds. These Boards actually had superseded the power of either the former colonial powers or the national governments of emerging African states. Wolfe showed how this acephalous organization was one which could neither be joined nor resigned from, based as it was on overlapping membership in which no one membership could be seen as *primarily* related to the whole (Wolfe 1962).[3]

---

[3] In further discussion of this important paper, it is useful to make two points. The control broke down as the Belgian Miners Union Minière attempted to excise the old forms of nationally based exclusive power, and the disorders in the Congo have been a continuing sequelae. Wolfe's paper, in a revised form was turned down by several social science journals, an indication of how ideologically culture-bound the social sciences are becoming.

A practical version of the acephalous model within which the components are not sufficiently identified to make warfare or revolution possible, is provided by the U.S. and Canada Eastern electric power grid. Had this model fulfilled its requirements, it would have provided an acephalous self-regulatory mechanism of very high functional ability.[4]

Our new models for world organization can be asked to meet the following negative requirements: (1) absence of forms of organization providing any mutually exclusive self-identifications; (2) absence of self-perpetuating, accelerating systems involving positive feedback runaways; (3) absence of the kind of hierarchical, linear, or branching structures, in which the component units can be seen as of the same sort—and so rivalrous—or as presenting organizational lines of fission.

As positive requirements, new models should:

1. Provide order as well as prevent major wars.

2. Provide for the distribution of the essentials and goods of life among *all* the peoples of the planet, in such a way that their common and shared species membership is not violated and so accompanied by denial.

3. Distribute centers of power over organizational functions that will necessarily be world-wide, such as control of food, banking, communication, policing, travel and migration, and protection of the natural environment, so that no two centers coincide geographically. The structures that express these functions should be as structurally dissimilar as possible, in such dimensions as size, internal relationship between organizational levels, number of constituent regions, in order to reduce possibilities of symmetrical conflict among them. None of these structures should command other than professional loyalties.

4. Establish the conditions for self-identification with a small geographically located group, within which all the component individuals can be personally known to each other, to underwrite

---

[4] Analysis of the 1965 breakdown only serves to underline the importance of the model. It broke down because of a mixture of automatic and human functions (including mutually contradictory considerations of load and cost) and inadequate automatic checks, and the consequences of the break down were aggravated by the extra lack of imagination—prevalent in many fields in the United States—by which a separate source of power to restart the generators had not been provided.

each growing child's need for identity and security. These needs have been well spelled out (Erikson 1959, 1964; Soddy 1961).

5. Establish the conditions for a variety of mutually over-lapping and non-exclusive identifications with larger groups of many kinds, without any single or overriding loyalty.

Finally, there are conditions of order without which it would be impracticable to discuss such new world-wide arrangements, the non-fulfillment of which might seriously prolong the present state of world-wide anarchy, small wars and disorder. It will be necessary:

1. To formalize ways of preventing nuclear war (Kurtz and Kurtz 1967).

2. To establish adequate technological and political means to halt the rapid pollution and deterioration of the biosphere.

3. To establish the technology and the ethics to halt the present rate of population increase and to restore it to a balance with food supplies and human resources of maturity and skill.

4. To increase food production without intensification of the present consequences in the destruction of the biosphere.

5. To establish a world-wide secondary spoken language that will equalize the positions of speakers of all languages large and small (Mead 1965b)—this means the adoption of a politically negligible natural language as a secondary spoken language—and some form of glyphic and written communication which will be independent of lexicographic considerations, like Chinese, but more formal, simpler, and easier to learn and to execute.

6. To find ways in which young males, in an increasingly urbanized environment, can validate their courage and physical competence (Mead 1959) as substitutes for the validations once provided by exacting natural environments and war, in order to prevent the consequences in urban violence that we see all over the urban world today (Mead 1963c).

7. To develop a means of controlling large masses of people which will be effective but non-lethal.

Into all such plans, we should build methods of assaying the unanticipated by-products of taking first steps in any given direction (Bateson 1958). Although general systems theory—as the sophisticated successor of cybernetics—has provided us with both a cross-disciplinary and cross-ideological medium of communication, it has not been self-conscious enough in allowing for changes when it itself is applied. Our knowledge of biological behavior of all sorts, and particularly of human behavior is so imperfect that long term planning without allowance for multiple feedback often does more harm than good.

DECISION MAKING ON WAR
AND PEACE

SEYMOUR MELMAN

D R. MEAD'S ABLE PAPER defines the role of the nation state in war making, and the capability of leaders to foster processes of dehumanization and legitimation of war making. Dr. Mead has also identified a series of desirable characteristics of governmental and non-governmental policies for securing social structures and processes in which conflicts could be resolved without recourse to war. In Dr. Mead's paper these have been defined without focusing on the institutions and ways of a particular war-making society. Therefore these analyses prescribe a general approach that must be utilized in designing a social alternative to war. However, the nature of social alternatives, for a particular society must always be defined in terms of the decision processes and institutional ways of that war-making society.

In these comments I approach the problem of alternatives to war from the vantage point of the specific conditions of American society. This approach suffers from no defect of being a "case study." The United States in its current federal budget allocates $87 billion for war making, or more than two-thirds of the total budgeted outlay of the federal government. This military budget of the United States amounts to half or more of the total world outlay for military purposes in the current fiscal year. With respect to American society these comments ask: who needs a war system; what are some of the grossly unsatisfactory conditions (problems) generated by operation of the war system; what are conceivable alternatives to the war system.[1]

Military organizations press for commitments to the war system

---

[1] The analyses given here may also be read as a response to the main propositions of the recently published "The Report from Iron Mountain: on the Possibility and Desirability of Peace."

from their own society so that the military groups may maintain
or extend their organizations, and their accompanying decision
power. They do this in the name of defending the nation from
external attack and operating a system that can win military vic-
tories. Since the Second World War these prognoses and promises
of the military institution can no longer be fulfilled, for the military art has been transformed. In nuclear war there is no known
way of scoring any meaningful gain by any side. There is no basis
in knowledge for disproving the proposition that nuclear war
would involve, if not the termination of the race, then the termination of entire societies. "Conventional" wars are no longer
fought to a military conclusion. Since the Second World War
every armed conflict between states has been terminated by political intervention of single states, groups of states, or the
United Nations. No military conflict between states has been permitted to run to a military conclusion. Everywhere, on occasion
of each international conflict, there has been the pervasive fear
of involvement by the great powers and rapid escalation into nuclear conflict with loss for all.

Also, since the Second World War the development of the
military and related technologies has proceeded in such fashion
as to make possible more lethal and always cheaper weapons,
with their technology publicly available to a widening range of
nation states. Chemical and biological warfare techniques (see
Science and Citizen for Aug.–Sept. 1967) now includes techniques
which give these technologies the competence of a "poor man's
atom bomb." As a result unique military advantage may no longer
be achieved only by states of greatest material wealth.

Modern military forces both nuclear and conventional can be
used to threaten or destroy, but no longer to defend or to win a
politically meaningful victory. Thereby, the innovators of military
technology and the operators of military systems have checkmated
themselves as a consequence of their own success in the search
for more lethal military technologies. Whatever else may be done
by a "Department of Defense," this much is clear: that department and its armed forces cannot defend the shores of the United
States nor insure continuity of human life in this land following
a nuclear exchange; neither can these armed forces use their
"conventional" weaponry to insure politically meaningful "victory" in conventional military operations. Therefore, the remain-

ing military strategy for improving the military security of nation states—large and small—is now disarmament.

Political decision makers who operate with policies that use military power to extend their decision making at home and abroad need the maintenance and extension of military institutions. But these policies are frustrated by the highly destabilizing consequences of military priorities in developed as well as in developing countries. Thus, in the United States military priorities now preclude significant economic development at home. Domestic rebellions against conditions of life will probably continue until the rebelling populations are either exterminated, imprisoned, or satisfied in their culturally validated economic demands by major economic development programs. For example: 7.5 million American families in poverty require for economic development not less than $30,000 per family in the form of varied development investment. Therefore a capital fund of $215 billion, at minimum, is required for meaningful economic development in the United States. This fund and the manpower and other resources it represents is unavailable within the framework of sustained military priority in money, manpower, and other resources.

The same military priority in the United States precludes allocation of meaningful resources for economic development in Asia, Africa and Latin America. In 1962 I calculated in the little book "The Peace Race" that $22 billion a year would suffice for capital investment purposes of every sort in the pursuit of economic development for all of Asia, Africa and Latin America. At the present time, with more than $30 billion a year being spent on the war in Vietnam alone, the United States is using up in this way more than the entire capital fund required for world-wide economic development. The present U.S. military priority therefore nurtures political instability wherever governments in developing lands are unable to marshal resources for a meaningful pace of economic development.

The priority in material goods and money given to the military services has many consequences for the quality of life within American society. For example: the speed and destructiveness of modern military technologies are used to justify military and allied political activities by covert methods which, inescapably, undermine legality in the behavior of government not only overseas but at home as well. Practices of this quality therefore contradict the formal structure of government as a government of limited powers, and generates conflict with all those who bear allegiance to these traditional concepts.

Industrial managers over military work within government and in private industry need the maintenance and extension of military organizations. The government management so involved is mainly the industrial managing organization operating in the Department of Defense. These managements are placed in opposition to the rest of society insofar as there is any desire to perform major domestic economic development. A shift to civilian priority would require the dismantling, retraining, and regrouping of the men now engaged in military industrial management—governmental and private.

About 3.3 million men in the armed forces and 6 million civilian employees in private industry are now locked into the war system by the nature of the goods and services they help to produce. For these men too the maintenance and extension of the war system is a professional-economic requirement. But these men are by and large readily transferable or trainable to work performed on behalf of civilian goods and services production. A shift to civilian priorities could rapidly generate annual outlays in areas of marked civilian underdevelopment in the United States of as much as $76 billion per year, or more—equivalent to about 9½ million jobs each year.

Vigorous pursuit of the war system soothes and nourishes the psyches of Americans who are involved in extreme, verging on paranoid, anti-communist fears. Recent experience, however, suggests that certain events can have dramatic impact in overriding fears of long standing. Thus, following the Cuban missile crisis of October 1962 the prospect of an "end of the world" impelled many Americans to approve policies of detente between the United States and the Soviet Union that were instituted immediately thereafter by Messrs. Kennedy and Khrushchev.

A considerable number of American intellectuals earn their livelihood by developing military technologies involving both the natural and the social sciences. However honored and well supported these men may be in their work, it remains a sustaining source of frustration to be locked into the service of managements that persistently extend their decision power, in order to operate military systems that can no longer be used to win. In the presence of wide pressures for changes in national priorities, and changing job opportunities, it may be expected that the scientists and engineers who have grown into servicing the war system will find ways of retraining or transferring their competence toward the service of civilian arts.

On the matter of national states as sustaining sources of military conflict: For a foreseeable future it is reasonable to expect that national states, large and small, will continue to exist and that sharp conflicts will arise between them. The issue then is: is it conceivable to police such conflicts in a way that will severely limit recourse to military power? I know of no science that would lead one to exclude such possibilities. Under conditions of a slowed arms race and initial steps of disarmament by the great powers, all states would find themselves under pressures—economic and political—wielded by the great powers, to refrain from the use of military force for settling disputes.

Under these conditions it would become conceivable to institute systems of international police forces which would operate with the same sort of automatically triggered reliability, impartiality and speed that is now visible in the operation of a good metropolitan police force. It is technically feasible to design such international police forces to prevent or halt conflict between smaller and medium sized states.

The crucial precondition for this is agreement among the great powers to agree that military power is no longer a competent way of settling their own disputes. One major step in this direction was made after the Cuban missile crisis when Messrs. Kennedy and Khrushchev are reported to have agreed that neither the United States nor the Soviet Union would make nuclear war on purpose. The subsequent frantic search for further technical devices that might give military superiority in nuclear and other weaponry represents, even for the big powers, the terminal period of military power as an efficient political instrument.

Within American society the war system is accepted via a structure of decision making in which the Department of Defense and allied groups in the Executive formulate orders which are issued to the population. These orders must be accepted and implemented for the orders to have the quality of effective decisions.

In this reasoning, alteration of the institutions which rely on war and war preparation, and the development of alternatives to war, requires, on the one side, growing reluctance among the

population to accept and implement war system orders, together with politically efficient action toward altering the domestic
war system institutions and replacing the policies which rely on
military power for political ends.

WE HAVE BEGUN TODAY to make a systematic anthropological contribution to the most pressing problem of our generation —the prevention of war. I use the term prevention of warfare rather than the term peace because the idea of peace includes the idea of war, of periods of alternation between recognized peace and recognized war. Our task today is the continuing, unremitting effort to establish forms of political, social and economic organization on a world-wide scale that will effectively prevent war, in which the continued expectation of war will become as outmoded as the continued expectation of an epidemic once the conditions under which a disease becomes epidemic are known. We belong to the first generation that has actually had a chance to consider the prevention of war because for the first time in history modern forms of warfare, particularly nuclear warfare, make warfare catastrophic for *all* of those who engage in it. For the first time in history, therefore, we may be able to muster sufficient political backing to support institutions for the prevention of war rather than institutions directed either towards political predation or defense against such predation. But first the peoples of the world will have to invent those institutions.

This symposium has been planned and carried out under two kinds of tension. There is the tension that is engendered by the threat of nuclear war, a threat which will challenge mankind's best efforts at war prevention throughout the conceivable future —for although we may succeed in destroying the stockpiles of bombs we cannot destroy the knowledge of how to make them. And second, particularly for the people of the United States and its associates, there is the problem of the Vietnam war and developing safeguards against the occurrence of similar limited wars.

The years in which we have so far prevented the occurrence of a world devastating nuclear war have faced us with new problems that arise when the great powers are immobilized, and the resulting smaller scale disasters of civil war, wars of liberation, and internal massacres of huge proportions are a characteristic of this kind of uneasy world truce.

The responsibilities and tasks of anthropology as a discipline concerned with man's past, his present and his future development have been outlined in the course of this symposium. This is only a beginning of making a systematic attack on the whole question but it is, I think, a good beginning.

We have to explore the origins of war, in man's long history, bringing to bear all that we know of pre-history and pre-hominoid man. We have to explore the continuities and discontinuities between the behavior of human beings and the behavior of other primates, other mammals and other living creatures. We are going to have to relate our knowledge of human culture and human capacities for learning with the findings of psychology and physiology and investigate more seriously than we did today, the problem of whether human beings have any innate predispositions and needs which have been served by warfare in the past and for which other forms of gratification and expression must be devised. We will need to pay particular attention, I believe, to the need of young males to validate their strength and courage, and to the differences between the sexes which have been expressed throughout human history in the conspicuous unwillingness of most human societies to arm women. We are going to have to organize all that we know about the consequences of war in population changes, and in disease, and changes in ecological balance. We will need to bring to bear our unique and detailed acquaintance with a variety of social forms, from which it may be possible to derive new models for social order, models that are superior to those which could be developed from within our own limited historical tradition. These are all anthropological tasks; the nature of prehistoric warfare, the nature of primitive warfare, the relationship of warfare to the rise of civilization and to the maintenance of civilizations, the significance of changes in forms of warfare, changes in weapons and forms of social organization, and how these have changed the nature of human social life.

If we are to perform these tasks, if we are to meet these responsibilities, we need to systematize our approach, develop some agreed upon and usable definitions, codify our current knowledge and work out research designs within which our particular competencies will be relevant and useful. The task of bringing to bear all of the human sciences on the most crucial problem of our time is not, of course, a task for anthropologists alone. It is a task that we share with all of the other human sciences, with all the biological sciences, and with Science as a whole. In devoting this symposium to our share of the responsibility, we are beginning to set our own house in order, to become sufficiently clear about what we have to offer, so that we may take part in an enterprise which must involve the contributions of each human culture and each relevant scientific discipline. And in the course of considering warfare we must also consider the problems of control of violence, a question that is almost as pressing as the prevention of war itself, because without the control of violence the order that men have built, without which science itself would not be possible is in danger, and also because, as Bronowski has so beautifully said in *The Face of Violence,* "Violence is the sphinx by the fireside, and she has a human face."

BIBLIOGRAPHY

Abel, T.
  1941 The elements of decision in the pattern of war. *Amer. Soc. Review*
  6:853–859.
Ackerknecht, E.
  1965 *History and Geography of the Most Important Diseases*. New
  York: Hafner.
Ackerman, Charles
  1964 Structure and statistics: the Purum case. *Amer. Anthrop.* 66:53–63.
Altmann, S. A.
  1962 A field study of the sociobiology of rhesus monkeys, *Macaca mu-
  latta*. *Ann. N. Y. Acad. Sci.* 102:338–435.
  1967 (ed.) *Social Communication Among Primates*. Chicago: University of Chicago Press.
Andrews, R. J.
  1963 The origin and evolution of the calls and facial expressions of the
  primates. *Behaviour* 20:1–109.
Ardrey, Robert
  1966 *The Territorial Imperative*. New York: Atheneum.
Baal, J. van
  1966 *Dema*. The Hague: Martinus Nijhoff.
Barker, James P.
  1953 Memoria sobre la cultura de los Guaika. *Bol. Indig. Venezolano*,
  1:Nos. 3–4:433–488.
Barnes, J. A.
  1954 *Politics in a Changing Society: A Political History of the Fort
  Jameson Ngoni*. Capetown: Oxford University Press.
Barnicot, N. A.
  1965 Natural selection and transmissible disease. *Nature* 208:535–536.
Bateson, Gregory
  1946 The pattern of an armaments race. *Bull. Atomic Sci.* 2:10–11;
  26–28.
  1947 Atoms, nations and culture. *International House Quarterly*, Spring:
  47–51.
  1958 *Naven, Second edition*. Stanford: Stanford University Press.
  (Originally published 1936.)

Beals, Ralph
1967 International Research Problems in Anthropology. *Current Anthrop.* Vol. 8.
Beals, R. L., and H. Hoijer
1965 *An Introduction to Anthropology, Third Edition.* New York: Macmillan.
Beattie, J. H. M.
1959 Checks on the abuse of political power in some African states: a preliminary framework for analysis. *Sociologus* 9:97–115.
Bender, L., and P. Schilder
1936 Studies in aggressiveness IV. *Genetic Psychology* Monograph No. 18:254–261.
Benedict, Ruth
1934 *Patterns of Culture.* Boston: Houghton Mifflin.
1948 Appraisals of the conference. In: Quincy Wright (ed.), *The World Community.* Chicago: University of Chicago Press, pp. 303–315.
1959 The natural history of war. In: Margaret Mead, *An Anthropologist at Work.* Boston: Houghton Mifflin, pp. 369–382.
Bennett, J. H., F. A. Rhodes, and H. N. Robson
1959 A possible genetic basis for kuru. *Amer. J. Human Genetics* 11:169–187.
Berkowitz, L.
1962 *Aggression: A Social Psychological Analysis.* New York: McGraw-Hill Book Company.
1965 The concept of aggressive drive: some additional considerations. In: L. Berkowitz (ed.), *Advances in Experimental Social Psychology,* Vol. 2. New York: Academic Press, Inc., pp. 301–329.
Bernard, J., T. H. Pear, R. Aron, and R. C. Angell
1957 *The Nature of Conflict.* Belgium: UNESCO.
Bierce, Ambrose
1925 *The Devil's Dictionary.* New York: Boni. (Originally published 1911.)
Biocca, Ettore
1965 *Yanomamö.* Bari: Leonardo da Vinci.
Boas, Franz
1888 The central Eskimo. *Bur. Amer. Ethnol.* Sixth Ann. Rept. 1884–1885, pp. 399–669.
1940 The limitations of the comparative method of anthropology. In: F. Boas, *Race, Language and Culture.* New York: Macmillan, pp. 270–280.
Bock, Kenneth E.
1966 The comparative method of anthropology. *Comp. Studies Soc. Hist.* 8:269–280.
Bohannan, Paul J.
1964 *Africa and Africans.* New York: Natural History Press.
Borgman, Donald M., and Sandra L. Cue
1963 Sentence and clause types in Central Waica (Shiriana). *Internat'l J. Amer. Ling.* 29:222–229.

Borgman, Donald M., Sandra Cue, Sue Albright, Merril Seeley, and Joseph
E. Grimes
1965 The Waican languages. *Anthrop. Ling.* 7:1–22.
Bronowski, J.
1967 *The Face of Violence.* New York: World Publishing. (Originally
published 1954.)
Broom, Robert, and G. W. H. Schepers
1946 *The South African Fossil Ape-man: The Australopithecinae.* Trans-
vaal Museum Mem. No. 2.
Brown, Robert
1963 *Explanation in Social Science.* Chicago: Aldine.
Brown, Roger, and E. H. Lenneberg
1954 A study in language and cognition. *J. Abnor. Soc. Psych.* 49:454–
462.
Bryant, A. T.
1929 *Olden Times in Zululand and Natal: Containing Earlier Political
History of the Eastern Nguni Clans.* New York: Longmares, Green &
Co.
Bureau for Native Affairs, Hollandia, Netherlands New Guinea
1958 Anthropological research in Netherlands New Guinea since 1950.
Oceania 19:132–163.
Burton, J.
1964 The nature of aggression as revealed in the atomic age. In: Carthy
and Ebling (ed.), *The Natural History of Aggression.* London: Academic Press, pp. 145–149.
Buss, A. H.
1961 *The Psychology of Aggression.* New York: John Wiley and Sons,
Inc.
Calhoun, J. B.
1948 Mortality and movement of brown rats (*Rattus norvegicus*) in artificially supersaturated populations. *J. Wildlife Management* 12:167–172.
Cancian, Francesca
1960 "Functional Analysis of Change," *Amer. Soc. Rev.* 25:818–827.
Carneiro, Robert L.
1961 Slash-and-burn cultivation among the Kuikuru and its implications
for cultural development in the Amazon Basin. *Antropologica Supp.*
No. 2:47–67, Caracas.
Carpenter, C. R.
1942 Sexual behavior of free-ranging rhesus monkeys. *J. of Comp. Psy.*
33:113–142.
1964 *Naturalistic Behavior of Nonhuman Primates.* University Park:
Pennsylvania State University Press.
Carthy, J. D., and F. J. Ebling (eds.)
1964 *The Natural History of Aggression.* London: Academic Press.
Cartwright, D.
1950 Emotional dimensions of group life. In: M. L. Reymert (ed.), *Feelings and Emotions:* the Moosehart Symposium, New York: McGraw-
Hill Book Company, Inc., pp. 439–447.

Chagnon, Napoleon A.
    [ms.]   *Yanomamö Warfare, Social Organization and Marriage Alliances,*
            Ann Arbor: University of Michigan. Doctoral Thesis, 1966.
    1967   Yanomamö—the fierce people. *Natural History,* Vol. 76:22–31.
    in press, a.   *Yanomamö: The Fierce People,* Case Studies in Cultural
            Anthropology. New York: Holt, Rinehart and Winston.
    in press, b.   The feast. *Natural History.*
Chamla, M.-C.
    1964   L'accroissement de la stature en France de 1880 à 1960; comparai-
            son avec les pays d'Europe. *Bull. Mem. Soc. Anthrop. Paris,* ser. 11,
            6:201–278.
Colby, Eldridge
    1931   Conscription. In: Edwin R. A. Seligman (ed.), *Encyclopedia of
            the Social Sciences.* Vol. 4. New York: Macmillan, p. 220.
Collias, N. E.
    1944   Aggressive behavior among vertebrate animals. *Physiol. Zoo.*
            17:83–123.
Collins, Paul
    1965   "Functional Analyses in the Symposium 'Man, Culture, and Ani-
            mals.'" In: Anthony Leeds and Andrew P. Vayda, (eds.) *Man, Culture,
            and Animals: The Role of Animals in Human Ecological Adjustments.*
            Washington: American Association for the Advancement of Science
            (Publication No. 78), pp. 271–282.
Collins, Paul, and Andrew P. Vayda
    [ms.]   "Functional Analysis and Its Aims." In: *Anthropology and Aus-
            tronesia* [Festschrift for E. S. Craighill Handy], publication arrange-
            ments pending.
Cook, S. F.
    1946   Human sacrifice and warfare as factors in the demography of pre-
            colonial Mexico. *Human Biology,* 18:81–102.
Coser, Lewis A.
    1956   *The Functions of Social Conflict.* New York: Free Press Paper-
            back.
    1963   Violence and the social structure. In: J. Masserman (ed.), *Vio-
            lence and War,* Vol. 7 of *Science and Psychoanalysis.* New York:
            Grune and Stratton.
Coult, A. D., and A. E. Hammel
    1963   A corrected model for patrilateral cross-cousin marriage. *S. W.
            J. Anthrop.,* 19:287–296.
Count, E. W.
    1958   The biological basis of human society. *Amer. Anthrop.,* 60:1049–
            1085.
Crow, J. F.
    1958   Some possibilities for measuring selection intensities in man. In:
            J. N. Spuhler (ed.), *Natural Selection in Man.* Detroit: Wayne State
            University Press, pp. 1–13.
Darwin, C.
    1872   *The Expression of the Emotions in Man and Animals.* London:
            Murray.

Davie, Maurice R.
1929 *The Evolution of War: A study of its role in early societies.* New Haven: Yale University Press.
Deutsch, Karl W.
1963 *Nationalism and social communication, Second edition.* Cambridge: Massachusetts Institute of Technology.
DeVore, Irven (ed.)
1965 *Primate Behavior.* New York: Holt, Rinehart and Winston.
DeVore, Irven, and S. L. Washburn
1963 Baboon ecology and human evolution. In: F. Clark Howell and Francois Bourliere (eds.), *African Ecology and Human Evolution* Wenner-Gren Publications in Anthropology, No. 36. Chicago: Aldine Publishing Co., pp. 335–367.
Dollard, J., L. Doob, N. Miller, O. Mowrer, and R. Sears
1939 *Frustration and Aggression.* New Haven: Yale University Press.
Duffy, James
1961 *Portuguese Africa.* Cambridge: Harvard University Press.
Durbin, E. F. M., and J. Bowlby
1939 *Personal Aggressiveness and War.* New York: Columbia.
Durkheim, Emile
1963 *Incest: The Nature and Origin of the Taboo.* Edward Sagarin (trans.), New York: Lyle Stuart. (Originally published 1897.)
Eibl-Eibesfeldt, I.
1967 Concepts of ethology and their significance in the study of human behavior. In: H. W. Stevenson, E. H. Hess, and H. L. Rheingold (eds.), *Early Behavior,* New York: Wiley, pp. 127–146.
Eisenberg, J. F.
1966 The social organization of mammals. *Handbuch Zoo.* 10:1–92.
Ekman, P.
1965 Communication through nonverbal behavior: a source of information about an interpersonal relationship. In: T. S. Tomkins and C. Izard (eds.), *Affect, Cognition, and Personality.* New York: Springer Publ. Co., pp. 390–443.
Erikson, Erik H.
1959 *Identity and the Lifecycle.* New York: International Universities Press.
1964 *Childhood and Society, revised and enlarged edition.* New York: Norton.
1967 Ontogeny of ritualization in man. In: J. Huxley (Organizer), *A Discussion of Ritualization of Behaviour in Animals and Man. Phil. Trans. Royal Soc. London,* Ser. B, 251:247–526.
Etkin, W.
1954 Social behavior and the evolution of man's mental faculties. *Amer. Nat.* 88:129–142.
1963 Social behavioral factors in the emergence of man. *Human Biology,* 35:299–311.
Evans-Pritchard, E. E.
1951 *Kinship and Marriage Among the Nuer,* London: Oxford University Press.

Ewers, J. C.
  1955   *The horse in Blackfoot Indian culture.* Smithsonian Institution, *Bur. Amer. Ethnol. Bull.* 159.
Faris, Robert E. L.
  1955   *Social Disorganization, Second edition.* New York: Ronald Press.
Fearing, F.
  1950   Group behavior and the concept of emotion. In: L. M. Reymert (ed.), *Feelings and Emotions:* the Moosehart Symposium, New York: McGraw-Hill Book Company, pp. 448–451.
Foerster, Heinz von (ed.)
  1950–1956 *Cybernetics,* (5 volumes). New York: Josiah Macy, Jr., Foundation.
Forde, C. D.
  1934   *Habitat, Economy and Society.* New York: Harcourt, Brace.
Fortes, M., and E. E. Evans-Pritchard
  1940   *African Political Systems.* New York: Oxford University Press.
Fried, Morton H.
  1966   On the concepts of "tribe" and "tribal society." *Trans. N. Y. Acad. Sci.,* Ser. 2, 28:527–540.
Fuller, J. L., and W. R. Thompson
  1960   *Behavior Genetics.* New York: John Wiley and Sons, Inc.
Gajdusek, D. C., C. J. Gibbs, and H. Alpers
  1965   *Slow, Latent, and Temperate Virus Infections.* Bethesda: U. S. Department of Health, Education, and Welfare.
Gardner, Robert
  1964   Dead birds. Cambridge: Peabody Museum, Harvard University. Distributed: New York, Contemporary Films, 16 mm.; 83 min.; sound; color.
Gearing, Fred
  1958   The structural poses of 18th century Cherokee villages, *Amer. Anthrop.,* 60:1148–1157.
  1962   Priests and warriors: social structure for Cherokee politics in the 18th century. *Amer. Anthrop. Assoc. Mem.* No. 93.
Gesell, A.
  1950   Emotions from the standpoint of a developmental morphology. In: L. M. Reymert (ed.), *Feelings and Emotions:* the Moosehart Symposium, New York: McGraw-Hill Book Company.
Gluckman, Max
  1963   *Order and Rebellion in Tribal Africa.* New York: Free Press.
Golding, William G.
  1959   *Lord of the Flies.* New York: Putnam. (Originally published 1955.)
Goodenough, F. L.
  1931   Anger in young children. *Inst. Child Welfare Mono.* Ser., No. 9. Minneapolis: University of Minnesota Press.
Goodhart, C. B.
  1960   The evolutionary significance of human hair patterns and skin colouring. *Adv. Sci.* 17:52–59.

Gorer, Geoffrey
1966a Man has no killer instinct. *The New York Times Magazine,* November 27:47 ff.
1966b Cultural community and cultural diversity. In: Geoffrey Gorer, *The Danger of Equality and other Essays.* London: Cressett, pp. 48–62.
1967 Ardrey on human nature. *Encounter* 28:66–71.
Hafez, E. S. E. (ed.)
1962 *The Behaviour of Domestic Animals.* Baltimore: Williams and Wilkins.
Haldane, J. B. S.
1952 The origin of language. *Rationalist Annual,* pp. 38–45.
1953 Animal populations and their regulation. *New Biology* 17:9–26.
1959 Disease and evolution. *La Ricera Scientifica Supple.* 19:68–76.
Hall, K. R.
1964 Aggression in monkey and ape societies. In: Carthy and Ebling (eds.), *The Natural History of Aggression.* London: Academic Press, pp. 51–64.
Harding, Thomas
1960 Adaptation and stability. In: Marshall D. Sahlins and Elman R. Service (eds.), *Evolution and Culture.* Ann Arbor: University of Michigan Press, pp. 45–68.
Harley, G. W.
1941 *Native African Medicine.* Cambridge: Harvard University Press.
Hasluck, M.
1967 The Albanian blood feud. In: Paul Bohannan (ed.), *Law and Warfare.* New York: Natural History Press, pp. 381–408.
Hebb, D. O.
1966 *A Textbook of Psychology, Second edition.* Philadelphia: W. B. Saunders, Co.
Helms, Mary
[ms.] *Britain, Spain, and the Miskito Kingdom: A Functional Analysis.*
Henry, Jules
[ms.] *Social and Psychological Preparations for War.*
Hickerson, Harold
1962 The southwestern Chippewa: an ethno-historical study. *Amer. Anthrop. Assoc. Mem.* No. 92.
1966 The genesis of bilaterality among two divisions of Chippewa. *Amer. Anthrop.* 68:1–26.
Hirsch, J. (ed.)
1967 *Behavior-Genetic Analysis.* New York: McGraw-Hill Book Company.
Hobhouse, L. T.
1956 The simplest peoples. Part II, Peace and order among the simplest peoples. *Brit. J. Soc.* 7:96–119.
Hobhouse, L. T., G. C. Wheeler, and M. Ginsberg
1915 *The Material Culture and Social Institutions of the Simplest Peoples: An Essay in Correlation.* London: Chapman and Hall.
Hockett, C. F., and Ascher, R.
1964 The human revolution. *Cur. Anthrop.* 5:135–168.

Hoffman, F. S.
  1967   Pentagon holds economic sword. *The Minneapolis Tribune*, October 15, 1967, pp. 1A and 14A.
Holloway, R. L., Jr.
  1966   Cranial capacity, neural reorganization, and hominid evolution: a search for more suitable parameters. *Amer. Anthrop.* 68:103–121.
  in press, a.   The evolution of the human brain: some notes toward a general theory. *General Systems*, Vol. 12.
  in press, b.   Review of Ardrey: *Territorial Imperative. Pol. Sci. Quart.*
  in press, c.   The evolution of the primate brain: some aspects of quantitative relations. *Brain Research.*
Hooton, E. A.
  1920   Indian village site and cemetery near Madisonville, Ohio. *Peab. Mus. Amer. Archae. and Ethnol. Papers*, Vol. 8, No. 1.
  1930   *The Indians of Pecos Pueblo.* New Haven: Yale University Press.
Hunt, George T.
  1940   *The Wars of the Iroquois: A Study in Intertribal Trade Relations.* Madison: University of Wisconsin Press.
Hunt, H. R.
  1930   Some biological aspects of war. *Eugenics Res. Assoc. Mono. Ser.*, No. 2, New York: Galton Publishing Co.
Huxley, Sir Julian (organizer)
  1967   A discussion on ritualization of behaviour in animals and man. *Phil. Trans. Roy. Soc. London*, 251:247–526.
Imanishi, K.
  1957   Social behavior in Japanese monkeys, *Macaca fuscata. Psychologia: Internat'l J. Psych. Orient* 1:47–54. (Reprinted in: C. H. Southwick [ed.], *Primate Social Behavior*. Princeton: 1963, D. Van Nostrand and Company.)
Jenness, Diamond
  1967   Hunting bands of eastern and western Canada. In: Roger C. Owen, James J. F. Deetz, and Anthony D. Fisher (eds.), *The North American Indians: A Source Book*. New York: Macmillan.
Jones, V. C.
  1948   *The Hatfields and the McCoys.* Chapel Hill: University of North Carolina.
Kato, H., W. J. Schull, and J. V. Neel
  1966   A cohort-type study of survival in the children of parents exposed to atomic bombings. *Amer. J. Human Genetics* 18:339–373.
Kimura, K.
  1967   A consideration of the secular trend in Japanese for height and weight by a graphic method. *Amer. J. Phys. Anthrop.* 27:89–94.
Krzywicki, Ludwik
  1934   *Primitive Society and its Vital Statistics.* London: Macmillan.
Kulischer, E. M.
  1943   *Europe on the Move.* New York: Columbia University Press.
Kurtz, Howard, and Harriet Kurtz
  1967   Global compassionate power. *Renewal.* June 3–17.

Langer, E.
1967 Chemical and biological warfare (1): The research program. *Science* 155:174–179.
1967 Chemical and biological warfare (2): The weapons and policies. *Science* 155:299–303.

Leach, E. R.
1951 The structural implications of matrilateral cross-cousin marriage. *J. Roy. Anthrop. Inst.* 81:23–55.
1965 Letter to the Editor, *Man,* 12:25.
1966 Don't say "boo" to a goose. *N. Y. Rev. Books.* Dec. 15.
1967 Ritualization in man in relation to conceptual and social development. In: Huxley (Organizer), A discussion of ritualization of behaviour in animals and man. *Phil. Trans. Roy. Soc. London.* 251:403–408.

Lee, Richard B.
[ms.] *What "Hunters" do for a living: or, How to make out on scarce resources.*

Leeds, Anthony
1963 The Functions of War. In: Jules Masserman (ed.), *Violence and War: with Clinical Studies,* Vol. VI of *Science and Psychoanalysis.* New York: Grune and Stratton, pp. 69–82.

Leeds, Anthony, and Andrew P. Vayda, eds.
1965 *Man, Culture, and Animals: The Role of Animals in Human Ecological Adjustments.* Washington: American Association for the Advancement of Science (Publication No. 78).

Lehman, D. S.
1953 A critique of Konrad Lorenz's theory of instinctive behavior. *Quart. Rev. Biol.* 28:337–363.

Lenneberg, E. H.
1967 *Biological Foundations of Language.* New York: John Wiley and Sons, Inc.

Lewin, Leonard C.
1967 On the possibility and desirability of peace. *Esquire.* December, pp. 129–137, 222 ff.

Livingstone, F. B.
1958 Anthropological implications of sickle cell gene distribution in West Africa. *Amer. Anthrop.* 60:553–562.

Lorenz, Konrad
1966 *On Aggression.* New York: Harcourt, Brace and World.
1967 Ritualization in the psycho-social evolution of human culture. In: Huxley (Organizer), A discussion of ritualization of behaviour in animals and man. *Phil. Trans. Roy. Soc. London.* 251:278–284.

Lorimer, F.
1946 *The Population of the Soviet Union.* Geneva's League of Nations.

Lowie, R. H.
1920 *Primitive Society.* New York: Boni and Liveright.
1954 *Indians of the Plains.* New York: McGraw-Hill Book Company.

McNeil, E. B. (ed.)
1965 *The Nature of Human Conflict.* Englewood Cliffs, New Jersey: Prentice-Hall.

Malinowski, Bronislaw
  1948   An anthropological analysis of war. In: B. Malinowski, *Magic, Science and Religion, and other essays*. Glencoe: The Free Press. (Originally published 1926.)
Mark, L. L.
  1967   Patrilateral cross-cousin marriage among the Magpie Miao: preferential or prescriptive. *Amer. Anthrop.* 69:55–62.
Martin, W. Edgar
  1953   *Basic Body Measurements of School-Age Children.* Washington: U. S. Department of Health, Education, and Welfare, Office of Education.
Mason, W. A.
  1967   Motivational aspects of social responsiveness in young chimpanzees. In: H. W. Stevenson, E. H. Hess and H. L. Rheingold (eds.), *Early Behavior: Comparative and Developmental Approaches.* New York: John Wiley and Sons, Inc.
Masserman, Jules H. (ed.)
  1963   *Violence and War: with Clinical Studies,* Vol. VI of *Science and Psychoanalysis.* New York: Grune and Stratton.
Matthiessen, Peter
  1962   *Under the Mountain Wall.* New York: Viking.
Mauss, Marcel
  1954   *The Gift.* Glencoe: The Free Press. (Originally published 1925.)
May, J.
  1960   The ecology of human disease in culture, society and health. In: Vera Rubin (ed.), *Ann. N.Y. Acad. Sci.* 84:789–794.
Maybury-Lewis, David H. P.
  1965   Prescriptive marriage systems. *S. W. J. Anthrop.* 21:207–230.
Mayr, E.
  1959   Darwin and the evolutionary theory in biology. In: B. J. Meggers (ed.), *Evolution and Anthropology: A Centennial Appraisal.* Washington: Anthropological Society of Washington, pp. 1–10.
Mead, Margaret
  1940   Warfare is only an invention—not a biological necessity. *Asia* 40:402–405.
  1948   World culture. In: Quincy Wright (ed.), *The World Community.* Chicago: University of Chicago Press, pp. 47–56, discussion pp. 57–94.
  1959   Cultural contexts of puberty and adolescence. *Bull. Phila. Assoc. Psych.* 9:59–79.
  1963a   *Sex and Temperament in Three Primitive Societies.* New York: Morrow. (Originally published 1935.)
  1963b   Violence in the perspective of culture history. In: Jules H. Masserman (ed.), *Violence and War.* New York: Grune and Stratton, pp. 92–106.
  1963c   The psychology of warless man. In: Arthur Larson (ed.), *A Warless World.* New York: McGraw-Hill, pp. 131–142.
  1964a   A savage paradigm. *Film Comment.* 2:14–15. (Review of "Dead Birds," a film made by Robert Gardner.)

1964b Cultural factors in the cause and prevention of pathological homicide. *Bull. Menninger Clinic* 28:11–22.
1965a *And Keep Your Powder Dry.* New York: Morrow. (Originally published 1942.)
1965b The future as the basis for establishing a shared culture. *Daedalus,* Winter:135–155.
in press. Incest. In: *International Encyclopedia of the Social Sciences.* New York: Macmillan. (To be published, 1968.)
Mead, Margaret, and Rhoda Metraux
1965 The anthropology of human conflict. In: Elton B. McNeil (ed.), *The Nature of Human Conflict.* Englewood Cliffs, New Jersey: Prentice-Hall, pp. 116–138.
Medawar, P. B.
1960 *The Future of Man.* New York: New American Library.
Meggitt, M. J.
1958 The Enga of the New Guinea highlands: some preliminary observations. *Oceania* 28:253–330.
1962 Growth and decline of agnatic descent groups among the Mae Enga of the New Guinea highlands. *Ethnology* 1:158–165.
1965 *The Lineage System of the Mae Enga of New Guinea.* New York: Barnes and Noble.
Migliazza, Ernesto
1965 Fonologia Máku. *Bol. Mus. Paraense Emilio Goeldi, Anthropologia* 25:1–19.
Migliazza, Ernesto, and Joseph E. Grimes
1961 Shiriana phonology. *Anthrop. Ling.* 3:31–41.
Mozley, A.
1953 *A Background for the Prevention of Bilharzia.* London: H. K. Lewis.
Murdock, G. P.
1934 *Our Primitive Contemporaries.* New York: Macmillan Co.
Murphy, Robert F.
1957 Intergroup hostility and social cohesion. *Amer. Anthrop.* 59:1018–1035.
Murphy, Robert F., and Yolanda Murphy
1960 Shoshone-Bannock subsistence and society. *Anthrop. Records.* 16: No. 7. Berkeley and Los Angeles: University of California Press.
Nagel, Ernest
1956 *Logic Without Metaphysics.* Glencoe, Ill.: Free Press.
Needham, Rodney
1962 *Structure and Sentiment.* Chicago: University of Chicago Press.
1965 Terminology and alliance. *Sociologus,* Part I, 16:141–157; Part II, 17:39–53.
Neel, J. V.
1963 *Changing Perspectives on the Genetic Effects on Radiation.* Springfield, Illinois: C. C. Thomas.
Neel, James V., and Napoleon A. Chagnon
in press. The demography of two tribes of primitive, relatively unacculturated American Indians. *Proc. Nat'l Acad. Sci.*

Nieboer, H. J.
  1900 *Slavery as an Industrial System: Ethnological Researches.* The
  Hague: Martinus Nijhoff.
Otterbein, Keith F.
  1967 The evolution of Zulu warfare. In: Paul Bohannan (ed.), *Law
  and Warfare: Studies in the Anthropology of Conflict.* New York: Natural History Press, pp. 351–358.
Piaget, J.
  1926 *The Language and Thought of the Child.* New York: Harcourt,
  Brace.
  1929 *The Child's Conception of the World.* New York: Harcourt, Brace.
  1954 *The Construction of Reality in the Child.* New York: Basic Books.
Pospisil, L.
  1958 *Kapauku Papuans and Their Law.* Yale University Publications in
  Anthropology, No. 54. New Haven: Yale University Press.
Radcliffe-Brown, A. R.
  1964 *The Andaman Islanders.* New York: Free Press. (Originally published 1922.)
Rheingold, H. L.
  1967 A comparative psychology of development. In: H. W. Stevenson,
  E. H. Hess, and H. L. Rheingold (eds.), *Early Behavior.* New York:
  Wiley, pp. 279–294.
Richardson, Lewis F.
  1939 Generalized foreign politics. *British J. Psych. Mono. Supp.* No. 23.
  1960 *Arms and insecurity.* Nicolas Rashevsky and Ernesto Trucco
  (eds.), Chicago: Quadrangle Books.
Rodrigues, Aryon Dall'Igna
  1960 Über die Sprache der Surára und Pakidái. Appendix to: *Die Surára
  ünd Pakidái,* Hans Becher, *Mitteilungen aus dem* Museum für Volker-
  kund in Hamburg, 26. Hamburg.
Ross, Alexander
  1956 *The Fur Hunters of the Far West.* Norman: University of Okla-
  homa Press. (Originally published 1824.)
Sahlins, Marshall D.
  1963 Poor man, rich man, big man, chief: political types in Melanesia
  and Polynesia. *Comp. Studies Soc. Hist.* 5:285–303.
  1963 Review article: Remarks on social structure in Southeast Asia.
  J. Poly. Soc. 72:39–50.
  1965 On the ideology and composition of descent groups. *Man.* 12:
  104–107.
Schapera, I.
  1951 *The Knoisian Peoples of South Africa.* London: Routledge and
  Kegan Paul. (Originally published 1930.)
Schilder, P.
  1942 *Goals and Desires of Man.* New York: Columbia University Press.
Schiller, C. H. (ed.)
  1957 *Instinctive Behavior.* New York: International Universities Press,
  Inc.

Bibliography251

Schneirla, T. C.
1965 Aspects of stimulation and organization in approach/withdrawal processes underlying vertebrate behavioral development. In: D. S. Lehrman (ed.), *Advances in the Study of Behavior*. Vol. I. New York: Academic Press, pp. 1–74.

Schrier, A. M., H. F. Harlow, and F. Stollnitz (eds.)
1965 *Behavior of Nonhuman Primates*. Vols. I and II. New York: Academic Press.

Scott, J. P.
1958 *Aggression*. Chicago: University of Chicago Press.
1962 Hostility and aggression in animals. In: E. L. Bliss (ed.), *Roots of Behavior*. New York: Harper and Brothers, pp. 167–178.
1967 The evolution of social behavior in dogs and wolves. *Amer. Zoo.* 7:373–381.

Scott, J. P., and J. L. Fuller
1965 *Genetics and the Social Behavior of the Dog*. Chicago: University of Chicago Press.

Secoy, Frank Raymond
1953 Changing military patterns on the Great Plains. *Mono. Amer. Ethnol. Soc.*, No. 21. New York: J. J. Augustin.

Seitz, Georg
1963 *People of the Rain Forests*. A. J. Pomerans (transl.) London: Heinemann.

Service, Elman R.
1962 *Primitive Social Organizations*. New York: Random House.
1963 *Profiles in Ethnology*. New York: Harper and Row.

Shimizu, K.
1966 Epidemiological study on malignant lymphoma among A-bomb survivors in Hiroshima. *Hiroshima. J. Med. Sci.* 15:201; 211.

Snow, C. E.
1948 Indian knoll skeletons of Site Oh 2, Ohio County, Kentucky. *U. Ken. Repts. Anthrop.* 4: No. 3: Part 2.

Soddy, Kenneth (ed.)
1961 Cross-Cultural Studies in Mental Health, *Identity, Mental Health, and Value Systems*. New York: Humanities Press.

Southwick, C. H.
1967 An experimental study of intragroup agonistic behavior in rhesus monkeys. *Behaviour* 28:182–209.

Spencer, B., and F. J. Gillen
1927 *The Arunta*. Vol. 2. London: Macmillan and Company, pp. 443–455.

Spuhler, J. N.
1959 Somatic paths to culture. In: J. N. Spuhler (ed.) *The Evolution of Man's Capacity for Culture*. Detroit: Wayne State University Press, pp. 1–13.

Stevenson, Robert F.
[ms.] *Population Density and State Formation in Sub-Saharan Africa*. Doctoral Thesis, Columbia University.

Steward, Julian H.
1938   Basin-Plateau Aboriginal Sociopolitical Groups. *Bur. Amer. Ethnol. Bull.* No. 120.
1946–48   South American cultures: an interpretative summary. In: Julian H. Steward (ed.), The Comparative Ethnology of South American Indians, Vol. 5 of *Handbook of South American Indians, Bur. Amer. Ethnol. Bull.* No. 143.
Steward, Julian H., and Louis C. Faron
1959   *Native Peoples of South America.* New York: McGraw-Hill Book Company.
Steward, Julian H., and Erminie W. Voegelin
[ms.]   *The Northern Paiute Indians.*
Stewart, K. M.
1947   Mohave warfare. *S. W. J. Anthrop.* 3:257–278.
Storr, A.
1964   Possible substitutes for war. In: J. D. Carthy and F. J. Ebling (eds.), *The Natural History of Aggression.* New York: Academic Press, pp. 137–144.
Stott, D. H.
1962   Cultural and natural checks on population growth. In: Ashley Montagu (ed.), *Culture and the Evolution of Man.* New York: Oxford University Press, pp. 255–376.
Struhsaker, T. T.
1967   Auditory communications among Vervet monkeys. In: Altmann (ed.), *Social Communication Among Primates.* Chicago: University of Chicago Press, pp. 281–324.
Swanton, John R.
1946   The Indians of the Southeastern United States. *Bur. Amer. Ethnol. Bull.* No. 137.
Sweet, Louise E.
1965a   Camel pastoralism in North Arabia and the minimal camping unit. In: Anthony Leeds and Andrew P. Vayda (eds.), *Man, Culture, and Animals: The Role of Animals in Human Ecological Adjustments.* Amer. Assoc. Adv. Sci. Publication No. 78:129–152.
1965b   Camel raiding of North Arabian Bedouin: a mechanism of ecological adaptation. *Amer. Anthrop.* 67:1132–1150.
Tax, Sol (ed.)
1967   The Draft: A Handbook of Facts and Alternatives. Chicago: University of Chicago Press.
Thalbitzer, William (ed.)
1914   The Ammassalik Eskimo, Part I. *Meddelelser om Grønland* 39:1–755. Copenhagen.
1923   The Ammassalik Eskimo, Part II. *Meddelelser om Grønland* 40:113–564. Copenhagen.
Thompson, David
1916   *David Thompson's Narrative of his Explorations in Western America, 1784–1812.* Toronto: Champlain Society Publication No. 12.
Thorpe, W. H.
1963   *Learning and Instinct in Animals, Second Edition.* London: Methuen and Co., Ltd.

Times (London)

1967 Do eagles fight storks? August 10:6.

Turney-High, Harry Holbert

1949 *Primitive War: Its Practice and Concepts.* Columbia, South Carolina: University of South Carolina Press.

Tylor, Edward B.

1871 *Primitive Culture* (two volumes). London: John Murray.

1888 On a method of investigating the development of institutions; applied to laws of marriage and descent. *J. Roy. Anthrop. Inst.,* 18:245–269.

Underhill, Ruth M.

1953 *Red Man's America: A History of Indians in the United States.* Chicago: University of Chicago Press.

Vansina, J.

1962 A comparison of African kingdoms. *Africa,* 32:324–335.

Vansina, J., R. Mauny, and L. V. Thomas

1964 *The Historian in Tropical Africa.* London, Ibadan, Accra: Oxford University Press.

Vayda, Andrew P.

1960 Maori warfare. *Polynesian Soc. Maori Mono.,* No. 2. Wellington: Polynesian Society.

1961 Expansion and warfare among swidden agriculturalists. *Amer. Anthrop.* 63:346–358.

1967 Research on the functions of primitive war. *Peace Research Soc. Intern'l Papers,* Vol. 7.

in press, a. Foreword to *Pigs for the Ancestors: Ritual in the Ecology of a New Guinea People* by Roy A. Rappaport. New Haven: Yale University Press.

in press, b. "The Study of the Causes of War, with Special Reference to Head-Hunting Raids in Borneo," *Ethnohistory.*

Vayda, Andrew P., and Anthony Leeds

1961 Anthropology and the study of war. *Anthropologica,* n.s., 3:131–133.

Vayda, Andrew P., A. Leeds, and D. B. Smith

1961 The place of pigs in Melanesian subsistence. In: Viola E. Garfield (ed.), Symposium: Patterns of Land Utilization and Other Papers. *Proc. Amer. Ethnol. Soc.* Seattle: University of Washington Press.

Warner, W. L.

1930 Murngin Warfare. *Oceania* 1:457–494.

1937 *A Black Civilization.* New York: Harper and Brothers.

Wedgwood, Camilla H.

1930 Some aspects of warfare in Melanesia. *Oceania* 1:5–33.

Weisenfeld, S. L.

1967 Sickle cell trait in human biological and cultural evolution. *Science* 157:1134–1140.

Wheeler, Gerald C.

1910 *The Tribe and Intertribal Relations in Australia.* London.

Whiting, John W. M.

1944 The frustration complex in Kwoma society. *Man* 44:140–144.

Wiedner, Donald
1964   *A History of Africa South of the Sahara.* New York: Random House.
Williams, F. E.
1939   *Orokaiva Society.* London: Oxford University Press.
Wilson, J.
1967   When lawmakers wear uniforms: strength in reserve. *Minneapolis Tribune.* Nov. 19, p. 1c.
Wissler, Clark
1936   Changes in population profiles among the Northern Plains Indians. *Anthrop. Papers Amer. Museum of Natural History* 36:1–67.
Wolf, H. G.
1960   Stressors as a cause of disease in man. In: J. M. Tanner (ed.), *Stress and Psychiatric Disorders, the Proceedings of the Mental Health Research Fund 2nd Conference.* Oxford: Blackwells, pp. 17–31.
Wolfe, Alvin W.
1962   *The team rules mining in Southern Africa.* Toward Freedom 11.
1963   The African mineral industry: Evolution of a supranational level of integration. *Social Problems* 11:153–164.
Wood, J. W., K. G. Johnson, Y. Omcri, S. Kawamote, and R. J. Keehn
1937   Mental retardation in children exposed in utero to the atomic bombs in Hiroshima and Nagasaki. *Amer. J. Public Health* 57:1331–1338.
World Conference on Church and Society
1967   *Christians in the Technical Revolutions of Our Time.* Geneva: July 12–26, World Council of Churches.
Worsley, Peter M.
1961   The analysis of rebellion and revolution in modern British social anthropology. *Science and Society* 25:26–37.
Wright, Quincy
1965   *A study of War, Second Edition.* Chicago: University of Chicago Press.
Wynne-Edwards, V. C.
1962   *Animal Dispersion in Relation to Social Behaviour.* Edinburgh: Oliver and Boyd.
1964   Population control in animals. *Sci. Amer.* 211:68–74.
1965   Self-regulatory systems in populations of animals. *Science* 147: 1543–1548.
Zawodny, J. K. (ed.)
1966   *Man and International Relations,* (two volumes). San Francisco: Chandler Publishing Company.
Zerries, Otto
1964   Waika: Die Kulturgeschichtlich Stellung der Waika-Indianer des oberen Orinoco im Rahmen der Völkerkunde Südamerikas. *Ergebnisse der Frobenius-Expedition 1954/55 nach Südost-Venezuela.* Munich.
Zinsser, Hans
1935   *Rats, Lice and History.* Boston: Little, Brown and Company.

Aberle, David, xv, 24, 97–100
Aboriginal types of evolutionary stages, 164, 167
Acephalous control, and structural impossibility of rebellion or revolt, 225–26
Adams, Robert M., 22
Aerobiology, research in, 74
African primitives, effects of European expansion on warfare of, 164–65
Aggression: warfare as postulated instinct for, 11–12, 13, 33–34; and "displacement activities," 11, 30, 38, 48; different forms and organizational features of, 18; biological or genetic consequences of, 18–19; uninhibited, man as victim of, 18, 19; of humans, instinctive, innate, or learned nature of, 29, 32–36; species-specific theory of, for humans, 29, 36–42; human, compared to that of other animals, 29, 30, 31, 48; and socio-economic conditions, 30; definitions of, 32, 36, 42; and intent of, 32–33; and cue functions or environmental stimuli, 33, 34; range of stimuli that can produce, in humans, 34–36; as potential asset, 36; of non-human animals, stimuli evoking responses of, 37, 38; and appeasement function of postures and vocalizations, 38; and "frustration-aggression" hypothesis, 39; in children, development and control of, 40; and evolution, 42–48; utilization of, by states for their own ends, 47; comparisons of micro-behavior patterns of same kind, 52; approaches to comparative studies of aggressive behavior, 51–52; comparisons at general functional level, 51–52; activities of, as homologous across mammalian phyla, 52–53; inhibitors of aggressive activities, 53; releasors or excitors of aggressive actions, 53; intensity of aggressive behavior during normal states of excitement and at high intensities, 55; conflicts and aggressive behavior among animals of same species, 55–56; regulation of, 57, 58
Aggressive instinct of animals, man as heir to behavior patterns of, 18

Airborne infection, research in, 74
Alland, Alexander, Jr., xv–xvi, 65–75, 81–82
Allison, John, 60
Alternatives to war, 85, 215–28; and specific conditions of American society, 229–34
American Anthropological Association: Washington annual meeting of (1967), x; Pittsburgh annual meeting of (1966), x; Washington Symposium (1967) on anthropology and war, x, xi–xiii; and war in Vietnam, xi; and study on ethics involved in research, 212
Annihilation, possibility of, in future warfare, 16, 20, 23, 24–25, 221, 222, 230
Anthropological contributions to subject of alternatives to war, 225
Anthropologists: and political neutrality, xii, 211; comparative silence of, on causes, nature, and effects of warfare, 109–10; and research for government, 211, 212; responsibilities and tasks of, in attacking problems of war prevention, 235–37
Anti-communist fears, and support of U.S. war system, 202–3
Applied approach to problems of health and culture, 76–77
Archaic Civilization, as aboriginal evolutionary stage, 167
Armed Services, manpower requirements of, 210
Arming of women, 219–20, 236
Atomic warfare: and mutations to deleterious genes, 4–5. See also Nuclear warfare

Banditry, 215
Barker, James P., 116
Bateson, Gregory, 225
"Battles" between labor and capital, 215
Behavior: comparative studies of, 51; and physiological functions, relationships between, 51; comparison of, across orders and genera of organisms, 51; plurality of determinants of, 52–53; aggressive, see Aggression

Behavioral adjustments to disease, 65–
67, 79
Behavioral approach to problems of
health and illness, 77
Benedict, Ruth, 225
Biological capacity of man, 19
Biological consequences of social malfunctions that lie behind war, 20–21
Biological effects of modern warfare
on combatant populations, 3–8
Biological warfare, 73–75, 81–82, 230;
genetic effects of, 24, 25; described
as "humanitarian," and as "war without death," 65, 73, 79; and arsenal of
biological weapons, 74; and risks for
noncombatants in populations, 74–
75; defined as "public health in reverse," 75, 79
Biosocial organizations of nonhuman
primates, 53–54
Biosphere, halting pollution and deterioration of, 227
Birth malformations in wartime, 4–5
Birth rate in wartime, 4, 5
Body size differences, warfare as contributing factor to, 10–11
Bohannan, Paul, xvii
Brain of man: organization and development of, as species-specific, 37;
evolution of, 42–43, 44–45, 47; increase in growth of, and increased
dependency period of children, 44,
56
Built-in biological aggression, warfare
as extension of, 218, 219

Cannibalism, and transmission of virus
infections, 10
Care of young, extension of period of,
44, 56
Carpenter, C. R., xv, 49–58, 60
Carstairs, Dr. Morris, 78
Cerebral cortex of man, evolutionary
enlargement of, 43
Chagnon, Napoleon A., xvii, 109–59,
168
Channeling manpower, Selective Service document on, 203–4
Chemical warfare, 73–74, 230; biological and social imbalance produced
by, 79–80
Children, species-specific development
of ego structure of, 40
Civilian population, debilitating effects
of war on, in Vietnam, 80, 81–82
Civilian priorities, and potential effects
of shift to, in U.S., 232
"Civilized" warfare, 3; and class or
group interests, 186–87
Civil war within national states, 222,
236

Cognitive reorganization related to evolution of brain, 44, 47
Cohesion of human societies: and role
affiliations, 40–41; as function of
war, 100–2
Communication: and symbol systems,
42, 44, 45, 47; and establishing of
world-wide secondary language, 227
Comparative method in study of primitive peoples and modern states, 165–
66
Competition concept of warfare, 100
Congress: and congressional committees, and the making of laws, 206,
208–9, 210; reserve officers in, 209
Conquest warfare, 95–96
Conscription: systems of, 198, 209; *see
also* Draft
Controlling large masses of people, developing effective but nonlethal
means of, 227
Conventional warfare, 230, 231
Conventional weaponry in use in Viet-
nam war, 73
Cooperation for survival, and evolution
of human social structures, 44
Courage and physical competence of
young males, ways for validating,
227, 236
Cranial capacity, evolutionary expan-
sion of, 43
Criteria for distinguishing warfare
from other types of conflict, 215–16
Critical issues concerning the human
condition, 31
Crop diseases, as weaponry of war, 73
Cuban missile crisis, 232, 233
Cultural artifact, warfare as, 219–20
Cultural ecology: definition of, 110,
111; of the Yanomamö, critical aspect of, 113–14
Cultural evolution, 160; in South Amer-
ica, 111–12; war as feature of, 169
Cultural practices, and disease suscep-
tibility, 66

Davie, Maurice R., 109
Death rate of population in wartime,
4, 5
Decision making on war system, and al-
terations of structure of, in U.S.,
233–34
Defense Department: national support
of, 210; and futility of, in nuclear
exchange, 230; and impossibility of
insuring victory in conventional war,
230; industrial managing organization operating in, 232
Defoliation of forest land in Southeast
Asia, and epidemiological patterns,
69, 71, 79

Demographic variables, regulation of, as function of primitive war, 86, 89, 90

Demography: minimal effects of modern warfare on, 5, 20; random effect of future warfare on, 16

Department of Health, Education and Welfare, 75

Dependency period of children, extension of, 44, 56

Deterrence, as function of primitive war, 87–88

Diamond, Stanley, xviii, 183–88, 190, 191

Diets, inadequate, in Southeast Asia, and increase in risk of epidemics, 71

Disarmament, universal, 181, 231, 233

Disease: and warfare, 65–82; behavioral and genetic adjustments to, 65–67, 79; and continuation of wartime risks after return to normal conditions, 71–73

Disequilibrating warfare, 99

Dissociated persons, war as impersonal evil done by, 187–88, 191

Domestication of the male, evolutionary behavior adaptation of, 44

Domination concept of warfare, 100

Draft: as violation of American values of freedom and equality, 195, 207; deferments, 195, 203–4; feasible alternatives to, 196, 203–4, 206, 207; as system of military manpower procurement, 196–97; in feudal-type societies, 198; impatience with system as a whole, 198; inequities in, 198; opposition to, not new, 202–3; prosecution of draft dodgers, 203; voluntary professional army as alternative to, 203, 207; and Congress and congressional committees, 205–6, 208–9, 209–10; preference of Pentagon for, over alternatives, 206; reason for imposition of, 209; conflict over, 209

Draft, The: A Handbook of Facts and Alternatives (ed., Tax), 196, 206

Ecological niche, equilibrium in, 14, 56, 92–93

Ecological relationships, and health patterns, 66, 76

Economic development in U.S., effect of military priorities on, 230–32

Economic variables, maintaining of, as function of primitive war, 86–87, 88–89, 90–91

Economic warfare, 221

Egalitarian Society, as aboriginal evolutionary stage, 167

Ego structure of human child, species-specific development of, 40

Electric power grid of U.S. and Canada, acephalous control of, 226

"Emic" approach to problems of health and culture, 76

Endocrine relationships, and evolution of man, 44, 45, 56–57

England, plague epidemic in, 68

Environment: conditions in, leading to warfare, 12; adaptation to, and genetic and behavioral adjustments to disease, 67

Epidemics, association of with war, 65

Epidemiological patterns in Southeast Asia, factors affecting, 71–73

Equilibrium, maintenance of, as function of war, 97, 98, 99, 100, 103, 105

Ethnocentrism: fallacies of, 93; and the *waiteri* complex of the Yanomamö, 128, 129

"Etic" approach to phenomena of health and illness, 77, 78, 82

European expansion, and adaptive political-military responses, 161, 162, 164

Evolution of man; influence of warfare on forces of, 6, 7, 9–10; importance of social adaptations in history of, 36; variables involved in, 43–44; paradox of, 47; disease as agent in, 65

Evolution of War, The (Davie), 109

Expansion concept of warfare, 100, 112

Extermination, wars of, 25

Extra-group aggressional tendencies, 47

Facilitation of attention, and evolutionary neural reorganization, 45–46, 56–57

"Fail-safe" systems for prevention of war, 181, 184, 188

Female, sexual receptivity of, and evolutionary behavior adaptation, 44

Feuds among primitive peoples, 94, 95

Fighting, forms of, among primitive peoples, 94–95

Finney, Joseph C., 59

Fish, killing of, in Vietnam streams, 79

"Flight from grief," primitive wars as devices of, 88

Folk medicine. *See* "Native" drugs

Food crops, destruction of, in Vietnam by spraying of herbicides, 79

Food production, increasing of, 227

Fort Detrick center for biological warfare research, 73, 74

"Frustration-aggression" hypothesis, 39, 40, 41, 42, 47

Functional explanations as part of scientific models, 25

Functions of war, 85–91, 92, 99, 100–1, 102, 103, 104, 105; in the past and in modern society, 220–21, 222

Gangland warfare, 215
Genetic adjustments to disease, 65–67
Genetic damage by radiation, 4–5, 6, 16, 23
Genetic evolution: minimal effects of modern warfare on, 6, 16, 20, 23–24; effect of warfare on primitive populations, 9–10, 17–18
Goiaz, Antonion, 116
Goldberg, Richard, 190
Gorer, Geoffrey, 225
Great Basin-Plateau Shoshone societies, warfare of, 162–63
Group or class interests, modern wars fought for, 186–87
Guerrilla warfare, 215

Hallinan, Matthew, 190
Hate, as component of war, 174–75, 182, 187
Health patterns, dependence of, on ecological relationships, 66
Heckert, Carolyn, 168
Herbicides, damage from spraying of, in Vietnam, 79
Hierarchical Society, as aboriginal evolutionary stage, 164, 167
Hoebel, E. Adamson, xviii, 208–10
Holloway, Ralph L., xiv, 29–48
Homeostasis, maintenance of, as function of war, 97, 98, 99, 100
Homicide among primitive peoples, 94, 95
Horse-raiding parties of American Indian Plains, 95
"Humanitarian" warfare, 65
Human sacrifice in pre-conquest Mexico, demographic effects of, 17

Identification and solidarity, sense of, and reinforcement through war, 59
Impersonal evil: done by good persons, war as, 182, 187–88, 191; done by dissociated persons, war as, 188, 191
Impersonality of war, 177–78
Indians of the Americas: warfare as controlling factor in size of population, 9; and wars of extermination, 25; vengeance parties and horse-raiding parties of, 95; wars of Iroquoian Confederacy, 161–62; Great Basin-Plateau Shoshone societies, warfare of, 162–63; Sac and Fox Indian war, 179–80, 187; conquest of North American Indians, 187. *See also* Yanomamö
Inequalities in goods or resources,

regulation of, as function of war, 86–87, 88–89, 95, 99, 100
Infanticide: as factor in control of population size in primitive groups, 14, 20; of the Yanomamö, 139, 168
Inhibition of constant monitoring, and evolutionary neural organization, 45–46, 56–57
Instinct of aggression in man, 11–12, 12–13, 33–35, 218
Institutional complex of war, 57, 60–61, 100–1
Intellectual functions, increased efficiency of, and evolution of the brain, 44–45, 56
Interests served by war, 178–80
Intergroup aggression, 3
Internal massacres, 236
International police forces, 233–34
Intersocietal offenses, regulation of, as function of war, 89
Intragroup commitments, and frustration and power, 47
Intragroup killing distinguished from extragroup warfare, 216, 217–18
Intrasocietal hostility, diversion of, onto substitute objects, 88
Intraspecies antagonism of nonhuman primates, and ecological niche theory, 56
Invention, warfare as, 219–21
"Inverted U function," 46
Iroquoian Confederacy, wars of, 161–62

Land, redistribution of, as result of primitive war, 87, 104
Langer, Elinor, 73, 74
Language, establishing of a world-wide secondary, 227
Language abilities, as species-specific patterns of neural and behavioral development, 39–40, 56
Law-making system of U.S., 204–7, 208–9
Learning, importance of, in genesis of fixed action patterns, 34, 52–53
Lebensraum argument for war, 12, 20
Leeds, Anthony, 100–1
Lesser, Alexander, xvii, 23, 92–96
Levine, Jack, 100
Liberation, wars of, 236
Limited wars, 186, 187, 235
Livingstone, Frank B., xiii–xiv, 3–15, 24–25
Losing a war, as a crime, 189
Luth, Dietrich, 189

Male, domestication of, and evolutionary behavior adaptation, 44

Manpower procurement by U.S.: process of decision making, relevant to, 195. *See also* Draft

Mass hysteria, and war, 178

Massacres, internal, 236

Material foundations of war, 102, 104

Mayer, Jean, 79

Mead, Margaret, xix, 215–28, 235–37

Melman, Seymour, xviii, 229–34

Mexico, pre-conquest, demographic consequences of warfare and human sacrifice on population, 9, 17

Microbiological warfare. *See* Biological warfare

Migration, influence of warfare on, 6, 9–10

"Militant enthusiasm," concept of, 41 *n*

Militarism, deformations produced by, in political, social, and economic institutions, 22

Military art, transformation of, since World War II, 230–31

Military budget of U.S., 229

Military industrial management, government and private, 232

Military manpower procurement. *See* Draft

Military organizations, and the war system, 229–30

Military pay made comparable to civilian pay, 207, 210

Military power as way of settling disputes, and agreement among the great powers against use of, 233

Military priorities in U.S.: and precluding of economic development, 231; and consequences for quality of life in American society, 231–32

Military technologies, and American intellectuals engaged in developing of, 232–33

Minerals in Africa, acephalous control of, 225–26

Missionaries, contact of, with the Yanomamö, 116

Mistake, war by, 179–80, 187

Mobilization: state of, 173–75, 186; process of, 175–86; training for, 176–77, 181; for nuclear war, 183, 186; for war in highly industrialized states, 183

Multi-nationality, development of, 222–23

Mutual cooperation in economic tasks, and cohesion of human societies, 40

National boundaries, as component of warfare, 222

National service system, including military and other functions, as alternative to present draft, 203–4, 210

Nationhood, concepts of, as replacement for nationalism, 223

Nation-states: modifications of present concepts of, 222–23; and international organizations built on, 223; military security of, and disarmament, 230–31, 233

"Native" drugs: effect of, on specific disease agents, 66, 78; and reduction of anxiety, 78–79

Natural selection: influence of warfare on, 6, 10; and changes in genetic characteristics, 6

Nazi Germany, and psychopathology of administrative personnel, 180, 184–85, 189

Nonterritorial warfare of the Yanomamö, 110–11, 113, 158–59; psychological explanations of, 112–13

Nuclear age, and relations of warfare to the biology of man, 23

Nuclear warfare: and threat of annihilation, 23, 24–25, 221, 222, 230, 235; effects of, on small populations, 24, 25; mobilization for, 183, 186; as component of modern culture, 221; and efforts for establishment of international order after World War II, 222; formalizing ways of preventing, 227

Nuremberg Trials, 188, 189, 190

Nurturance, social and emotional, species-specific pattern of, 39–40

Nutritional standards, lowering of, in Southeast Asia, and lower resistance to diseases, 71

Occupational deferments, and the draft, 203–4

Optimal levels of arousal of organism, 45–46

Outlawing of war, as obsolescent and destructive to all participants alike, 222

Pacifists, 181, 202–3

Past war as psychological preparation for the next, 189–90

Pathological nature of war, 97, 99

Paul, Benjamin, xvi, 76–80

Peace, condition of, 101

Peace Corps, 207

Pentagon, influence of, with congressional committee staffs, 205

People, redistribution of, as result of primitive war, 87

Personnel, armed forces and civilian, in U.S. war system, 232

Perversion of administrative process, war as result of, 180

Pharmacopoeias of non-Western societies, 66
Plague: etiology of, 67; European epidemics of, in 13th to 16th centuries, 67–68, 80; in Southeast Asia, 68–70, 79–80
Polgar, Steven, 24, 81–82
Police forces, international, 233
Political-economic arrangements in this interconnected world, alternatives to, 222
Political tool, discarding war as, 222
Population: modern warfare as negligible force in controlling size of, 5, 16, 20; of primitive peoples, warfare as factor controlling size of, 8–9, 14, 16, 17, 87; of American Indians, warfare as controlling factor in size of, 9; dislocation and relocations in Southeast Asia, effect of, on epidemiological patterns, 71, 79–80; halting present rate of increase of, 227
Power, structured on world-wide sharing basis, need for, in prevention of war, 31
Predation and aggression, difference between, 18
Prescientific peoples: effective behaviors of, in combating and preventing disease, 66; and genetic and behavioral adjustments to disease, 66–67; and public health, 67
Prescriptive marriage system, 14, 155, 156, 157
Prevention of war, 31, 85, 181–82, 227, 235
Preventive medicine, and adjustment to disease, 65, 66, 77–78
Primitive peoples: and existence of warfare among, 93, 94; forms of fighting among, 94–95
Primitive war: hypothesized functions of, 85, 86–89; comparisons of, with civilized war, 89–90, 93–94, 95, 98, 185–86; tests of hypotheses on functions of, 90–91; essential features of, 110. *See also* Yanomamö, warfare
Psychological development, species-specific patterns of, 39
Psychological preparations for war, 173–82; state of mobilization, 173–75; process of mobilization, 174–76, 186; training for mobilization, 176–77, 182; impersonality of war, 177–78; interests served by war, 179–80; prevention of war, 181–82
Psychological variables, regulation of, as function of primitive war, 88, 89, 90, 112
Psychological warfare, 215, 221
Psychopathology of administrative personnel, war as result of, 180, 184–85, 189, 190–91
Public health: as matter of policy, 65; in prescientific populations, 67; impairment of facilities of, by warfare, 70–71; in Southeast Asia, and lack of effective measures of, 70–71; evolution of, 81–82
Punishment for crimes, and principles of freedom and equality, 195

Raboy, David, 24
Radiation, deleterious effects of, 4, 6, 16, 23
Rage expression and control, developmental patterns of, 40
Rat elimination in Southeast Asia, 69
Recruitment of military manpower. *See* Draft
Report from Iron Mountain, The, xvi, 229 *n*
Reproductive physiology and behavior, and evolution of man, 43–44, 56
Reserve officers in Congress, 209–10
Revolutions, and necessity of providing for realization of full human potential, 47
Ritualization in animals and man, 33 *n*
Robinson, Scott, 211
Role affiliations, and cohesion of human societies, 40–41
Role differentiation, and frustration and power, 47

Sac and Fox Indian war, 179–80, 187
Sarles, Harvey, 97
Satisfactions offered by war, 59, 60
Selective Service: document on "channeling" of manpower, 203–4. *See also* Draft
Self-determination, right of groups to, 223–24
"Sentiment structure" in species-specific patterns of human behavior, 41–42, 44, 46
Service, Elman, xvii, 160–67, 169
Sexes, distinction between, in use of tools and weapons, 219–20, 236–37
Sex ratio, regulation of, as function of primitive war, 86–87, 89, 139–40
Sexual dimorphism of man, evolutionary decrease in, 43
Sexual receptivity of the female, evolutionary behavior adaption of, 44
Sickle cell anemia, 6–7, 11–12
Social adaptations, importance of, in evolutionary history of man, 36
Social changes of drastic and world-wide nature, need for, in prevention of war, 31
Social consequences of warfare, 23

Social control, and development of symbolization, 42, 44, 45, 47

Social invention, warfare as, 219–21

Social malfunction, biological consequences of, 20

Social relationships, and causes of modern warfare, 190

Social structures, evolution of, 44–45, 47, 56–57

Socio-economic conditions of humanity, 30, 31

Socio-political units, size of, and external vs. internal threats, 161

Socio-political variables, regulation of, as function of primitive war, 90

Soil pollution in Vietnam, from spraying with herbicides, 79

South American primitives, military responses of, to Iberian conquest, 163–64

South Vietnam: rate of population growth in, 5; plague incidence in, 69–70. *See also* Southeast Asia; Vietnam

Southeast Asia: plague in, 69–70, 79; and infectious diseases and parasites, 70; ecological situation in, 70; imposition of modern warfare on, and problems of health of population, 70–71; factors affecting epidemiological patterns in, 71–73. *See also* South Vietnam; Vietnam

Sovereignty of states, and making of war, 96

Space race, as substitute for war, 11

Spartan system of military manpower procurement, 196–97

Species-specific behavior, concept of, 39, 50

Sports, as alternative to harmful aggression, 11, 30, 38–39

State organization, war as basic aspect of present system, 168

States, and utilization of aggression for their own ends, 47

Stature, changes in, in wartime, 4, 19

Stefaniszyn, Father, 189–90

Stockard, Dr. Joe, 69

Strategic resources of warfare, 102

Stress: associated with relocation in Southeast Asia, and lowered resistance to disease, 71; in civilian populations, 72–73

Student deferments, and the draft, 195, 203–4

Symbol systems of man, 37, 45, 47, 218; and social control through communication, 42, 44, 45, 47

Tariff wars, 215

Tax, Sol, xviii, 195–207, 211–12

Taxation, and principles of freedom and equality, 195

Taxonomy of behavior, 51–52

Tension: regulation of, as function of war, 88; engendered by threat of nuclear war, and by Vietnam war, 235–36

Territorial demands, as factor in warfare, 19, 20, 112

Theology of revolution, 224

Therapeutic procedures, and adjustment to disease, 65–66

Thieme, Fred, xiv, 16–21, 23–24, 25

Threat behavior, and threat features, 10

Toolmaking, and cognitive reorganization related to brain growth and reorganization, 44

Tribe and Intertribal Relations in Australia, The (Wheeler), 94

United Nations, 96, 201, 230

United States wars: reasons for, 199, 208; analysis of twelve wars, 199–203 (*table*)

Universal disarmament, 181, 230–31, 233

Universities, collaboration of, in selective service system, 195

University of Chicago conference on the draft, 196, 203

Unstable ecological community, as environmental factor of warfare, 12–13, 19–20

Variables: interrelations, and regulations of, as function of primitive war, 88–89, 99; pre- and postwar values of, as functions of primitive war, 90; social and political, as functions of war, 100; systems as collections of, 102–3

Vayda, Andrew P., xii, xvi–xvii, 85–91, 102–5

Vendetta in remote parts of modern states, 215

Vengeance among primitive peoples, 94

Victory, as military conclusion in modern warfare, 230

Vietnam: damage in, from spraying of herbicides, 79; debilitating effects of war on civilian population, 80, 81; nature of war in, 186–87; and U.S. efforts for favorable end to war, 189; reaction to U.S. involvement in, 190; as most unpopular war in U.S. history, 199, 201–3; annual expenditure of U.S. on war in, 231; tension engendered by war in, 235–36. *See also* South Vietnam; Southeast Asia

Violence, problems of control of, 237

Voluntary system of military manpower procurement, 196–97; as alternative for draft, 203, 206–7

Wallace, Anthony F. C., xviii, 173–82, 191
War: different kinds of, 3; of the past, effects of, on present composition of human gene pool, 3, 8; negligible effects of, on size of human populations, 5–6, 16, 17, 20; as postulated instinct for aggression, 11–12, 13, 33–34; of the future, and possible annihilation of life, 16–17, 20, 23, 25, 222, 230; as one type of aggressive behavior between societies, 18, 19–20; selective effects of, on genetic characteristics within a population, 25; as organized extension of politics carried to different level, 29; at level of mass societies, explanation of, 47; and involvements of institutions, law, culture, and symbolic systems, 57, 60–61, 101; difficulty in defining unequivocally, 59; providing rationale and justification for, 60; as nonfunctional pathological condition of society, 85; definition of, 173, 183; and dormant potential of war psychology, in certain social values, 190; among subunits of a society, 215; as distinguished from other types of conflict, 215–18; positive or negative value placed on, 216; possible uses of, 220–21. *See also* Biological warfare; Chemical warfare; Nuclear warfare; Primitive war
Warrior caste system of military manpower procurement, 196–97
Water pollution in Vietnam, from spraying of herbicides, 79
Weapons, and development of military technologies, 230
Webb, Malcolm, 168–69
Wheeler, G. C., 94
Wolfe, Alvin, 225
World community of future as single hierarchical state, 223–24
World opinion, preparation of, for outlawing of war, 222
World organization, new models for: negative requirements, 226; positive requirements, 226–27; and conditions of order, 227
World state, as solution to war, 181, 186
World War II: and psychopathology of administrative personnel, 180, 184, 185, 190–91; roots and causes of, 184, 189
World-wide involvements in modern warfare, 102, 104
World-wide secondary spoken language, establishing of, 227

Yanomamö: case study of Indian tribe of southern Venezuela, 109–59; nonterritorial nature of warfare, 110–11, 113, 158; and stealing of each other's women by members of independent villages, 110; and inter- and intravillage conflicts, 112; cultural ecology of, and neighboring, hostile villages, 113; warfare, 114, 118–19, 129, 135, 139–41; population, 115–16; contact with outsiders, 116; economic geography of terrain, 117; settlement pattern of villages, 117; village mobility, and warfare, 118–19; village raiding, 118–19, 120, 136–39; and taking refuge with neighboring villages, 118–19; gardens, importance of, 119, 120, 123–24; and demands for women from allies, 119; alliances, intervillage, 120, 159; intervillage visiting and trading, 121; feasting alliances, 122, 123; intervillage exchange of women, 123, 124; sovereignty of villages, 124–25, 159; *waiteri* (ferocity) complex, 124–39, 141; village fissioning, 125, 136, 141; ethnocentrism of, 128, 129; socialization process, and encouragement of ferocity, 130–32; masculinity, emphasis on, 130, 139, 141, 168; wife-beating, 131, 132; contests for expressing ferocity, 132–38; chest-pounding duels, 132–33; side-slapping duels, 133; club fights, 133–34; spear fights, 134–35; related groups, and warfare, 135; treacherous feasts (*nomohoni*), 138–39, 141; demography, and warfare, 139–41; infanticide, 139, 168; sex-ratio, 139–40, 168; causes of death, 140–41 (*table*); social organization, 141–50; kinship system, 141–42; patrilineal descent, 142–43; lineages, 143–45; history of one cluster of villages, and political relationships with other groups, 150–55; marriage behavior in two villages, comparison of, 155–59; fighting of, distinguished from true warfare, 160